TSQ Transgender Studies Quarterly

Volume 2 ★ Number 1 ★ February 2015

Making Transgender Count

Edited by Paisley Currah and Susan Stryker

RESEARCH NOTE

MANIFESTOS

BOOK REVIEWS

Introduction

PAISLEY CURRAH and SUSAN STRYKER

Abstract In this introduction to the special issue of *TSQ: Transgender Studies Quarterly* on the theme "making transgender count," the authors delineate the senses in which trans people can count. On one hand, one makes trans count (in the sense of having its importance recognized) by counting it (making it visible through quantification). On the other hand, one *makes* (i.e., compels) trans count by forcing atypical configurations of identity into categories into which they do not quite fit—the proverbial square peg in a round hole. In this way, the *imperative to be counted* becomes another kind of normativizing violence that trans subjects can encounter and hence another problematic to be critically interrogated by the field of transgender studies. The tensions among what to count, whom to count, how to count, why to count, or whether to count or be counted at all are explored in this issue's articles. What makes the notion of trans* such a fecund point of departure for work in transgender studies is that the definitional lines of the concept are moving targets. That very instability frustrates the project of fixing embodied identities in time and space—a requisite operation for the potentially life-enhancing project of counting trans populations and better addressing their needs as well as for the necropolitical project of selecting certain members of the population for categorical exclusion as dysgenic. The essays in this issue do not resolve the tension between efforts to refine techniques of governmental reason and strategies of resistance, between attempts to sedentarize trans identities and movements that refuse such settling, or between universalizing imperatives to classify and local demands to reject incorporation into a global schematics of gender difference organized by male/female, man/woman, cis-/trans-, trans-/homo-, or white/color dichotomies. Some attempt to do both, while all ultimately fall on one side or the other of various problematics. Our goal in curating this issue has been less to gather a collection of articles that definitively settle these vexed questions than to stage a conversation in which the stakes of the game are made visible.
Keywords transgender, statistical citizenship, survey research, gender identity, census

Standardizing populations is one of the central tasks of modern states. But a map of a dominion's territory is of little state use if not accompanied by a detailed inventory of its peoples. To that end, states seek to enumerate populations with some specificity: number of people per household, age, sex, race, ethnicity, birthplace, work status, income, education, health status, languages spoken, and so on. Cataloguing the population according to its properties not only facilitates the exercise of the state's broad police powers to regulate the population, often to the detriment of minoritized groups, but can also, in the best-case scenarios, help ensure the safety, health, and welfare of the people.[1] *Enumeration* can be a somewhat misleading term for this process to the degree that it suggests one is merely counting objects that already exist, for the enumerative process in fact has the capacity to create what it purports only to name, causing new kinds of people to appear on the social map—sometimes drawing attention to their needs and redirecting resources to address those needs, sometimes concentrating recalcitrant, wayward, messy, incoherent, and noncompliant types of bodies and subjects deemed inconvenient to or obstructive of ends in categories that facilitate containment and control. Transforming "a social hieroglyph" of "exceptionally complex, illegible, and local social practices" into "a legible and administratively convenient format" requires the creation of standardized classifications and metrics for measuring them (Scott 1998: 3). To regularize a population is to flatten its zoetic confusions of movement and form, of time and space, of doing and being, into neat two-dimensional axes specifying static properties and numbers. This process requires, in short, fixing people and their purported attributes in place—"making up people," in Ian Hacking's now famous phrase (1986). But which properties should matter? Precisely what and who should be counted? Or should the counting practices themselves be resisted?

For people who share some perceived commonality, the decision to enable official recognition of the numerical sort can mark a group's entry into "statistical citizenship" (Hannah 2001: 516). That is why debates about population enumeration are often so politically charged. In the United States, for example, while the Census Bureau has collected data on the number of households with same-sex couples for some time, that information was released to the public for the first time only after the 2010 census. Previous administrations declined to make it available on the premise that doing so would violate the Defense of Marriage Act (Sherman 2009). In reversing this policy and releasing the numbers of same-sex households, the Census Bureau director appointed by President Obama proclaimed, "We understand how important it is for all groups to have accurate statistics that reflect who we are as a nation" (US Census Bureau 2011). While the 2010 decennial census did not yet ask about sexual orientation directly—if you were not partnered and living together, you were not counted—questions on sexual orientation were added to one of the federal government's largest data collection instruments, the US Centers for Disease Control's National Health Statistics Survey, in 2013 (Ward et al. 2014). Unfortunately, despite the urging of advocates, federal policy makers declined to add measures to identify trans respondents on that survey, continuing the exclusion of trans people from the official national imaginary.

In the absence of research conducted by government agencies, trans activists have been producing surveys and needs assessments of their communities for decades, documenting the characteristics of these populations, including their demographics (race, ethnicity, gender, education, income, and so on) and their experiences (access to transition and non-transition-related health care and the frequency and type of violence and discrimination they experience) (e.g., Singer, Cochran, and Adamec 1997; Wilchins, Lombardi, and Priesing 1997). The largest survey of trans people to date in the United States—the National Transgender Discrimination Survey (NTDS), conducted largely over the Internet by the National Center for Transgender Equality and the National Gay and Lesbian Task Force—generated a convenience sample of 6,456 transgender people (Grant, Mottet, and Tanis 2011: 15). (To learn more about how the survey identified transgender people as well as other aspects of it, see Reisner et al., Labuski and Keo-Meier, and Harrison-Quintana, Grant, and Rivera, in this issue.) It found that 47 percent had experienced an "adverse job outcome," 41 percent lacked an identity document that matched their gender identity, and 20 percent had served at one time in the armed forces (Grant, Mottet, and Tanis 2011: 3, 5, 30). Working off the NTDS findings, the Williams Institute, an LGBT think tank, claimed that ten states with strict voter identification laws could disenfranchise 24,000 transgender people in the November 2014 elections and that 149,800 transgender people have served or are currently serving in the military (Herman 2014: 1; Gates and Herman 2014: 1). These findings suggest that more resources should be directed to health care for transgender veterans and that policies for changing identity documents should be changed.

But using the NTDS results to make larger inferences about the number of transgender people in the United States affected by particular state policies or decisions about resource allocation, as these reports did, requires having credible statistics generated by random sampling about trans prevalence in large population-based surveys. Unfortunately, there are no large-scale, high-quality data on these questions. For the Williams Institute to produce the numbers cited above, demographer Gary Gates had to extrapolate from two state-level surveys and a handful of meta-level analyses to come up with an estimated transgender prevalence rate of 0.3 percent of the adult US population (about 700,000 transgender people, by this reckoning) (Gates 2011: 6). Gates himself notes that this methodology has "substantial limitations" (Chalabi 2014). Moreover, as Scout, a researcher and health policy analyst who works on LGBT issues, notes, findings based on community and regional surveys "just don't carry the same authority as federal data in grant applications, policy decisions, and resource allocation"; as a result, LGBT, trans, and health advocates have been "beating this drum for data collection" for years (Scout 2013). Regardless of how nonconforming people name themselves or are named by others, they are not yet represented in the official numbers of any state. Only Nepal and India have attempted to measure these subpopulations in national survey instruments (see Knight, Flores, and Nezhad's article in this issue; Nagarajan 2014).

We chose "Making Transgender Count" as the title of this special issue of *TSQ* because it contains a number of telling puns. On one hand, one makes trans count (in the sense of having its importance recognized) by counting it (making it visible through quantification). On the other hand, one *makes* (i.e., compels) trans count by forcing atypical configurations of identity into categories into which they do not quite fit—the proverbial square peg in a round hole. In this way, the *imperative to be counted* becomes another kind of normativizing violence that trans subjects can encounter and hence another problematic to be critically interrogated by the field of transgender studies. The tensions among what to count, whom to count, how to count, why to count, or whether to count or be counted at all are explored in the articles that follow. What makes the notion of trans* such a fecund point of departure for work in transgender studies is that the definitional lines of the concept are "moving targets" (Stryker, Currah, and Moore 2008: 13). That very instability frustrates the project of fixing embodied identities in time and space—a requisite operation for the potentially life-enhancing project of counting trans populations and better addressing their needs as well as for the necropolitical project of selecting certain members of the population for categorical exclusion as dysgenic. The essays in this issue do not resolve the tension between efforts to refine techniques of governmental reason and strategies of resistance, between attempts to sedentarize trans identities and movements that refuse such settling, or between universalizing imperatives to classify and local demands to reject incorporation into a global schematics of gender difference organized by male/female, man/woman, cis-/trans-, trans-/homo-, or white/color dichotomies. Some attempt to do both, while all ultimately fall on one side or the other of various problematics. Our goal in curating this issue has been less to gather a collection of articles that definitively settle these vexed questions in ways with which we might both agree than to stage a conversation in which the stakes of the game are made visible.

It is usually the case that people who conceptualize transgender as a fluid state of being resist efforts to quantify it. In this issue's lead article, "The (Mis)Measure of Trans," Christine Labuski and Colton Keo-Meier argue that "asking questions from within this instability" can generate more useful findings than bracketing that fluidity, the usual practice in quantitative analysis. The authors advise us to reject a number of a priori ideas that usually accompany empirical and quantitative research on this topic. By jettisoning the assumptions that transgender is a "stable and measurable 'thing,'" that trans and nontrans are mutually exclusive categories, that there are "aspects of trans identity . . . incommensurate with nontrans experience," researchers will be better able to identify the mechanisms at work in producing hierarchical social difference in a given milieu. Indeed, reifying transgender by attempting to measure the effects "it" produces can obscure situations in which other axes of identity and experience might matter more, such as race, gender, or sexual orientation. In other contexts, the authors point out, transgender and other such broad categories should be disassembled because they can function as "a proxy for something far more specific and amenable to measurement," something that could be better grasped by a more precise question about "what is to be learned from a specific . . . population." For example, rather than setting FTM as the independent variable, one might choose "'people assigned female at birth taking exogenous testosterone at X dose' or 'trans men who live in cities with large transgender populations.'" Drawing on the work of feminist science studies scholar Karen Barad and other "new materialist" approaches, the authors remind us that the conceptual apparatus of any particular trans research project (e.g., the definition of transgender, the tools for measuring phenomena, and the cultural, anatomical, or psychological frame of reference) is not external to causes and effects it observes but part of the phenomena it purports to measure (Barad 2007: 143).

In most publicly funded data collection, "sex/gender" is most definitely treated as an a priori. (Researchers not interested in trans populations typically use both terms interchangeably, making no distinction between the sex one is assigned at birth and one's gender identity.) It is generally measured by self-reports on survey instruments (circle *M* or *F*) or by telephone interviewers who decide (circle *M* or *F*) based on the interviewee's voice. Trans advocates can demand that birth sex and gender identity be disaggregated so that trans people can better be counted, but those demands need to be accompanied by assurances that there are reliable measures to identify this population. Members of the Gender Identity in US Surveillance (GenIUSS) Group at the Williams Institute, a multidisciplinary group of researchers interested in technical, political, and epistemological issues related to measuring trans populations, have been testing various questions to find out which ones work best. In "'Counting' Transgender and Gender-Nonconforming Adults in Health Research," some members of the GenIUSS Group (Sari L. Reisner, Kerith J. Conron, Scout, Kellan Baker, Jody L. Herman, Emilia Lombardi, Emily A. Greytak, Alison M. Gill, and Alicia K. Matthews) present their findings regarding what they consider to be the most effective questions for distinguishing "gender minorities" in population-based surveys. Interestingly, the group finds that general-population survey questions designed to capture data about gender minorities must, in order to prevent false-positive responses that mistakenly inflate transgender prevalence, be "geared toward the majority group" (cisgendered respondents) such that they are easy for them to answer correctly.[2]

The GenIUSS Group report also highlights another obstacle—the problem of transgender collectivities' being "too small" to count in the US context. They point out that government agencies tend to resist adding questions to general-population surveys that would glean information from any group thought to comprise less than 0.5 percent of the population. That means that individuals who share some potentially important commonality but number fewer than 1.6 million are not likely to be counted. In fact, the authors point out, "federally funded national surveys collect and report data on subpopulations and health conditions that affect far fewer than this number of citizens." For example, those who fall under the category Native Hawaiians and other Pacific Islanders have been counted in national surveys, and those data help health agencies direct the appropriate resources and information to those communities (AHRQ 2010; CDC 2014). Given that transgender people, especially trans women of color, have some of the highest known rates of HIV infection, according to reports from community groups and public health departments (CDC 2013), it would seem only logical to include "gender minorities" on general-population surveys.[3] Counting this population and deploying resources to those most in need within it—trans women of color—could do much to lower their morbidity and mortality rates. But those lives are not objects of the biopolitical project of measuring the population to foster life. Overlooking them in the state statistics suggests that these lives fall on the letting-die side of the biopolitical project.[4] Federal neglect of the health crisis among trans women of color epitomizes Ruth Wilson Gilmore's construction of racism as the "production and exploitation of group-differentiated vulnerability to premature death" (Gilmore 2007: 28).

In his contribution to this issue, T. Benjamin Singer observes how gender-variant and trans-identified people continue to be erased by medical knowledges and practices still organized around a naturalized gender binary. He makes a convincing case, however, that neither the violence of categorical exclusion nor the flattening effects of a unitary and reductive identity category (transgender) can account for what he actually found during fieldwork in community health settings and in analyzing trans-specific health care needs-assessment studies: a rapidly emerging, seemingly endless stream of emergent "embodiments and identities that exceed familiar sex and gender categorization," which Singer characterizes as constituting a proliferative matrix structured by the "generative capacity of the category transgender itself." His research refuses the facile dichotomy that would have us believe that activism, resistance, or liberatory critique can come only from outside institutional frameworks and that institutions can only homogenize and consolidate identities in reactionary ways. He goes so far as to suggest that even within the apparently immobilizing forces of institutions, even as institutional strategies attempt to contain unruly bodies and subjects within administratively useful categories, "bodies can and do exert an insurrectionary pressure upon the enumerative practices designed to produce and define them."

Given the growing call of trans advocates to develop metrics for measuring trans populations, Kristen Schilt and Jenifer Bratter set themselves the task of asking two questions of trans people: Do they want a transgender option on the census? If there were such an option, would they choose it? In their article, "From Multiracial to Transgender? Assessing Attitudes toward Expanding Gender Options on the US Census," they frame these questions with social-science findings on identity validation, which has been used to explain people's choices concerning whether or not to identify as multiracial. (A multiracial option was added to the US Census in 2000 when individuals were allowed to choose more than one racial category.) Their findings, based on a convenience sample of 167 individuals attending transgender or genderqueer conferences, produced some surprising results: 41 percent of the respondents supported adding a transgender option to the US census, but only 29 percent actually reported identifying as transgender on forms when given the option. The fact that forms (from doctors' offices, etc.) are not anonymous while the census is may account for part of that discrepancy. But digging deeper into these responses, the authors note that identity validation played an important role, as it had with individuals choosing the multiracial option. If one's gender identity was socially validated (by others), they were "far *less* likely to endorse adding a category to the US Census or to use such a category on official forms." But those whose gender identity was not validated socially, or those whose *trans*gender identity was validated, were more likely. These findings suggest that a significant proportion of people identified by social scientists and advocates as "transgender" might not want to be seen occupying a position outside the gender binary.

In 2007, the Blue Diamond Society petitioned the Nepalese government to repeal all laws and legal and institutional arrangements that discriminated on the basis of sexual orientation and gender identity. Responding to Blue Diamond's claim that "even the state has ignored us," the Supreme Court directed the government to recognize "third gender" (*tesro lingi*) people by, among other things, including that option on the census form (*Pant v. Nepal*, Writ No. 917 of the Year 2064 BS [AD 2007], translated in *NJA Law Journal*; see "Decision of the [Nepal] Supreme Court" 2008). Accomplishing that task, however, proved easier said than done. Nepal's attempt to add a third gender category to the national census—the first such attempt anywhere—was largely deemed a failure: the category was not clearly defined, the enumerators lacked training, and the census software used to tabulate the data was not retrofitted to include the third gender option. In

"Surveying Nepal's Third Gender," Kyle G. Knight, Andrew R. Flores, and Sheila J. Nezhad discuss their research on how the census might be improved in the future. Working with the Blue Diamond Society, they conducted focus groups to develop and refine a survey instrument that was used on 1,178 members of sexual and gender minorities in Nepal. One of their most significant findings was that *tesro lingi*, conceptualized as a catch-all category similar to transgender, may not be an adequate term for accurately representing all of the seven sex/sexuality/gender identity descriptors they found that people applied to themselves. Moreover, the neat analytic distinctions between sexual orientation and gender identity that have characterized much Western scholarship do not hold in the Nepali context. Instead, they point out, any locally relevant survey instrument has to account for "the fluidity and hybridity of sexual and gender terms used in Nepal (as elsewhere)."

Anna M. Kłonkowska's contribution to this issue, "Making Transgender Count in Poland: Disciplined Individuals and Circumscribed Populations," could also be titled "Making Transgender People Disappear in Poland." In this article, she documents how a medical model of transsexuality governs not just individual transgender lives but also their numerical representation in the population. As she notes, "transposed onto the regulatory realm, the norms governing whether, how, and when individuals in Poland may transition from one gender to another also become metrics for estimating the number of transsexuals in the population." As a result, only physically transitioned bodies come to matter, rather than gender identifications, behaviors, or self-presentation. For those who desire to transition physically, very few are able to overcome the many legal, medical, and bureaucratic obstacles. The inevitable result is that the vast majority of trans people in Poland simply are not "legible as trans," as the authors put it; out of a population of 38.5 million, only 203 people received a court order allowing them to change their gender marker between the beginning of 2009 and the end of 2012. Kłonkowska's work, based on interviews with trans people in Poland, documents their strategies of resistance and assimilation and provides a vital counterpoint to the official ignorance with respect to trans lives.

Large entities such as government agencies and private insurance companies have a stake in smoothing out differences between members of a population such that individuals become more or less interchangeable units, represented and manipulated in standardized ways. In contrast, smaller, community-based health and social-service organizations want and need to know who their patients/constituents are in order to give them the particular kind of care they need. But because delivering that care requires reporting data about their patients to outside agencies and corporations, LGBTQ health centers must come up with ways to balance the need for specificity in one context with the need for homogenization in another. In "Counting Trans* Patients: A Community Health Center Case Study," Natalie Ingraham, Vanessa Pratt, and Nick Gorton discuss how Lyon-Martin Health Services in San Francisco has responded to this dilemma. In addition to relying on the two-step method (asking about the sex assigned at birth and current gender identity), clinicians at Lyon-Martin have developed other strategies that allow them to respect their patients' gender identities and to translate the data in ways that are legible to outside entities. Any solutions, however, are only provisional. Seemingly mundane yet often intractable technical matters, such as codes in electronic medical records or insurance company billing software, can thwart service-provider attempts to recognize and validate the self-understanding and self-presentation of their patients or constituents.

The violence of global and globalizing categories is made evident in Hale Thompson and Lisa King's contribution to this issue. In "Who Counts as 'Transgender'? Epidemiological Methods and a Critical Intervention," they show how collapsing a wide range of differently gendered subjects under the transgender category makes invisible the economic, political, and social processes that "contribute to the marginalization and invisibility of trans and gender-nonconforming individuals within the HIV prevention and treatment complex." In relation to HIV, fixing "transgender" in place as a discrete category reinforces the idea that it is being "transgender" that causes vulnerability to premature death, rather than the many structural forces that increase trans people's "risk of risk" and create conditions for what Lauren Berlant has called "slow death" (Berlant 2007: 754). Disability rights activists have long rejected the idea that disability originates in individual bodies and have favored instead a model that understands disability as an effect of legal, social, medical, and physical landscapes that privilege the normatively able-bodied. Drawing on the same logic, Thompson and King argue that the target of interventions should be the normalizing institutions, discourses, and apparatuses rather than trans people themselves.

The social norms embedded in information systems comprise a crucial but often overlooked area of contestation. In a research note, "Information Systems and the Translation of Transgender," Jeffrey Alan Johnson expands on the discussion begun in Ingraham, Pratt, and Gorton's article and examines how the complexity of gender nonconformity gets erased in the sociotechnical processes of the "translation regime" through which data systems interpret and construct the world. He uses Utah Valley University's data systems as a case study. At one point, the system included "U" (for "unspecified") as a value in its gender field, in addition to "M" and "F." After state legislators became aware of an effort to install unisex restrooms in support of gender-nonconforming students at Utah Valley University, the U was "deprecated" (removed). In this political context, U values were no longer seen as a way to represent individuals who did not see themselves as *M* or *F*; the *U* values were instead seen as "bad data." Although there are no technical barriers to expanding gender possibilities, that the *U* did not mesh with the Utah System for Higher Education's data standards (*M* or *F* only) also provided a technical justification for the political decision policing the gender binary.

In the "Manifestos" section that closes the special issue–themed articles, we present two appraisals of efforts to make transgender count. In "Boxes of Our Own Creation: A Trans Data Collection Wo/Manifesto," Jack Harrison-Quintana, Jaime M. Grant, and Ignacio G. Rivera reflect on their experiences working on the National Transgender Discrimination Survey, the largest survey of trans people to date in the United States. Most significantly, they discuss the qualifying questions through which the NTDS constituted the "transgender" population. With its survey instrument based on a grassroots research process, the questions were meant to serve as a "radical welcome" to participate in what would turn out to be an important tool for trans advocacy in the United States. The 6,456 trans and gender-nonconforming people who decided to respond helped to create "the largest quantitative data set on trans experience anywhere in the world."

Switching attention from the output to the input side of the survey process, from the utility of the findings to the interests of those contributing the data, the Reverend Megan M. Rohrer, a longtime San Francisco–based activist, offers an alternative view. In "The Ethical Case for Undercounting Trans Individuals," they point out that asking vulnerable individuals to answer surveys about their bodies, their identities, and their behaviors can leave them "feeling pathologized, overexposed, and abnormal." Moreover, because needs-assessment data collection often takes place in social-service settings where trans people are seeking food, shelter, or medical care, they might perceive requests to answer questions as a necessary part of a transaction in which they risk being denied a necessity. Rohrer argues that vulnerable people, people who are low- or nondisclosers, and people who might be classified by others as trans but who do not identify as such should have the right not to be counted. Finally, because the attempt to quantify trans communities requires radically minimizing or erasing our many differences by imposing a static and neat order upon them, Rohrer suggests we forgo trying to "capture in statistics" a "community that cannot be generalized."

Paisley Currah teaches political science and gender studies at Brooklyn College and the Graduate Center of the City University of New York and is general coeditor of *TSQ: Transgender Studies Quarterly*.

Susan Stryker is associate professor of gender and women's studies and director of the Institute for LGBT Studies at the University of Arizona and general coeditor of *TSQ: Transgender Studies Quarterly*.

Acknowledgments

We are deeply grateful to those who contributed to the editorial process of "Making Transgender Count": the anonymous reviewers whose comments and suggestions were invaluable; Somjen Fraser, Jeff Mathias, and Amaya Perez-Brumer, whose timely help at crucial stages in the editorial process was invaluable; and our diligent and ever-patient editorial assistant, Abraham Weil, whose title should actually be *TSQ* Whip.

Notes

1. At its origin, the term *statistics* is inseparable from political knowledge. It comes to us from the German *Statistik*, coined in 1748 by Gottfried Achenwall to describe a state's empirical knowledge of itself, which, in Chenxi Tang's summary, includes "the number, physical and moral characteristics of the population" as determined through deployment of "a system of categories, in which particular objects and phenomena are made visible, identified, and properly classified" (Tang 2008: 31).

2. The initial idea for a special issue of *TSQ* organized around the theme "making transgender count" emerged from conversations within the GenIUSS Group, in which both editors have participated. We are not coauthors of the GenIUSS article published herein, "'Counting' Transgender and Gender-Nonconforming Adults in Health Research," and we neither endorse nor contest its methodology and policy recommendations. We gratefully acknowledge financial support from the Williams Institute during *TSQ*'s start-up fundraising campaign.

3. A Centers for Disease Control (CDC 2014) fact sheet states, "Because data for this population are not uniformly collected, information is lacking on how many transgender people in the United States are infected with HIV."

4. For Michel Foucault, it is racism that accounts for the splitting of a population into those whose lives matter and those whose lives do not (Foucault 2003: 254–58).

References

AHRQ (Agency for Healthcare Research and Quality). 2010. "Table 2-5: Selected Characteristics of the NHOPI Population in the United States." United States Department of Health and Human Services. www.ahrq.gov/research/findings/final-reports/iomracereport/reldatatab2 -5.html.

Barad, Karen. 2007. *Meeting the Universe Halfway: Quantum Physics and the Entanglement of Matter and Meaning*. Durham, NC: Duke University Press.

Berlant, Lauren. 2007. "Slow Death (Sovereignty, Obesity, Lateral Agency)." *Critical Inquiry* 33, no 4: 754–80.

CDC (Centers for Disease Control and Prevention). 2013. "HIV among Transgender People." www.cdc.gov/hiv/risk/transgender/index.html.

———. 2014. "HIV among Native Hawaiians and Other Pacific Islanders in the United States." www.cdc.gov/hiv/risk/racialethnic/nhopi/index.html.

Chalabi, Mona. 2014. "Why We Don't Know the Size of the Transgender Population." FiveThirty EightLife, *FiveThirtyEight* (blog), July 29. www.fivethirtyeight.com/features/why-we -dont-know-the-size-of-the-transgender-population.

Foucault, Michel. 2003. *"Society Must Be Defended": Lectures at the Collège de France, 1965–76*. Translated by David Macey. New York: Palgrave.

Gates, Gary J. 2011. "How Many People Are Lesbian, Gay, Bisexual, and Transgender?" Williams Institute. williamsinstitute.law.ucla.edu/wp-content/uploads/Gates-How-Many-People -LGBT-Apr-2011.pdf.

Gates, Gary J., and Jody L. Herman. 2014. "Transgender Military Service in the United States." Williams Institute. williamsinstitute.law.ucla.edu/wp-content/uploads/Transgender-Military -Service-May-2014.pdf.

Gilmore, Ruth Wilson. 2007. *Golden Gulag: Prisons, Surplus, Crisis, and Opposition in Globalizing California*. Berkeley: University of California Press.

Grant, Jaime M., Lisa A. Mottet, and Justin Tanis. 2011. "Injustice at Every Turn: A Report of the National Transgender Discrimination Survey." Washington, DC: National Center for Transgender Equality and National Gay and Lesbian Task Force. www.thetaskforce.org /downloads/reports/reports/ntds_full.pdf.

Hacking, Ian. 1986. "Making Up People." In *Reconstructing Individualism*, edited by Thomas C. Heller, Morton Sosna, and David E. Wellbery, 222–36. Palo Alto, CA: Stanford University Press.

Hannah, Matthew G. 2001. "Sampling and the Politics of Representation in US Census 2000." *Environment and Planning D: Society and Space* 19, no. 5: 515–34.

Herman, Jody L. 2014. "The Potential Impact of Voter Identification Laws on Transgender Voters in the 2014 General Elections." Williams Institute. williamsinstitute.law.ucla.edu/wp -content/uploads/voter-id-laws-september-2014.pdf.

Nagarajan, Rema. 2014. "First Count of Third Gender in Census: 4.9 Lakh." *Times of India*, May 30. timesofindia.indiatimes.com/india/First-count-of-third-gender-in-census-4-9-lakh /articleshow/35741613.cms.

"Decision of the [Nepal] Supreme Court on the Rights of Lesbian, Gay, Bisexual, Transsexual, and Intersex (LGBTI) People [*Pant v. Nepal*]." 2008. *NJA Law Journal* 2, no. 1: 261–86. www .gaylawnet.com/laws/cases/PantvNepal.pdf.

Scott, James C. 1998. *Seeing Like a State*. New Haven, CT: Yale University Press.

Scout. 2013. "Déjà Vu: National Surveys Leave Trans People Behind." *Huffington Post*, June 13. www.huffingtonpost.com/scout-phd/national-health-interview-survey-transgender_b _3428446.html.

Sherman, Jake. 2009. "White House Looks to Include Same-Sex Unions in Census Count." *Wall Street Journal*, June 19. online.wsj.com/articles/SB124537164093129827.

Singer, T. Ben, Mary V. Cochran, and Rachel Adamec. 1997. "Final Report by the Transgender Health Action Coalition (THAC) to the Philadelphia Foundation Legacy Fund." Philadelphia: Transgender Health Action Coalition.

Stryker, Susan, Paisley Currah, and Lisa Jean Moore. 2008. "Introduction: Trans-, Trans, or Transgender." *WSQ* 36, nos. 3–4: 11–22.

Tang, Chenxi. 2008. *The Geographic Imagination of Modernity*. Palo Alto, CA: Stanford University Press.

United States Census Bureau. 2011. "Census Bureau Releases Estimates of Same-Sex Married Couples," September 27. www.census.gov/newsroom/releases/archives/2010_census/cb11 -cn181.html.

Ward, Brian W., et al. 2014. "Sexual Orientation and Health among U.S. Adults: National Health Interview Survey, 2013." *National Health Statistics Reports*, no. 77, July 15. www.cdc.gov /nchs/data/nhsr/nhsr077.pdf.

Wilchins, R., et al. 1997. *The First National Survey on TransViolence*. New York: Gender Public Advocacy Coalition.

The (Mis)Measure of Trans

CHRISTINE LABUSKI and COLTON KEO-MEIER

Abstract This essay considers the utility of research questions that articulate aspects of transgender lives to the nontransgender populations with whom they share a wide range of bodily and lived experience. By foregrounding transgender's instability as a research variable, the authors argue for more precise methodological orientations in trans research, particularly regarding gender and sexual orientation. Drawing on their own data with trans men whose sexual attractions have shifted during transition, they argue against unidimensional interpretations of this experience. Feminists and critical race scholars suggest that race and gender frequently function as "proxies": variables that reduce the complexities of biosocial bodily experience to more quantifiable forms of data. The authors argue that much of the research conducted with transgender persons suffers from similar reductions, narrowing the epistemological frameworks through which these populations are subsequently investigated and understood. By contrasting the National Transgender Discrimination Survey's focus on the measurable experience of discrimination with research that makes broader claims regarding "the transgender population," the essay invites researchers to develop a set of best practices that resemble those of feminist science studies scholars.

Keywords methodology, transgender research, feminist science

This essay weighs the risks and benefits of quantifying a group of individuals who are made vulnerable by, actively challenge, and gain political recognition from the categories rendered "real" by quantitative research. Acknowledging the necessity of data like those produced by the National Transgender Discrimination Survey (NTDS) (Grant et al. 2011), we consider the utility of research questions that articulate aspects of the transgender experience to the nontransgender populations with whom they share a wide range of bodily and lived experience.

We define transgender as dynamic, unstable, and porous, and we use these characteristics to explore the relative use of measuring transgender people. How, in other words, can we quantify an experience that Judith Butler (2001: 627) has called "becoming . . . itself"? As a start, we turn to a set of "good practice guidelines" (Springer, Stellman, and Jordan-Young 2012) developed to promote better science about sex and gender.[1] We believe that these guidelines, which insist on carefully delineated claims that consider robust and explicit alternative mechanisms, offer a beginning standard by which trans researchers can gauge their quantitative research instruments and results. We hope to generate a productive and interdisciplinary dialogue about the difficulties inherent in producing the "right" kinds of research about transgender populations: how to produce useful and meaningful data about an unstable category and how to capture the experience of being trans for the widest variety of readers in ways that benefit transgender people.

We depart from and extend Jamison Green's (2006) assertion that trans people are "just like anyone" (500) by suggesting that transgender is one of many intersectional and socially hierarchical experiences. By reorienting research questions toward methodologies that do *not* assume nonconstructed differences between transgender and nontransgender people, we redirect quantitative research projects away from fixed understandings of trans toward those that are generative and evolving in nature.

A Background Story

Measuring "the transgender population" presented a challenge for us when we were invited to contribute a chapter to a handbook on sexuality demographics (Meier and Labuski 2013). Like many contributors to this journal, we were energized by what trans lives make obvious: that sex and gender are profoundly unstable realities whose "assumed concordance" (Karkazis 2008: 12) is more ideological than material. And though our goal was to represent trans people in the most comprehensive and useful ways possible, we were acutely aware that such a project was riddled with complexity. Like any unit of scientific analysis, transgender is a category through which a wide variety of multidimensional individuals are gathered, many of whom have little in common aside from their gender-diverse bodies and practices.

A related problem was that the term *transgender* is variably defined and that, for many, this diverse nomenclature is a central feature of being trans (Stryker, Currah, and Moore 2008).[2] And though we were at pains to represent a category that we saw as both multiple and evolving, we were stymied by how to best render categorical resistance to an audience of demographers. Katherine Rachlin (2009) argues that "researchers must be able to clearly define the subgroup of interest for their study" (266), a challenge made difficult by two related issues: first, a growing number of trans people explicitly resist categories that stabilize gender in any way, rendering conventional quantitative methods unwieldy; second, many transgender individuals know exactly "who they are" (Valentine 2007), regardless of whether categories exist to represent them.

Quantifying the so-called trans population also risked allying with forms of legitimacy and conformity through which many trans people have thus far been marginalized (Vidal-Ortiz 2002; Califia 2012). Collected data can be used to downplay or background the concerns of trans people, and standardizing the categories of pre- and postoperative could relegate many trans persons to a quasi-legitimate status. Finally, we grappled with questions of methodology—that is, "the more deeply embedded premises . . . [that] underpin how research questions are asked [and] how studies are constructed" (Spanier and Horowitz 2011, 45). We knew that our explanatory framework needed to capture a lived experience that was simultaneously real and contingent, measurable yet elusive, and vulnerable to misrepresentation while capable of representing itself.

In the end, we agreed with researchers like Rachlin (2009), who describe an "urgent need" for data that can "positively impact the lives of transgender people" (261). We knew that demonstrating the prevalence of trans people, however imperfectly, could contribute to both heightened awareness of and more affirming attitudes toward trans people (Silverschanz 2009). The NTDS makes the consequences of transphobia clear: in addition to higher rates of suicide attempts and emotional distress, a full three-quarters of respondents experienced discrimination, bullying, and violence in their lifetimes. In this context, any and all evidence of the statistical prevalence of a population that some would prefer remain invisible is a political and human rights necessity.

[handwritten margin note: consequence of transphobia]

But we also knew that if our "numbers" did not come with a context, that is, did not translate into a more meaningful understanding of transgender lived experience, then we would have gotten only part of it right. Moreover, if population prevalence rates—of any percentage—led to even well-intentioned misunderstandings that transgender was a stable and measurable "thing," then we were aligned with a reification project that reflected neither our own understandings of the term nor our politics about it. Ultimately, we wanted to hold close the generative nature of trans while still communicating the ways in which the experience could be "captured" for the benefit of trans people worldwide.[3]

Intra-researcher Complexity

Further complicating our efforts was the fact that we defined transgender differently. For Colton Keo-Meier, transgender is a lived reality that becomes stable while it destabilizes man, woman, male, and female, while for Christine Labuski, the instability of these categories exists on the same relative plane. In this latter framework, transgender people and bodies offer as many insights about a dynamic and evolving human condition as they do about alternative gender systems; they help to reveal the instability of bodies—period. Evolution here is not linear, with trans bodies positioned in between less perfect and more perfect human forms. It is, rather, a way to think about the durable and inextricable relationships between bodies and cultural practice; the physical and physiological changes that signify trans—including prosthetics, pronouns, dress, and

[handwritten margin note: differ definitions]

surgery—are in a relationship with discourses and material realities involving gender, genitals, bodies, power, and sex.

In short, we were—and continue to be—of two minds concerning the nature of trans. One of us, a transgenderqueer male psychologist, understands transgender to be fairly stable across history and culture: trans people have existed across time and space and, aside from cultural variation, reflect a similar mode of gender incongruence that can—though need not—be addressed with medical interventions or other modes of bodily adaptation. The other, a nontransgender female cultural anthropologist, understands trans to be as local and contingent as any other cultural practice or bodily state and that regardless of the existence of gender nonconformers in other times and places, how people transition in the contemporary United States reveals as much about the political economy, belief systems, and physical environment of that time and place as it does about the process of living gender differently.

As individuals, we embrace these somewhat divergent perspectives. But as researchers and coauthors, we recognize the conceptual difficulties they index. Located in psychology and anthropology, we engage with almost mutually exclusive literatures and frame problems in different ways. In this context, what is the nature of the concept at hand? Can we produce work that "matters" to both of us and to our disciplines? To be sure, conceptual instability is not a problem unique to trans scholarship. But because the current question concerns measurement, we are preoccupied by its translatability and utility. It is because transgender renders other categories unstable that we must properly attend to its own contingencies.

We suggest, then, that we think about trans people being "just like anyone" by focusing on their intersections with other social hierarchies. These hierarchies—race, immigration status, physical ability—leave almost all of us both well and poorly positioned in our various worlds; how this multidimensionality maps onto the material experiences of trans *and* nontransgender people is part of what interests us here. How, for instance, do transgender men of color experience black male incarceration rates in the United States? How do trans women negotiate street harassment from perpetrators who see them as female but not (necessarily) trans? These articulations evidence an alternative methodology for trans research, one that does not reduce the reality of transgender to a genetic sequence, a neuroanatomical site, or childhood behavior patterns; one that allows us to describe and construct "men and women who are also trans people" in addition to a "transgender population."

Conventional quantitative methods cannot address these entangled forms of difference; this is not news. But unpacking this assertion further helps to open transgender research questions up to many other dimensions of identity. Dean

Spade (2006) argues that the ways he was "different" as a child, including being Christian and on welfare, were neither more nor less relevant to his transgender identity than were his surgical or childhood behavioral histories: "Why should I engage this idea that my gender performance has been my most important difference in my life? It hasn't, and I can't separate it from the class, race, and parentage variables through which it was mediated" (319). By attending to these imbrications, we hope to demonstrate how trans can fruitfully attach to other forms of identity, not to dilute or mitigate the sometimes urgent realities of being trans but to remind those of us who ask questions for a living that more precise answers may come from analyses that do not render trans and nontrans as mutually exclusive categories.

Counting the Problems

In this section, we more carefully examine some of the problems with quantitative research that does not foreground transgender's conceptual instability. We believe that trans—like all other bodies and forms of identity—can and should be researched as an identity coconstituted by its social milieu. We seek to incorporate Susan Stryker's (2006b) assertion that "encounter[s] [with] the transsexual body [reveal] the constructedness of the natural order" (254) into a methodological orientation useful to quantitative researchers, a set of strategies that the final section of this essay will describe.

The NTDS

Developed and carried out by the National Center for Transgender Equality and the National Gay and Lesbian Task Force, the purpose of the NTDS was to "bring the full extent of discrimination against transgender and gender non-conforming [GNC] people to light" (Grant et al. 2011: 1). At 220 pages, the NTDS is the largest set of quantitative data about transgender persons in the United States, and it tells a difficult story: three-quarters of respondents report discrimination, bullying, and violence at the hands of classmates, health care providers, police officers, public officials, bosses and coworkers, teachers, and family members. These experiences were associated with increased rates, when compared with national averages, of drug and alcohol abuse, interrupted education, incarceration, mental health problems, and suicidality. The survey also demonstrated significant racial intersections, with transgender people of color experiencing much higher rates of poverty and police harassment than their white counterparts. There is no question that the NTDS represents a major achievement in quantitative research design, that it has produced vital empirical data about being trans in the contemporary United States, and that these data will be analyzed by trans and legal scholars, social scientists, and activists for decades. What we wish to explore further is how the NTDS stabilized the term *transgender* in order to produce their data.

Not surprisingly, the NTDS thought big and included "those who transition from one gender to another (transsexuals), *and* those who may not, including genderqueer people . . . and those whose gender non-conformity is a part of their identity" (2011: 12). Notably, the authors handled gender's inherent variability with a series of questions that addressed the *act* of nonconformity rather than its specific content, including a self-assessment ("do you consider yourself transgender?"); two questions contrasting birth-assigned and currently lived gender; a list of terms with which respondents could identify; and two questions about social interactions ("people can tell" and "I tell people"). The data were then cleaned in order to eliminate respondents who did not meet the researchers' definition of transgender.

Though the NTDS collected data regarding surgery, hormones, and other transitional practices, these data were not used to define transgender. And though this strategy reflects a set of admirable assumptions about research subjects' capacities for self-representation, problems arise when other researchers make different choices—for example, by explicitly tying inclusion criteria to respondents' having "made strides to accommodate" another gender (Vidal-Ortiz 2002: 225). Such "strides" are variously defined and may or may not include behaviors in which cisgender people also engage (e.g., cross-dressing). Our concerns here are not with the NTDS, whose tight focus reflected a methodological orientation toward lived experience rather than ontology. But for researchers interested in what *constitutes* transgender, survey instruments that do not more specifically define the population in question may invite more confusion than clarity. As it stands, trans scholars hoping to make empirically based claims have a variable— and at times contradictory—set of definitions through which they must wade (Lombardi 2009).

David Valentine, for example, defines transgender as "a plastic category . . . that clarifies a newly emergent model of gender and sexuality" (2012: 201), while Stryker calls it "a wide variety of phenomena that call attention to the fact that 'gender' as it is lived, embodied, experienced, performed, and encountered, is more complex and varied than can be accounted for by the currently dominant binary sex/gender ideology of Eurocentric modernity" (2006a: 3). For Sandy Stone, the transsexual body is an intertextual one whose "troubling and productive multiple permeabilities of boundary and subject position" must be negotiated (1998: 300). These definitions make sense to most readers of this journal because they highlight the complexities that confound quantitative analyses. But for those attempting to count, measure, operationalize, define, or generate empirical data, these definitions are more or less unusable.

Who and What Is Transgender? And Who Defines It?

Our concerns echo those of other researchers (Meezan and Martin 2009b) who insist that we delineate "why we are studying this particular group at this particular point in time" (Wheeler 2009: 307), and who lament the fact that producing and maintaining trans as a singular entity can complicate the use of comparative data. In research she conducted with a group of trans men, for example, Rachlin (2009) limited her claims by strictly defining her research population: she combined a "a gender signifier" (birth-assigned female and male identified) and "a behavior" (considering surgery) (267). She compares this process with that of a colleague whose inclusion criteria for transitioning ranged from surgery to pronoun use. Though both used definitions specific to their research questions, their lack of concordance compromised their ability to generate widely useful data.

Indeed, inclusion criteria run the gamut, from expansive and sometimes vague advertisements for "anyone who does not identify strictly as their 'male' or 'female' birth sex" (Kuper, Nussbaum, and Mustanski 2012: 246) to subcategorical—and narrowly imagined—lists of trans-related attributes. Other studies simply report efforts to work with a "transgender community" (Rosser et al. 2007) (or "key members" of it: Paxton, Guentzel, and Trombacco 2006), whose interests are imagined to be homogeneous and represented as separate from those of the researchers. Still others, illustrated most consistently by Valentine (2007, 2012), question aspects of the category itself, arguing that its relevance is largely structural and institutional.

We argue that research design should begin with questions that specify what is to be learned from a specific transgender population—for example, the quantifiable experience of discrimination reported by the NTDS. What do questions about hormone use or surgery target, for example? Do they always inform the issue at hand? Do they preclude other, potentially more relevant, dimensions of bodily experience? If, for example, libido shifts during or after transition, how to best understand the various roles played by genitals, hormones, erotic attention, and the social environment? What role do we think these factors play in *any* person's libido, and what are our assumptions regarding differences among trans, GNC, and cis libidos? Do we imagine that exogenous hormones affect trans and cis persons in the same ways? Are we willing to expand our findings to nontransgender persons? And if not, why not? Again, we must be clear about *what* we want to know from transgender respondents and *who* we think our data represent—them, other people, or all of the above.

If both trans and cisgender people experience shifts in erotic attraction over the course of their lives, a finding from our own research with trans men

(Meier et al. 2013), how might we discern whether there are distinct mechanisms at work? Kristen W. Springer, Jeanne Mager Stellman, and Rebecca Jordan-Young (2012) argue that such mechanisms "must be articulated" in order to avoid "*a priori* expectations of . . . difference" (1822). This is not to discount the possibility of biologically measurable differences between these two groups, particularly regarding hormones. But because hormones are not used by all trans people, and because investigations of this experience are not (yet) standardized, we cannot extrapolate hormone use to transgender as a scientific variable. And we most certainly cannot do so if the hormone users in question differ along other dimensions that might contribute to varied bodily experience, such as sex/gender, race, or concomitant biological conditions.

Though a full accounting of how race might intersect with the bodily dimensions of transgender is beyond the scope of this essay, it is important to note that it remains largely undertheorized, including in quantitative analyses. By demonstrating that respondents of color fared worse along almost every measure in their survey, the NTDS has given researchers the opportunity to elucidate the details of these patterns and to develop theory about *how* transgender and race interact as compounding—and measurable—biocultural stressors. Darrell P. Wheeler (2009) argues that across the research in trans health, "there are differences in outcomes based on or linked to race" (303) but that these outcomes are rarely unpacked. Urging us to keep our focus intersectional, he notes the "serious concerns" among some LGBT African Americans "about the appropriateness and utility of research findings to the[ir] lives" (304). Our methodological orientation is one way to address Wheeler's concerns; research that includes transgender *alongside* other dimensions of identity and experience—for example, "people of color who are also trans" and "trans people who are also people of color" as equally unstable but distinctly nuanced populations—has the potential to address rather than evade these concerns.

Becoming (More) Precise

More precise definitional criteria, rather than supplanting direct questions about transgender experience, can allow us to look at existing themes in novel ways. If, for example, research on being trans at work demonstrates how profoundly work is structured along gendered lines (Schilt 2006), why not reframe the issue by aggregating rather than segregating trans and cis respondents, viewing "trans at work" and "gender at work" as two separate but related dimensions of a wider phenomenon? In this section, we look at two aspects of transgender that we believe are especially amenable to such efforts: sexual orientation and gender.

Sexual Orientation

Perry Silverschanz (2009) notes that "research has shown that lesbians and transgender people are less likely to seek medical care [because of] distressing interactions with medical providers" (3) and recommends LGBT-specific training modules as a remedy. The NTDS data support his argument by demonstrating "widespread provider ignorance" about transgender patients and severe levels of discrimination in the United States health care system, all compounded by race, income, and education (Grant et al. 2011: 72–86). Though we too want to educate providers, we begin our discussion with Silverschanz because of the imprecise nature of his concerns. What, we ask, is the underlying factor at work in these disparities, and how exactly does it connect lesbian and transgender individuals? If the inadequate care of these groups is related to their "sexual minority" status, why are gay men or bisexual people not struggling with this issue?

Here, the concept of sexual minority serves as a "proxy" (Springer, Stellman, and Jordan-Young 2012: 1818) for related factors that are more limited and/or precise. Though NTDS respondents reported alarming rates of discrimination in health care settings, the survey also found that trans men were more likely to postpone care than were trans women due to both financial insecurity and "discrimination and disrespect" (Grant et al. 2011: 76). Our proxy question here is about the more complicated natures of both transgender *and* health disparities and whether women—including (cis and trans) lesbians—articulate, as research variables, with trans men who have "female" genitalia and reproductive organs. Might these trans men's past experiences of being perceived as female patients overlap with the experiences of cisgender lesbians and (some) GNC or other cisgender heterosexual women? Might (some of) their lived experiences as women play a role in their increased economic precarity? And what role, if any, does sexual orientation play in any of this? What is the precise definition of "sexual minority" that adequately attends to these multidimensional strands of analysis?

These questions inform our own questions regarding sexual orientation and trans men, who, according to the NTDS, were more likely than trans women to describe themselves as queer (46 percent and 7 percent, respectively [Grant et al. 2011: 29]). Our research (Meier et al. 2013) demonstrates that shifts in attraction patterns are common among this group (35 percent of our sample) and that many eschew binary classificatory schemas (straight/gay) that do not correlate with their day-to-day experience. These multi-directional shifts in so-called sexual orientation, which have yet to be adequately described, theorized, or predicted, cut across all subgroups of trans men, including those whose gender identity or sexual orientation felt stable before transitioning. Though variables such as the use of exogenous testosterone and being seen as male by partner(s) have received some attention (Devor 1993, 1997; Schleifer 2006; Meier et al. 2013), the respective roles played by surgery, nonsurgical transitioning aids, community support (or the lack of it), mental health variables, relationships with other trans people, or the ability to openly transition at work or school—all of which are amenable to quantitative analysis—have barely begun to be outlined or described.

Moreover, reports of trans men's low levels of same-gender attraction (APA 2000; Bockting, Benner, and Coleman 2009) are worth reexamining. Fifty-one percent of our respondents reported current attractions to both men and women, and 17 percent reported exclusive attractions to men. These percentages may reflect a stable pattern of attraction; they may also be related to political and social developments in a community increasingly comfortable describing same-gender attractions. What is even more likely, however, and also suggested by our data, is that these attractions are part of a more fluid spectrum of desire, some of which is made available by the transitioning process itself. Additionally, and for a variety of reasons, fewer than 10 percent of trans men have had gender affirmation surgery involving their external genitalia (Meier et al. 2011), and many involve their vaginas and vulvas in their sexual activity. Less costly hormone supplements and body modifications (e.g., breast binders and prosthetic genitalia) make it increasingly possible to live and be perceived as male, shaping a population that is widely varied, both anatomically and experientially. In this milieu, "LGBT researchers" must be willing to consider what it means for the category of "gay man" to include people with vulvas, particularly if a vulva precludes entry into that category for others.

Finally, the shifting terms employed by researchers make interdisciplinary interpretation difficult, leading non–trans specialists to wonder about things like *which* trans men and women are gay, exactly? Does the definition stem from anatomical "sex"—that is, genitalia and secondary sex characteristics—or from gender identity and expression? What about sexual behavior? Do we presume sexual orientation to be stable, or is it "fluid" in the ways described by Lisa Diamond (2009), whose claims are especially interesting in that they involve greater fluidity in "women"? Though her research was with cis women, what questions does it help us to ask about trans women? To return to our good-practice guidelines, what is the *mechanism* or social phenomenon that we would want fluidity to inform?

Gender

Though the issue of how gender theory informs and is informed by transgender studies is beyond the scope of this essay, we want to note two separate though interrelated issues, the first being gender's social asymmetry. The lived experiences of women, though variously intersected, are generally subordinate to those of men, meaning that acquiring a male identity involves accessing (more) power compared to transitioning to a female or nonbinary one. Gendered asymmetry exists in virtually every social space that might be empirically measured; it is also lived out by the body, in that women's bodies are held to much stricter aesthetic standards, leading to stark differences in the bodily alterations in which different kinds of transgender people engage. "The fact is," argues Valentine, "that the history of medical research and attention, surgical sophistication, kinds of surgeries, access to surgeries, and cultural meanings of female-to-male and male-to-female surgeries are not equivalent" (2012: 205).

Research involving transgender people who identify *as a particular gender* must attend to these differences and acknowledge gender as a hierarchically ordered social dimension; analogizing the trans woman and trans man experience risks erasing both their "interpenetration" and their "power-laden differences" (Valentine 2012: 198).[4] Closer methodological scrutiny can guide researchers as to whether questions and results should be broken down by gender identity: Is the research about the workplace, a site where gendered asymmetries exist for non-transgender people? Is it about bodily aesthetics or the pressure to have cosmetic surgery? Is it about sexual assault, military service, or other areas where maleness and femaleness are experienced in sometimes acutely different ways? Again, we do not suggest that these experiences do not *also* contain transgender dimensions. But when an accurate understanding of gender is not built into the research design, results are more likely to misrepresent the issue under investigation (Schiebinger 2014).

Second, transgender can be investigated, theorized, and lived as an opting out of a priori gender identities, a phenomenon to which the NTDS was extremely attentive. Whether this signifies different "kinds" of transgender people remains to be seen, but reckoning the differences between trans women and trans men should compel us to think in more precise ways about the source and direction of sexual difference and dimorphism. Female, male, intersex, and all other bodies—both cis and trans—overlap and diverge along numerous paths—neurological, behavioral, hormonal, sociocultural, and genetic. The trans+gender experience can therefore provoke questions about evolution, the hormonal environment, bodily adaptation, epigenetics, biological stability, and what Jane Bennett (2010: viii) calls "vitality." Thinking in these terms invites research questions about trans-specific bodily practices as well as how trans bodies exist alongside other enhanced, augmented, or altered cyborg bodies—what Micha Cárdenas (2012) refers to as "the transreal"—in addition to the social worlds in which they are embedded.

Foregrounding gender in our research design can also help us to think more expansively about normative gender regimes. This argument has recently been made by Valentine (2012), who insists that theoretical models of gender that fail to denaturalize the nontransgender, or "NT," experience leave transgender individuals "bear[ing] the full weight of binary gender" (189). Developing his argument specifically around the process of sex reassignment surgery (SRS), Valentine insists that binary gender norms are shored up less by transsexuals seeking SRS than by gender theorists who do not actively question why NT people leave their genitals alone. In other words, Valentine suggests that gender categories are (re)produced by the decision to opt out of genital reassignment, a decision that many transgender people also avoid. Research design that starts here can open the category of transgender to anyone willing to alter their body in ways that trouble normative gender regimes, a process that Spade calls "mutilating gender" (2006: 315). This might include women who forego breast reconstruction after a mastectomy or "take hormones and become sexy 'bearded ladies'" or anyone who does not "prioritize how their genitals will look to others" (323). What we want to stress here is that both trans and nontrans people can engage in this mutilation and that researchers must account for all of the ways in which they do.

mutilating gender

Regardless of whether trans constitutes its own gender, some suggest that many trans people nonetheless "do gender" differently. Salvador Vidal-Ortiz (2002) describes alternative forms of masculinity pursued by trans men, attributing this to a "burden of sexism" they disproportionately bear (191); he and others also find trans men using dress to distinguish themselves from "dykes" (Halberstam 1998) or engaging in stereotypical forms of sexuality that "shore up" their masculinity. This behavior is unsurprising given the number of trans people who "have no intention of undermining present gender inequalities" or binaries (Schact 2002: 161), people who want "quite simply to *be*" male or female (Prosser 1998: 32) and do not wish to yield the "apparent naturalness of sex" to nontransgender people.

Whether we refer to this group as nondisclosing (colloquially, "stealth"), passing, or under the radar, they pose interesting problems for quantitative analyses, as they could be counted among both transgender and nontransgender populations. In some ways, they may be "easier" to measure given their unambiguous identities as male or female, though it is the unmarked quality of their gender identities that may keep them from even completing a survey like the NTDS. Important questions remain regarding the relationship of these subpopulations to an apparently growing number of queer and GNC transgender people; to our minds, they represent a fruitful area for quantitative inquiry.

A final point in this discussion is the role that feminist analysis can and should play in our methodologies. Though feminism's relationship to transgender studies has at times been an ambivalent one (Stryker, Currah, and Moore 2008; Enke 2012), there is a long history of scholarship from both areas working toward what Stephen Whittle (2006) refers to as "a better set of values in which gender loses some of its power of oppression" (202). Research designs that do not attend to the ways in which power is unevenly distributed across *all* bodies risk allowing transgender to "contain all [the] gender trouble" (Stryker 2004: 214) and, potentially, all of its radicality. And, though the NTDS paid close attention to the ways in which distinctly gendered participants experienced discrimination, the reporting of its qualitative data did not consistently interrogate the normative gender performed by some respondents.

In describing their experience with school-based discrimination, for example, one participant wrote that they were "harassed . . . bullied [and] forced to wear dresses to school" (Grant et al. 2011: 46). What we find missing from this account is a discussion—however brief—noting that gender-specific clothing is also problematic for some cis girls. And though, again, we are attuned to the "geometric" (Wheeler 2009: 302) forms of marginalization borne by trans children, particularly those marked by other forms of social stigma, we nevertheless want to ask whether part of our job as researchers and methodologists is to construct instruments through which our respondents can reflect on the normative arrangements that our research actively questions. Whittle (2006) argues that trans people have taught many feminists to "queer the pitch by highlighting, clarifying, deconstructing and then blowing apart . . . all the things we know about sex" (202); we seek only to extend this project to include cis girls and boys who may also need support and advocacy in resisting the gender norms through which their own nontransgender status will otherwise eventually be naturalized.

This would also be true for research with trans men who report that having sex as a man is often more pleasurable than it was as a woman (Vidal-Ortiz 2002; Dozier 2005). In her research with vulvar pain patients, Labuski (2013) found that the majority of her cis female respondents harbored longstanding feelings of distress regarding the relative importance of their specific sexual needs, making room for a broader discussion between trans and feminist scholars about how female eroticism is subordinated along gendered lines. If we are to fully resist the gender categories made real by the institutionalizing practices of medicine, schools, the media, and the state, then our research instruments must make room for our respondents to denaturalize gender in all its guises, including its structured hierarchies.

New Habits

William Meezan and James I. Martin argue that LGBT research "should be socially responsible" (2009a: 424); Rachlin, in the same volume, adds that we should "contribute not just to a greater understanding of transgender populations, but also to their quality of life" (2009: 264–65). Though our prescriptive agenda leans more toward research conduct and less toward social policy, we agree that our research should better the lives of our participants: not only should we seek to mitigate the potential harms to which so many trans people are routinely exposed, we should strive to illuminate the ways in which transgender persons can advance our understandings of human rights, bodily vulnerability, biocultural adaptability, gender, racialization and other forms of intersectional identity, and discrimination. More pragmatically, we also argue that transgender persons have experiences that are unique to their form(s) of identity as well as common to other populations, both of which can be measured using the methodological orientation developed here. In this section, we outline two ways this might be done.

In an essay titled "Two Questions about Race," anthropologist Alan Goodman (2006) argues that race is "no longer the right way to describe [human] biological variation." Asserting that the term is part clumsy shorthand, part folk tale, and part unstable scientific concept, Goodman cautions us about all the things we ask race to do. Reminding us that 94 percent of human variation cannot be statistically explained by race and that genetic variation is greater within so-called racial groups than it is across them, Goodman concludes that race is an unsuitable concept for scientific inquiry, a "blunt and dull instrument" that should be replaced with more precise concepts and corresponding terminology.

This assertion answers just one of Goodman's questions, however: "Is race a useful categorization to describe human biological variation?" We are more interested in his second—"Is race a useful categorization for tracking sociopolitical injustices?"—in that it indexes our collective motives for "making transgender count." By answering in the affirmative, Goodman offers concise and pragmatic advice regarding how to think about transgender's complexity. Transgender is biological in many of the ways that "race" is, in that none of its bodily markers (e.g., altered genitalia, hormonal fluctuation) are unique to trans individuals, nor are they demonstrable across all the types of people who identify as trans. The point here is that de-essentializing transgender need not compromise our efforts to document and measure its lived experience. And though linguistic variation challenges our abilities to accurately represent these populations, we agree with Goodman that "new vocabulary and concepts" can help our efforts achieve greater precision. As long as the term remains contingent, our research, writing, and activism can continue to address transgender's unstable nature while simultaneously recognizing how it meaningfully organizes experience.

Though a long tradition of opposing the material to the discursive has led to some stagnant and fixed conceptions of the body, new materialist discourse and theory (Bennett 2010; Barad 2007) remind us that the bodily dimensions of being trans—anatomical variation, hormonal fluctuation, technological augmentation—are precisely what make this population so dynamic, "fascinating" in their diversity (Goodman 2006), "far less implicated in physical norms, and far more diversely spread across rich and complex structuration of identity and desire, than it is now possible to express" (Stone 1998: 301). Though it remains critical to acknowledge, in the manner of the NTDS, the ways in which trans folks are persistently and structurally marginalized, we must also begin asking questions from within this instability—diving into the dynamic bodies and lives of transgender persons and opening them out to other categories of experience.

Our second solution comes from feminist science studies, specifically Springer, Stellman, and Jordan-Young's "good practice guidelines" (2012: 1817) that caution against unexamined uses of the terms *sex* and *gender*. Insisting that biological differences between men and women virtually always bear the traces of (social) gender, these authors call for more methodologically explicit delineations of whether and how sex/gender functions as an independent variable. In the case of cardiovascular disease, for example, numerous studies have described differences between males and females regarding risk and susceptibility. But what the guidelines illustrate is that other mechanisms often dictate sex-specific risk (or protection), including—in the studies they highlight—height and muscle mass. "Women," as they show, possess neither suboptimal glucose metabolism patterns nor diminished arterial elasticity; it is shorter people and people with less muscle mass who do. In these two cases, imprecision regarding the nature of the research question leads not only to improperly reassured short men and unnecessarily alarmed tall women but also to a general public underinformed about the relevance and stability of measurable sex-based differences.

Thus guided, we can consider how transgender might also function as a proxy, a variable reducible to other categories or experiences. In our own research, "trans man" might constitute a proxy for something far more specific and amenable to measurement: "people assigned female at birth taking exogenous testosterone at X dose" or "trans men who live in cities with large transgender populations," both of which address but do not homogenize the transgender experience. Were our research focus to shift to, say, the relationship between libido and genital alteration, we could use these guidelines to decide whether and how to include genitally altered nontransgender people.

The good-practice guidelines unsettle and displace the terms *sex* and *gender* in scientific—specifically clinical—research; Springer and colleagues also insist that alternative hypotheses, especially those involving social factors, be analyzed, accommodated, and/or disproved. And though it is their specific strategies that make the guidelines so appealing—they read like a literal "how to"—it is their methodology that we want to highlight. Stressing the intersectional nature of their orientation, they use the "new materialist" (Coole and Frost 2010) language of "irreducibl[e] entangle[ment]" (Springer, Stellman, and Jordan-Young 2012: 1818) to describe the relationships between biology and culture. This language helps us reassess research designs that attempt to measure the transgender experience outside its social milieu. With what other social factors is the aspect of transgender that we are investigating entangled? And what steps do we need to take in order to ensure that we have properly taken those factors into account?

Conclusions

Bonnie B. Spanier and Jessica D. Horowitz (2011) begin their methodological essay by asking, "What are the biologically recognizable differences between gay people and straight people[?]" (43), in order to illustrate a research question fundamentally grounded in two beliefs: first, that such differences exist; second, that they are amenable to measurement. We conclude with this provocation in order to review our major concerns and to gesture toward some of their implications.

Submitting our research designs to a similar "scratch test"—that is, are they based on unexamined assumptions about the differences between transgender and nontransgender people or on the similarities between all transgender people—is an important first step in delineating the kinds and scope of claims we hope to make. Once our assumptions are explicit, claim-specific instruments can be designed, and limitations can be anticipated. To continue with our own example, if our interest is in the relationship between transitioning and changes in libido and erotic attraction, we must define both "transitioning" and "libido" in ways that are measurable, and these definitions must reflect the degree to which we believe such a shift is unique to transgender people. Moreover, we should be clear about whether we want our research to contribute to a wider body of knowledge; if so, our definitions should strive to establish criteria that can be replicated by other researchers. Reorienting our designs in this way can help us avoid research trajectories that overly essentialize transgender people; it can also make it possible to establish bodily and experiential links with nontransgender people, "bursting transgender wide open" (Stryker, Currah, and Moore 2008: 12) to any number of measurable dimensions.

Research programs that neglect to elaborate the *specific* phenomena that the transgender experience is meant to illuminate risk substituting the category "trans" for any number of sociocultural processes—medical vulnerability (Grant et al. 2011), bodily integrity (Loeb 2008), racialized gender (Roen 2001), or misogyny (Serano 2012)—that exist within the broader population. These displacements obscure our perspective on the aspects of trans experience that are peculiar to these individuals and groups, and at the same time they circumscribe our research questions to the aspects of trans identity that we, perhaps erroneously, believe to be incommensurate with nontrans experience. "Similarity," argue Springer, Stellman, and Jordan-Young, "should . . . be considered with the same level of sophistication and attention given to explaining differences" (2012: 1822). Established similarities—however partial—can also be the basis for political solidarity (Feinberg 1992).

The degree to which we understand transgender in neurobiological, cultural, anatomical, behavioral, and/or psychological terms will determine the investigative angles and trajectories along which we trace and then establish a series of associations, hypotheses, findings, and even predictions, many of which will eventually articulate with public policy and popular media. We raise these concerns not to dissuade any of us from trans-related research topics but to highlight the significant limitations and potentially narrowed scope of the claims we might make with conventionally framed research questions. In short, how we, in Valentine's (2007) words, "imagine" the experience and reality of transgender will substantially shape the kinds of political and theoretical questions that we ask, both of and about these anything-but-uniform populations.

In heeding Valentine's call to "reach for a different imagination" regarding transgender experience (2012: 206), we are intrigued by the bodily states of hormonal instability, physiological precarity, and radical corporeal imaginaries that are perhaps less quantifiable—and less politically urgent—than some of what we have examined here. Nevertheless, we remain challenged to investigate and represent the lived experience of neither/nor (as well as both/and) that transgender individuals often embrace and embody—the "rich and rapidly proliferating ecologies of embodied difference" described by Stryker, Paisley Currah, and Lisa Jean Moore (2008: 12). These and other experiences articulate with a range of other individuals and social groups, many of whom do not (yet) perceive a shared interest with "the transgender population" but with whom precisely defined research projects can introduce and establish novel and even empathic forms of alliance.

Christine Labuski is an assistant professor of women's and gender studies at Virginia Tech, where she also directs the Gender, Bodies, and Technology initiative. Her ethnography, *"It Hurts Down There": The Bodily Imaginaries of Female Genital Pain*, is forthcoming.

Colton Keo-Meier is a clinical psychologist, researcher, and educator. He is a research coordinator at the Michael E. DeBakey Veterans Affairs Medical Center and an affiliate of Baylor College of Medicine. He teaches courses on human sexuality and transgender affirmative counseling at the University of Houston and at Southern Methodist University.

Notes

1.   We are aware of the literatures in critical and feminist science studies in which the project and practices of empirical/imperialist, capital *S* "Science" are shown to depend on and reproduce the very categories they claim to investigate (e.g., Harding 1986). Within this

context, looking to scientific data for legitimacy is a potentially misguided endeavor, as "Science" produces what it already imagines. Though we take them quite seriously, this essay brackets these critiques for the reasons made clear by the NTDS. The urgency that we and many others experience about their data, coupled with a growing number of scientists practicing from a queer and/or feminist perspective, makes us optimistic that "strongly inferential, empirical tests" (Gowaty 2003: 903) can be designed with transgender people in mind.

2.   See Jaime M. Grant et al., esp. 183–84, for a helpful discussion about terminology and the category "gender-not-listed-here."

3.   It is also important to note that qualitative research designs, such as the ethnographic methods in which Labuski is trained and that she typically employs, are particularly well suited toward accomplishing these aims. The present discussion is limited to specific insights about quantitative methods that our coauthorship has helped us to develop, but this does not mean that we do not recognize the crucial role that qualitative methods play in representing the complexity of social life.

4.   Valentine is citing Joseph 2002 here.

References

APA (American Psychiatric Association). 2000. *Diagnostic and Statistical Manual of Mental Disorders*. 4th ed., text revision. Washington, DC: American Psychiatric Association.

Barad, Karen. 2007. *Meeting the Universe Halfway: Quantum Physics and the Entanglement of Matter and Meaning*. Durham, NC: Duke University Press.

Bennett, Jane. 2010. *Vibrant Matter: A Political Ecology of Things*. Durham, NC: Duke University Press.

Bockting, Walter, Autumn Benner, and Eli Coleman. 2009. "Gay and Bisexual Identity Development among Female-to-Male Transsexuals in North America: Emergence of a Transgender Sexuality." *Archives of Sexual Behavior* 38, no. 5: 688–701.

Butler, Judith. 2001. "Doing Justice to Someone: Sex Reassignment and Allegories of Transsexuality." *GLQ* 7, no. 4: 621–36.

Califia, Patrick. 2012. *Sex Changes: Transgender Politics*. Berkeley, CA: Cleis.

Cárdenas, Micha. 2012. *The Transreal: Political Aesthetics of Crossing Realities*. New York: Atropos.

Coole, Diana, and Samantha Frost. 2010. *New Materialisms: Ontology, Agency, and Politics*. Durham, NC: Duke University Press.

Devor, Holly. 1993. "Sexual Orientation Identities, Attractions, and Practices of Female-to-Male Transsexuals." *Journal of Sex Research* 30, no. 4: 303–15.

Devor, Holly. 1997. *FTM: Female-to-Male Transsexuals in Society*. Bloomington: Indiana University Press.

Diamond, Lisa. 2009. *Sexual Fluidity: Understanding Women's Love and Desire*. Cambridge, MA: Harvard University Press.

Dozier, Raine. 2005. "Beards, Breasts, and Bodies: Doing Gender in a Sexed World." *Gender and Society* 19, no. 3: 297–316.

Enke, Anne Finn. 2012. "Introduction: Transfeminist Perspectives." In *Transfeminist Perspectives in and beyond Transgender and Gender Studies*, edited by Anne Finn Enke, 1–15. Philadelphia: Temple University Press.

Feinberg, Leslie. 1992. *Transgender Liberation: A Movement Whose Time Has Come*. New York: World View Forum.

Goodman, Alan. 2006. "Two Questions about Race." Social Science Research Council, *Is Race Real?* (blog), June 7. raceandgenomics.ssrc.org/Goodman.

Gowaty, Patricia. 2003. "Sexual Natures: How Feminism Changed Evolutionary Biology." *Signs* 28, no. 3: 901–21.

Grant, Jaime M., et al. 2011. "Injustice at Every Turn: A Report of the National Transgender Discrimination Survey." Washington, DC: National Center for Transgender Equality and National Gay and Lesbian Task Force.

Green, Jamison. 2006. "Look! No, Don't! The Visibility Dilemma for Transsexual Men." In *The Transgender Studies Reader*, edited by Susan Stryker and Stephen Wittle, 499–508. New York: Routledge.

Halberstam, Judith. 1998. "Transgender Butch: Butch/FTM Border Wars and the Masculine Continuum." *GLQ* 4, no. 2: 287–310.

Harding, Sandra. 1986. "From the Woman Question in Science to the Science Question in Feminism." In *The Science Question in Feminism*, 14–29. Ithaca, NY: Cornell University Press.

Joseph, Miranda. 2002. "Family Affairs: The Discourse of Global/Localization." In *Queer Globalizations: Citizenship and the Afterlife of Colonialism*, edited by Arnaldo Cruz-Malave and Martin Manalansan, 71–99. New York: New York University Press.

Karkazis, Katrina. 2008. *Fixing Sex: Intersex, Medical Authority, and Lived Experience.* Durham, NC: Duke University Press.

Kuper, Laura E., Robin Nussbaum, and Brian Mustanski. 2012. "Exploring the Diversity of Gender and Sexual Orientation in an Online Sample of Transgender Individuals." *Journal of Sex Research* 49, nos. 2–3: 244–54.

Labuski, Christine. 2013. "Vulnerable Vulvas: Female Genital Integrity in Health and Dis-ease." *Feminist Studies* 39, no. 1: 248–76.

Loeb, Elizabeth. 2008. "Cutting It Off: Bodily Integrity, Identity Disorders, and the Sovereign Stakes of Corporeal Desire in U.S. Law." *WSQ* 36, nos. 3–4: 44–63.

Lombardi, Emilia. 2009. "Varieties of Transgender/Transsexual Lives and Their Relationship with Transphobia." *Journal of Homosexuality* 56, no. 8: 977–92.

Meezan, William, and James I. Martin. 2009a. "Doing Research on LGBT Populations: Moving the Field Forward." In Meezan and Martin 2009b, 415–27.

———, eds. 2009b. *Handbook of Research with Lesbian, Gay, Bisexual, and Transgender Populations.* New York: Routledge.

Meier, S., and Christine Labuski. 2013. "The Demographics of the Transsexual Population." In *International Handbook on the Demography of Sexuality*, edited by Amanda Baumle, 289–327. New York: Springer.

Meier, S., et al. 2011. "The Effects of Hormonal Gender Affirmation Treatment on Mental Health in Female-to-Male Transsexuals." *Journal of Gay and Lesbian Mental Health* 15, no. 3: 281–99.

——— 2013. "Measures of Clinical Health among Female-to-Male Transgender Persons as a Function of Sexual Orientation." *Archives of Sexual Behavior* 42, no. 3: 463–74.

Paxton, Keisha Carr, Heather Guentzel, and Kellii Trombacco. 2006. "Lessons Learned in Developing a Research Partnership with the Transgender Community." *American Journal of Community Psychology* 37, nos. 3–4: 349–56.

Prosser, Jay. 1998. *Second Skins: The Body Narratives of Transsexuality.* New York: Columbia University Press.

Rachlin, Katherine. 2009. "The Questions We Ask: Conducting Socially Conscious Research with Transgender Individuals." In Meezan and Martin 2009b, 261–79.

Roen, Katrina. 2001. "Transgender Theory and Embodiment: The Risk of Racial Marginalisation." *Journal of Gender Studies* 10, no. 3: 253–63.

Rosser, B. R. Simon, et al. 2007. "Capturing the Social Demographics of Hidden Sexual Minorities: An Internet Study of the Transgender Population in the United States." *Sexuality Research and Social Policy* 4, no. 2: 50–61.

Schacht, Steven P. 2002. "Four Renditions of Doing Female Drag: Feminine Appearing Conceptual Variations of a Masculine Theme." In *Gendered Sexualities*, vol. 6 of *Advances in Gender Research*, edited by Patricia Gagne and Richard Tewksbury, 157–80. Oxford: Elsevier Science.

Schiebinger, Londa. 2014. "Analyzing Gender." genderedinnovations.stanford.edu/methods /gender.html (accessed December 1, 2014).

Schilt, Kristin. 2006. "Just One of the Guys? How Transmen Make Gender Visible at Work." *Gender and Society* 20, no. 4: 465–90.

Schleifer, David. 2006. "Make Me Feel Mighty Real: Gay Female-to-Male Transgenderists Negotiating Sex, Gender, and Sexuality." *Sexualities* 9: 57–75.

Serano, Julia. 2012. "Reclaiming Femininity." In *Transfeminist Perspectives in and beyond Transgender and Gender Studies*, edited by Anne Enke, 170–83. Philadelphia: Temple University Press.

Silverschanz, Perry. 2009. "What's 'Queer' Got to Do with It? Enlightening Mainstream Research." In Meezan and Martin 2009b, 3–16.

Spade, Dean. 2006. "Mutilating Gender." In *The Transgender Studies Reader*, edited by Susan Stryker and Stephen Wittle, 315–32. New York: Routledge.

Spanier, Bonnie B., and Jessica D. Horowitz. 2011. "Looking for Difference? Methodology Is in the Eye of the Beholder." In *Gender and the Science of Difference: Cultural Politics of Contemporary Science and Medicine*, edited by Jill A. Fisher, 43–66. New Brunswick, NJ: Rutgers University Press.

Springer, Kristen W., Jeanne Mager Stellman, and Rebecca Jordan-Young. 2012. "Beyond a Catalogue of Differences: A Theoretical Frame and Good Practice Guidelines for Researching Sex/ Gender in Human Health." *Social Science and Medicine* 74, no. 11: 1817–24.

Stone, Sandy. 1998. "The *Empire* Strikes Back: A Posttranssexual Manifesto." In *The Visible Woman: Imaging Technologies, Gender, and Science*, edited by Paula A. Treichler, Lisa Cartwright, and Constance Penley, 285–309. New York: NYU Press.

Stryker, Susan. 2004. "Transgender Studies: Queer Theory's Evil Twin." *GLQ* 10, no. 2: 212–15.

———. 2006a. "(De)Subjugated Knowledges: An Introduction to Transgender Studies." In *The Transgender Studies Reader*, edited by Susan Stryker and Stephen Wittle, 1–17. New York: Routledge.

———. 2006b. "My Words to Victor Frankenstein above the Village of Chamounix." In *The Transgender Studies Reader*, edited by Susan Stryker and Stephen Wittle, 244–56. New York: Routledge.

Stryker, Susan, Paisley Currah, and Lisa Jean Moore. 2008. "Introduction: Trans-, Trans, or Transgender?" *WSQ* 36, nos. 3–4: 11–22.

Valentine, David. 2007. *Imagining Transgender: An Ethnography of a Category*. Durham, NC: Duke University Press.

———. 2012. "Sue E. Generous: Toward a Theory of Non-Transsexuality." *Feminist Studies* 38, no. 1: 185–211.

Vidal-Ortiz, Salvador. 2002. "Queering Sexuality and Doing Gender: Transgender Men's Iden-
tification with Gender and Sexuality." In *Gendered Sexualities*, vol. 6 of *Advances in Gender Research*, edited by Patricia Gagne and Richard Tewksbury, 181–233. Oxford: Elsevier Science.

Wheeler, Darrell P. 2009. "Methodological Issues in Conducting Community-Based Health and Social Services Research among Urban Black and African American LGBT Populations." In Meezan and Martin 2009b, 300–314.

Whittle, Stephen. 2006. "Where Did We Go Wrong: Feminism and Trans Theory—Two Teams on the Same Side?" In *The Transgender Studies Reader*, edited by Susan Stryker and Stephen Wittle, 194–202. New York: Routledge.

Lack of research for the health of gender minorities.

"Counting" Transgender and Gender-Nonconforming Adults in Health Research

Recommendations from the Gender Identity in US Surveillance Group

SARI L. REISNER, KERITH J. CONRON, SCOUT, KELLAN BAKER,
JODY L. HERMAN, EMILIA LOMBARDI, EMILY A. GREYTAK,
ALISON M. GILL, and ALICIA K. MATTHEWS, The GenIUSS Group

Abstract *Gender minority* refers to transgender and gender-nonconforming people whose sex assigned at birth is different from their current gender identity. US health surveillance systems do not routinely include questions to identify gender minority respondents, resulting in a lack of representative health data that can be used to evaluate the health of gender minorities. This omission represents a missed opportunity to understand the health and well-being of transgender and gender-nonconforming people as well as to learn more about sex and gender differences that may be relevant for the health of all people—gender minority and majority alike. In 2011, the Williams Institute at the University of California, Los Angeles, School of Law convened the Gender Identity in US Surveillance (GenIUSS) Group, bringing together a multidisciplinary and multi-institutional group of experts to increase population-based data about gender minority people through the inclusion of gender-related measures (e.g., assigned sex at birth, gender identity, transgender status) in surveys, with a particular consideration for publicly funded data-collection efforts. Drawing on the expertise and experience of the GenIUSS Group, this article provides an overview of challenges and opportunities and makes eight recommendations for "counting" gender minority adults in health research, with an emphasis on adult population-based surveys.
Keywords transgender, gender minority, disparities, health surveillance, measurement

Gender minority is an inclusive umbrella term that refers to transgender and gender-nonconforming people—people whose sex assigned at birth (natal sex) is different from their current gender identity (IOM 2011). US health surveillance systems monitoring adult health do not routinely include questions to

Gender minority

TSQ: Transgender Studies Quarterly ∗ Volume 2, Number 1 ∗ February 2015   **34**
DOI 10.1215/23289252-2848877   © 2015 Duke University Press

identify gender minority respondents, resulting in a lack of representative health data that can be used to evaluate the health of gender minorities (IOM 2011). This omission represents a missed opportunity to better understand the health and well-being of transgender and gender-nonconforming people who disproportionately face social stressors such as transgender stigma, discrimination, and violence that negatively impact their health and well-being (Bockting et al. 2013; Bradford et al. 2013; Clements-Nolle et al. 2001; Clements-Nolle, Marx, and Katz 2006; Grant et al. 2011; Herbst et al. 2008; Kenagy 2005; Lombardi et al. 2001; Nuttbrock et al. 2010; Reisner et al. 2014a, 2014b, 2014c) as well as to learn more about how sex and gender may be relevant for the health of all people (Krieger 2003), gender minority and gender nonminority alike.

In 2011, a landmark report by the Institute of Medicine identified the lack of brief, validated tools with which to identify gender minority respondents in health research as a current barrier to monitoring the health of the gender minority population (IOM 2011). In 2011, the Williams Institute at the University of California, Los Angeles, School of Law convened the Gender Identity in US Surveillance (GenIUSS) Group, bringing together a national multidisciplinary and multi-institutional group of experts to increase population-based data about gender minority people through the inclusion of gender-related measures (e.g., natal sex, gender identity, transgender status) in surveys, with a particular consideration for publicly funded data-collection efforts. To achieve this goal, the group mapped the landscape of current practices in gender-related population research, assessed methodological and other challenges to data collection, and generated a set of recommendations for gathering scientifically rigorous data about the needs and experiences of transgender and gender-nonconforming individuals (GenIUSS Group 2013). GenUISS also funded two mixed-methods cognitive-testing studies of gender-related measures for use in population-based research (Lombardi et al., in preparation; Reisner 2013; Reisner et al. 2014d).

Drawing on the expertise and experience of the GenIUSS Group, this article provides an overview of opportunities, challenges, and recommendations for "counting" transgender and gender-nonconforming adults in US population health research. First, we situate transgender and gender-nonconforming adult health research within a framework of sex and gender health disparities. Second, we review considerations for measurement of gender identity in adult population-based surveys and offer recommendations of measures that identify gender minority respondents and will enable inclusive health surveillance efforts. This article contains eight recommendations proposed by the GenIUSS Group to guide inclusive sex and gender adult population-based research (see appendix). A full report and list of recommendations can be found elsewhere (GenIUSS Group 2014). Additional measures and recommendations pertaining to adolescents and youth specifically can also be found elsewhere (Conron et al. 2014; GenIUSS Group 2014).

Sex and Gender as Social Determinants of Health

Sex and gender are recognized globally as social determinants of health and well-being across a wide variety of geographic settings and contexts (Doyal 2001, 2003; Krieger 2003; Nieuwenhoven and Klinge 2010; Nowatzki and Grant 2011; Vlassoff 2007; WHO 2008). Social determinants of health are root causes of health disparities (WHO 2008). Health disparity refers to "a particular type of difference in health . . . in which disadvantaged social groups—such as poor, racial/ethnic minorities, women, or other groups who have persistently experienced social disadvantage or discrimination—systematically experience worse health or greater health risks than more advantaged social groups" (Braveman 2006). Reducing health disparities is a core aim of Healthy People 2020 (US Department of Health and Human Services 2010), the science-based roadmap with ten-year national measurable objectives and goals for improving the health of all Americans. Bettering the health of all people includes addressing health inequities in the United States—defined as unfair and avoidable differences in health—related to sex and gender (Gorman and Read 2006; Read and Gorman 2006). Gender minority people are positioned at the intersection of complex sex and gender pathways; that is, causal mechanisms that cause poor health are both sex and gender related (Reisner et al. 2014e). Thus learning more about the social determinants of gender minority people's health and well-being is an important task to inform health equity for everyone.

US population-level surveys do not utilize standardized questions to collect information about sex and gender (Conron et al. 2014). Most surveys measure sex with a self-reported demographic question (male or female). Some surveys rely on telephone interviewers to assess perceived sex or gender based on the vocal tone of respondents (Conron et al. 2012, 2014). The lack of standardized measures of both sex and gender impacts the empirical rigor of research on sex and gender differences in US population health by obfuscating differences between natal sex (biological) and gender (social) pathways. Underlying non-standardization of measures is a lack of conceptual clarity about sex and gender that fails to recognize that (1) sex and gender represent distinct constructs; (2) sex and gender are multidimensional and dynamic; and (3) gender identity is not synonymous with sexual orientation.

Recommendation 1: That standardized self-report questions about both sex and gender be included in all surveys of the US population.
Despite the imprecise and often interchangeable use of sex ("female" and "male") and gender ("woman" and "man") in the scientific research literature (Krieger

2003), sex and gender are not one and the same. *Sex* refers to biological differences among females and males, such as genetics, hormones, secondary sex characteristics, and anatomy (Haig 2004). The assignment of sex at birth (female or male) is made by medical providers and is typically based on the appearance of external genitalia. Sex is then labeled and categorized as female or male and is usually documented on a birth certificate to become a legal construct. *Gender* typically refers to cultural meanings ascribed to or associated with patterns of behavior, experience, and personality that are labeled as feminine or masculine (IOM 2011). The lack of recognition that sex and gender are distinct constructs can be seen in US population survey practice. Some surveys rely on interviewer judgment to assess the sex of respondents (Conron et al. 2012; Conron et al. 2014). For example, neither sex nor gender are self-reported on the Behavioral Risk Factor Surveillance System (BRFSS); rather, these constructs are noted by the telephone interviewer (as sex based on interviewer-perceived tone of respondent voice) and confirmed with the respondent if needed (Conron et al. 2012). This would be a source of significant measurement error for gender minority respondents. Thus, the consequences of these measurement techniques are inappropriate data collection on gender minority populations. They also can lead to error in other situations, such as with people who smoke, or who have unusually high or low speaking voices. Measuring sex and gender in US population surveys will contribute to understanding and ameliorating sex and gender health inequities.

Recommendation 2: That multiple aspects of gender be measured in US population-based research, including gender identity.

Gender is a multidimensional construct (Egan and Perry 2001) that requires additional empirical and theoretical attention. Understanding gender means attending to the psychological, social, and behavioral dimensions that influence individual health and well-being and contribute to population-level health disparities. A key dimension of gender that represents an underinvestigated social determinant of population health is gender identity (IOM 2011). Gender *identity* refers to a person's internal sense of being man, woman, transgender, or another gender. US population-level surveys do not routinely include survey items to identify transgender and/or gender-nonconforming respondents; therefore, there is a lack of routine health surveillance data to monitor health disparities by gender identity (Conron et al. 2014; IOM 2011). Representative data that allow comparisons between gender minority and majority people are essential to document health inequities as well as to reduce sex and gender health disparities in the United States (Schwartz and Meyer 2010).

Despite the dearth of probability-based national-level data on the health of gender minority people (Conron et al. 2012), local, regional, and national studies suggest that transgender and gender-nonconforming people face stigma, prejudice, violence, and institutionalized discrimination in areas of everyday life such as health care, housing, employment, education, and legal recognition of their gender. As a result of these social stressors and socioeconomic marginalization, gender minority people appear highly burdened by adverse health outcomes including psychological distress, suicidality, substance use and abuse, tobacco use, HIV, and sexually transmitted infections (STIs) (Bockting et al. 2013; Bradford et al. 2013; Clements-Nolle et al. 2001; Clements-Nolle, Marx, and Katz 2006; Conron et al. 2012; Grant et al. 2011; Hendricks and Testa 2012; Herbst et al. 2008; Kenagy 2005; Nuttbrock et al. 2010; Reisner, Bailey, and Sevelius 2014; Reisner et al. 2014b, 2014c). Negative health outcomes appear to be exacerbated for transgender- and gender-nonconforming-identified people who experience intersecting oppressions as members of other disadvantaged social groups (Bowleg 2012), for example, people of color and/or those who are economically marginalized and living in poverty (Garofalo et al. 2006; Herbst et al. 2008). In addition to adverse health outcomes among people who identify as transgender and gender nonconforming, the negative health sequelae of having a nonconforming gender expression have also been documented (D'Augelli, Grossman, and Starks 2006; Rosario, Schrimshaw, and Hunter 2008; Sandfort, Melendez, and Diaz 2007; Skidmore, Linsenmeier, and Bailey 2006; Toomey et al. 2010), including recalled childhood nonconforming gender expression measured retrospectively (Calzo et al. 2014; Roberts et al. 2012, 2013; Rosario et al. 2014). Together these data suggest the need for routine health surveillance that takes gender identity into account.

Gender pathways are multilevel and sociohistorically and culturally dependent, and they dynamically change over time. Understanding gender means not only conceptualizing and measuring different dimensions of gender but also considering its dynamic nature. Gender is relational and fundamental to the social structuring of power and privilege (Courtenay 2000). Dimensions of gender affect people's health and well-being at multiple levels of influence (Ferrant 2014). Thus, gendered pathways can be best conceptualized using a social-ecological model (McLeroy et al. 1988) whereby individual, interpersonal, organizational, community, and public policy levels influence population health (see fig. 1).

Gender is also sociohistorically and culturally dependent, meaning gender diversity manifests differently in various contexts and settings and over time. Dimensions of gender are dynamic and may change across a person's individual development; for example, a person's gender expression may change from young adulthood to middle age. These changes have implications for health across the life course (Pearlin et al. 2005). Dimensions of gender may also change over time

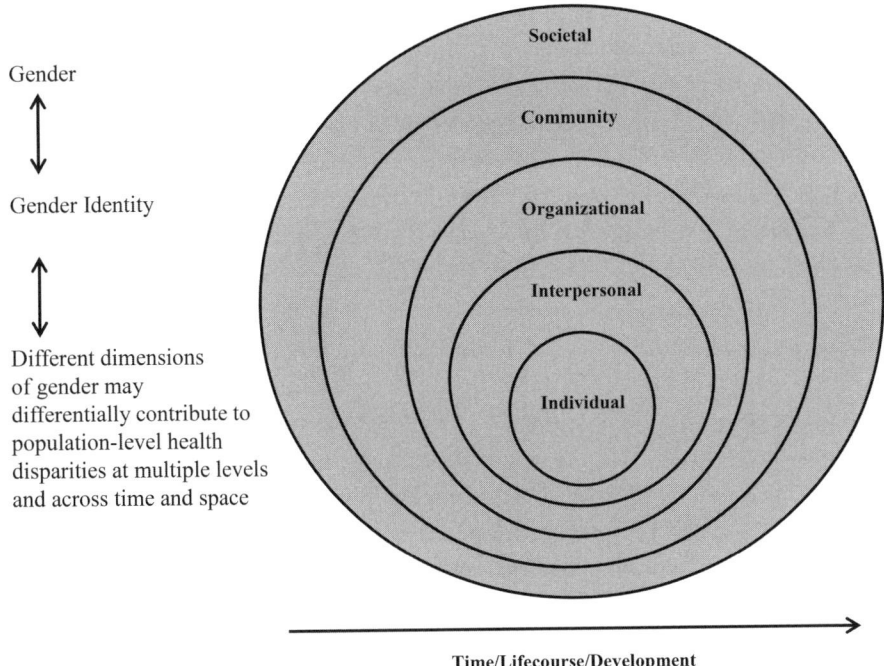

Gender

Gender Identity

Different dimensions of gender may differentially contribute to population-level health disparities at multiple levels and across time and space

Figure 1. Understanding gender as a social determinant of health

and throughout sociopolitical history—for example, intergenerational and age cohort shifts in gender-nonconforming expression or even what is acceptable as gender-nonconforming behavior (e.g., women wearing pants). These changes affect how gender diversity is conceptualized in population research. For example, over the past fifteen years there has been a paradigm shift in gender minority health research from a disease-based model (transgender and gender nonconforming as disorder) to an identity-based model (transgender and gender nonconforming as identity) (Bockting 2008, 2009). Conceptualizing transgender and gender-nonconforming people as having diverse, nonpathological gender identities and gender expressions rather than as "disordered" reformulates how a "case" is defined and measured in population research. Such redefinition of a case also affects prevalence estimates as to the number of gender minority people in the United States.

Recommendation 3: That questions specific to gender minorities be asked using skip patterns.

Gender minorities represent an underserved and underresearched population with specific medical and mental health needs (Grant et al. 2011; Grossman and D'Augelli 2006; Mayer et al. 2008), many of which remain unexplored. Collecting more high-quality data on the disparities associated with a transgender or gender-nonconforming identity and other social, economic, and health concerns of gender minority communities is essential if federal, state, local, and nonprofit agencies are to adequately serve transgender and gender-nonconforming people. Improved data are also necessary to allow researchers to better understand the backgrounds and needs of gender minority people and to help transgender advocates and their allies develop effective strategies for improving the circumstances of transgender and gender-nonconforming people's lives, including addressing inequities.

Many aspects of the needs and experiences of gender minority people remain unexplored (IOM 2011). Adding gender identity to surveys allows for skip patterns (a question or series of questions associated with a conditional response that can be skipped); thus questions specific to gender minorities can be asked. An example of questions that can be asked of gender minority respondents in skip patterns are those relating to gender affirmation (Sevelius 2013). Gender affirmation can be conceptualized across three domains: social (name, pronoun, disclosure of gender to others, passing), medical (hormones, surgery, etc.), and legal (name change, gender marker change, document amendments). All three domains may be relevant for the health of gender minority people and should be queried. Another example of questions for skip patterns are those relating to antitransgender discrimination (Bradford et al. 2013), resilience processes (Bockting et al. 2013), and coping (Budge, Adelson, and Howard 2013) in response to chronic adversity. Adding a gender minority–specific module of questions that a relatively small subset of respondents will be asked is a cost-effective endeavor. Although some cost will be incurred, this additional cost will be offset by the benefit of rendering visible the lives, experiences, and health of gender minority people.

Recommendation 4: A measure of gender identity does not replace sexual orientation (identity, attraction, behaviors). Measuring both gender identity and sexual orientation is recommended for US population-based surveys.

Gender identity is often mistakenly conflated with sexual orientation. As an example, the National Center for Health Statistics sexual identity question, which was added to the National Health Interview Survey (NHIS) in 2014 (CDC 2014), is an inadequate and inaccurate measure of gender identity. "Transgender" is one response option in a subset of "Something else" on the sexual orientation identity measure. The NHIS sexual orientation identity measure queries respondents as follows: "Which of the following best represents how you think of yourself?" with response options "Gay," "Straight, that is, not gay," "Bisexual," "Something else," "Refused," "I don't know the answer." If respondents answer "Something else," a subsequent question is asked that includes a response option for gender minority people: "What do you mean by something else?" with response options: "You are not straight, but identify with another label such as queer, trisexual, omnisexual or pansexual," "You are transgender, transsexual or gender variant," "You have not figured out or are in the process of figuring out your sexuality," "You do not think of yourself as having a sexuality," "You do not use labels to identify yourself," "You mean something else," "Refused," "Don't know."

There are several factors related to this measure that make it a decidedly poor measure for gender minority populations. A gender minority person who identifies their sexual orientation as any response option other than "Something else" will not be "counted" as a gender minority. Yet transgender and gender-nonconforming individuals, like anyone else, may identify as gay, straight, bisexual, or another sexual orientation; they may be attracted to people of any gender; and they may engage in sexual behaviors with people of any gender (Grant et al. 2011). The NHIS measure will likely underestimate the proportion of respondents who identify as transgender or gender nonconforming; thus we do not recommend this measure for population-based research in gender minority health. Survey designers should be aware that this question was not tested with the intention of capturing population prevalence estimates of gender minorities. This question assesses sexual orientation; thus a gender minority question should always accompany this measure.

Systematic data collection is key to the reduction of known health disparities (WHO 2008). After more than a decade of sustained effort by activists, researchers, and policy experts, there is now consensus around the importance of systematically collecting information related to sexual orientation (IOM 2011; SMART 2009). Similarly, precise measurement of sex and gender identity is needed in population-based research or else misclassification bias in sexual orientation-related data will occur. For example, a natal female who identifies her gender identity as a woman and who is sexually attracted to men may identify as "straight." However, a natal female who identifies his gender as a man and is sexually attracted to men may self-identify as "gay." Capturing sex only, without measurement of current gender identity, would result in misclassification of these sexual orientation identity data. In addition, the discriminatory treatment that some transgender and gender minority people suffer may be based in others' perceptions and understandings of gender identity and gender expression or sexual orientation (Gordon and Meyer 2007; Lombardi 2009). Therefore, data should be collected on sexual orientation and gender identity in order to fully study and understand the health disparities people face. Best practices for asking questions related to sexual orientation, including the three recommended dimensions of identity, attractions, and behaviors, have been described elsewhere (SMART 2009).

**General Considerations for Measurement of Transgender
and Gender-Nonconforming People on Population-Based Surveys**

Transgender and gender-nonconforming people live in communities across the country and complete general population surveys; however, they are invisible due to the absence of measures that would allow their responses to be identified and compared to those of gender majority respondents. The crucial first step in building the knowledge base about gender minority health is adding gender-related measures to publicly funded population surveys that can help characterize the needs of gender minority respondents and enhance the precision of the measurement of sex and gender differences in population health. The landscape of major federally supported surveys provides a key opportunity to gather demographic information about the US gender minority population as well as to gather information about the experiences of transgender and gender-nonconforming individuals across fields of inquiry where disparities affecting the gender minority population have been documented, including education, employment, health, military service, and criminal justice. Some of the largest and most important federally supported surveys in these fields include the American Community Survey, the Current Population Survey, the Survey of Income and Program Participation, the National Crime Victimization Survey, the National Health Interview Survey, the Behavioral Risk Factor Surveillance System, the National Inmate Survey, and the National Survey of Veterans. These surveys represent important sources of information about population-level health disparities in the United States, including by age, sex, and race/ethnicity. Adding gender identity to these and other publicly funded population surveys offers the unique opportunity to compare gender minorities and gender majorities.

*Recommendation 5: Build on "best practices" for asking about minority groups
on US population-based surveys: (1) gear questions asking about transgender
and gender-nonconforming status toward gender majority respondents;
(2) offer response options beyond binary "female"/"male" or "woman"/"man"
categories; (3) aggregate data over multiple years to ensure adequate
sample sizes.*

Three key issues related to collecting information about minority groups on population-based surveys are applicable and warrant consideration in the context of measurement of gender minority respondents. First, questions used to identify minority group members should be geared toward the majority group. Because a fairly small proportion of the US population is believed to be transgender (Conron et al. 2012; Gates 2011), it is imperative that questions included on general population surveys be easy for nonminority respondents to answer correctly. If even a small percentage of gender majority respondents incorrectly select answers that lead them to be classified as gender minority (scientifically termed "false positives"), the data collected will be of questionable utility.

Second, questions needed to identify minority group members must be acceptable to, and provide appropriate response options that resonate with, group members, even if the questions do not have the breadth and depth desired by minority group members. At the most basic level, this means offering more than two response options ("female"/"male" or "woman"/"man") on population-based surveys to allow for transgender and gender-nonconforming people to have an opportunity to identify themselves as gender minorities. This does not mean all gender minority people will select this option, as some do identify with the terms "female"/"male" or "woman"/"man." However, findings from the National Transgender Discrimination Survey (NTDS) (Grant et al. 2011), a community-based survey that sampled more than 6,400 US transgender adults, illustrate the importance of having a nonbinary response option in order to capture the diversity of gender identities and expressions that fall within the gender minority umbrella. In the NTDS, respondents were asked "What is your primary gender today?" with the responses "male/man," "female/woman," "part time as one gender, part time as another," and "a gender not listed here, please specify." More than one in ten respondents ($n = 860$) opted to write in a gender identity that was "not listed" (Harrison, Grant, and Herman 2011).

Third, the heterogeneity of gender minority identity and experience that is explored in community-specific surveys (Grant et al. 2011; Harrison, Grant, and Herman 2011) cannot be gathered in population-based surveys. Population-based surveys are intended to provide policy makers and public health planners with basic information about the needs and characteristics of geographically defined populations and of large sociodemographic groups within that population. Thus, unless they are designed to purposively oversample gender minority groups, population-based surveys typically do not have enough gender minority respondents to produce information about subgroups (e.g., female-to-male Latino young adults) within the gender minority population. As with any rare population data, aggregation over years is one of the primary methods for getting a sample size large enough to constructively analyze the health of transgender and gender-nonconforming people. For additional examples, approaches, and best practices associated with aggregation of data, please see the full GenIUSS report (GenIUSS Group 2014).

Recommended Measures for Gender Identity for Population-Based Surveys

Numerous examples exist of how to collect information about the gender minority population. Questions that would measure gender identity and enable survey respondents to be classified as gender minority or gender nonminority, often used in combination, include natal sex, gender identity, and transgender status. There are different strengths and limitations to measures and measurement approaches to gathering data about the health and sociodemographic characteristics of gender minority people. However, which questions to ask in order to produce data about the health needs and socioeconomic characteristics of transgender or gender-nonconforming respondents depends upon the goal of such an endeavor (i.e., purpose of data collection, outcome of interest, population that one wishes to generalize and serve), the measures already collected in existing surveys, and sample size considerations (GenIUSS Group 2014). Although future research is needed, particularly with more diverse, representative samples, there is already evidence of appropriate measures to include questions that classify gender minority and gender nonminority respondents in population-based surveys now.

Recommendation 6: When two demographic items can be added to an adult survey (or, in most instances, a standing measure of sex replaced and a measure of current gender identity added), inclusion of measures of assigned sex at birth and current gender identity is recommended.

Collecting information about assigned sex at birth (male, female) and current gender identity (e.g., man, woman, transgender) is often referred to as the two-step method to assess gender minority/gender nonminority status. First developed in 1997 by the Transgender Health Advocacy Coalition for use on a survey of transgender people in Philadelphia (Singer, Cochran, and Adamec 1997), the two-step method was subsequently adapted and used in the Washington Transgender Needs Assessment Survey (Xavier et al. 2005) and the Virginia Transgender Health Information Study (Bradford et al. 2013; Xavier, Honnold, and Bradford 2007). The two-step method uses two questions (assigned sex at birth and current gender identity) to cross-classify respondents as gender minority (discordant sex/gender responses) or gender nonminority (concordant sex/gender responses). The two-step method appears the most likely to have high sensitivity as well as high specificity with adults. Table 1 shows recommended measures for assigned sex at birth (a) and gender identity (b). It is unclear whether assigned sex at birth should precede or follow current gender identity; future studies should investigate ordering effects.

A 2013 study found that the two-step method was far more successful in identifying transgender respondents than a single, stand-alone gender identity item that offered a transgender response option (Tate, Ledbetter, and Youssef 2013). This study also found that some transgender individuals identify their gender as male or female and not as transgender and thus will be missed if a gender identity measure is used alone. Additional research by GenIUSS Group members that conducted cognitive testing of survey items supports the validity of a two-step method implemented using different response options (Conron,

Table 1. Recommended gender measures from the GenIUSS group

(a) Assigned sex at birth
What sex were you assigned at birth, on your original birth certificate? (check one)
- ☐ Male
- ☐ Female

(b) Current gender identity
How do you describe yourself? (check one)
- ☐ Male
- ☐ Female
- ☐ Transgender
- ☐ Do not identify as male, female, or transgender

(c) Transgender status
Some people describe themselves as transgender when they experience a different gender identity from their sex at birth. For example, a person who was born into a male body but who feels female or lives as a woman. Do you consider yourself to be transgender?
- ☐ Yes, transgender, male to female
- ☐ Yes, transgender, female to male
- ☐ Yes, transgender, gender nonconforming
- ☐ No

Note—Additional information for telephone interviewer if asked about definition of transgender:
Some people describe themselves as transgender when they experience a different gender identity from their sex at birth. For example, a person who was born into a male body but who feels female or lives as a woman would be transgender. Some transgender people change their physical appearance so that it matches their internal gender identity. Some transgender people take hormones and some have surgery. A transgender person may be of any sexual orientation— straight, gay, lesbian, or bisexual.
Note—Additional information for interviewer if asked about definition of gender nonconforming:
Some people think of themselves as gender nonconforming when they do not identify only as a man or only as a woman.

(d) LGBT identity
Do you think of yourself as (please check all that apply):
- ☐ Straight
- ☐ Gay or lesbian
- ☐ Bisexual
- ☐ Transgender, transsexual, or gender nonconforming
If yes to transgender, then probe:
- ☐ Transgender, male to female OR
- ☐ Transgender, female to male OR
- ☐ Gender variant
- ☐ Transsexual

Scout, and Austin 2008; Lombardi et al., in preparation; Reisner et al. 2014d). A two-step approach has also been used in online research by GenIUSS Group members in Latin America/the Caribbean, Portugal, and Spain (Reisner et al. 2014e). In 2011, the US Centers for Disease Control and Prevention added sex and gender identity data elements to the US HIV/AIDS surveillance system, including the Adult Case Report Form, as well as to its electronic case-reporting surveillance system, called the Enhanced HIV/AIDS Reporting System (eHARS) (CDC 2013a). A unique strength of the two-step method is that it takes into account both natal sex (biological) and gender (social) processes, which are key for health research and epidemiological studies of health (Krieger 2003).

A visual schematic of measurement using this method is shown in figure 2, illustrated using the two survey items and response options from the 2010 wave of the Growing Up Today Study (GUTS), a national cohort of more than sixteen thousand adolescents and young adults followed prospectively since 1996 (Reisner 2013). A gender minority person endorsing a male sex assigned at birth may identify their current gender identity as female (cross-sex identity), male-to-female transgender (transgender identity), or another gender identity (do not identify as male, female, or transgender); all individuals who fall into these categories can be counted as gender minorities. Further, differences by identity can be investigated, assuming adequate sample sizes. Thus cross-sex-identified respondents can be compared to transgender-identified respondents or to non-binary gender-identified people, or assigned female sex at birth can be compared to assigned male sex at birth. This item has been tested with "check one" instructions (Reisner et al. 2014d); however, based on the GenIUSS Group's collective experience in the field and work with gender minority communities, additional testing of this item using "check all that apply" instructions is suggested.

Since 2007, the Center of Excellence for Transgender Health at the University of California, San Francisco, has advocated the use of a specific two-step question protocol in health care settings where data are collected by a second party (e.g., a health provider) (Sausa et al. 2009). An applied example of how the two-step method can aid in culturally competent care in clinical settings and avoid epidemiological misclassification can be found in prostate health. Natal males have a prostate and natal females do not. Therefore, natal males need routine preventive prostate cancer screening regardless of their current identity (CoE 2011; Deutsch et al. 2013; Feldman 2007; Feldman and Goldberg 2006) and should also be in the denominator of a population prevalence estimate documenting utilization of preventive screening for prostate cancer.

Recommendation 7: When valid self-report measures of assigned sex at birth and current gender identity are not on a survey and cannot be added (or replace existing measures) and a valid measure of sexual orientation is already on a survey, then the Massachusetts Behavioral Risk Factor Surveillance System (BRFSS) stand-alone demographic item is recommended.

In 2007, a single-item measure of gender minority/gender nonminority status was added to the MA-BRFSS. The BRFSS is a national collaborative health surveillance effort between the CDC and state departments of public health. Each year, a

STEP 1: SEX

What sex were you assigned at birth, on your original birth certificate? (check one)

Male

Female

STEP 2: GENDER IDENTITY

How do you describe yourself? (check one)

Male

Female

Transgender

Do Not Identify as Male, Female, or Transgender

	Assigned Sex[a]	
	Male (male sex on original birth certificate) ♂	**Female** (female sex on original birth certificate) ♀
Current Gender Identity		
Male	**Cisgender Male[b]** (male birth sex, male gender identity) ♂	**Cross-Sex Male Identity** (female birth sex, male gender identity) ⚧
Female	**Cross-Sex Female Identity** (male birth sex, female gender identity) ⚧	**Cisgender Female** (female birth sex, female gender identity) ♀
Transgender	**Transgender Identity** (male birth sex, transgender identity) ⚧	**Transgender Identity** (female birth sex, transgender identity) ⚧
Do Not Identify as Male, Female, or Transgender	**Do Not Identify** (male birth sex, some other diverse gender identity) ⚧	**Do Not Identify** (female birth sex, some other diverse gender identity) ⚧

Figure 2. Conceptual overview: natal sex and current gender identity measurement using a two-step method in the Growing Up Today Study 1 (Reisner et al. 2014d).
[a]Infants born intersex are assigned either a female or male birth sex by a medical provider at birth.
[b]The term *cisgender* is used to refer to non-transgender individuals. The prefix *cis-* in Latin means "on this side of," opposed to *trans* or *ultra*, meaning across or beyond. Gender minority would be operationalized by collapsing people with a cross-sex identity, transgender identity, or who identify with a gender other than male, female, or transgender.

household probability sample of adults who can be reached by telephone is drawn using random digit dial methods. Topics such as health insurance coverage, cancer screening, and sexual behavior are assessed with core questions provided by the CDC. States may add supplemental questions to their own state surveys. A single-item measure that would permit respondents to be classified as gender minority and gender nonminority was initially developed by transgender community leaders and research allies for inclusion on the 2001 Boston BRFSS survey. Analyses of MA-BRFSS data collected between 2007 and 2009 indicate that 0.5 percent of eighteen- to sixty-four-year-old adults answered yes to this question and were classified as gender minority (Conron et al. 2012). The nonresponse rate (1.4 percent) for this item was very low; in fact, it was lower than the nonresponse rate for sexual orientation and much lower than the nonresponse rate for income on the same survey. A slightly modified version of this item is shown in table 1 (c) as well as a sexual orientation identity item; together, these questions were adopted by the Centers for Disease Control and Prevention in 2013 as an optional "sexual orientation and gender identity" module that states can include on their Behavioral Risk Factor Surveillance Surveys.

Recommendation 8: When valid self-report measures of assigned sex at birth and current gender identity are not on a survey and cannot be added (or replace existing measures), and a valid measure of sexual orientation identity is not already on a survey and cannot be added, then a stand-alone demographic item is recommended (without a write-in response option) that includes sexual orientation and gender identity. In 2008, the National Network for LGBT Tobacco Control (now the Network for LGBT Health Equity) developed and tested a single-item measure of gender identity and sexual orientation for Blue Cross Blue Shield of Minnesota. This question is a measure of LGBT status and queries about sexual orientation and transgender identity in a format that allows both aspects of identity to be independently reported through a "check all that apply" mechanism (table 1, d). In 2008, this measure was cognitively tested in a diverse sample (including oversamples of people of color, LGB, and transgender people) in Minnesota and has been part of the state's surveillance system since then. Importantly, this item successfully prevented false positives by steering gender nonminority respondents, including those who did not understand what *transgender* meant, away from the transgender response option.

Discussion

A critical first step in building the knowledge base about gender minority health is adding gender-related measures to publicly funded population surveys. These measures can help characterize the needs of transgender and gender-nonconforming respondents and gain precision in sex and gender differences in health more broadly. One of the challenges that has been raised related to transgender data collection is the relative value of adding measures that are only expected to collect data from 0.5 percent of the general population (Conron et al. 2012). This is an estimated 1.569 million US citizens. Federally funded national surveys collect and report data on subpopulations and health conditions that affect far fewer than this number of citizens (CDC 2013b).

To reduce the widening inequities in health across a variety of social determinants, including gender, the World Health Organization recommends that researchers "measure and understand the problem and assess the impact of action" (WHO 2008). Incorporating gender-related measures that allow for identification of gender minorities in national and federal surveys will allow public health data systems to document and understand a range of health disparities by transgender and gender-nonconforming identity and allow for the development of targeted public health efforts that are responsive to the lived realities of populations at the highest risk of poorer health. The potential "cost" of the few survey items that will need to be added is far outweighed by the public health benefits of the resulting knowledge.

The GenIUSS Group has identified additional gender-related measurement research that needs to be undertaken. Cognitive testing of survey measures in Spanish represents a key area for future measurement research. Research with more diverse samples is also needed, including by race/ethnicity and socioeconomic status. For example, anecdotal evidence and qualitative data (Hwahng and Nuttbrock 2007; Valentine 2007) show that there may be differences in nomenclature for transgender and gender-nonconforming identities based on race/ethnicity. Further research is needed to determine whether and how differences in the language of self-identity among people of color impacts our ability to accurately capture and reflect their experiences in population-based research. Another area of needed research is how to accurately identify intersex people on population surveys—people with a "difference of sexual development" or other intersex condition (GenIUSS Group 2014; IOM 2011).

We have focused on gender identity in this article. However, gender expression represents an important determinant of health (Calzo et al. 2014; Corby, Hodges, and Perry 2007; D'Augelli, Grossman, and Starks 2006; Egan and Perry 2001; Roberts et al. 2012, 2013; Rosario, Schrimshaw, and Hunter 2008; Rosario et al. 2014; Sandfort, Melendez, and Diaz 2007; Skidmore, Linsenmeier, and Bailey 2006; Toomey et al. 2010). People with gender-nonconforming gender expression may or may not self-identify as transgender, and they may or may not identify as sexual minority (Wylie et al. 2010). Survey respondents can be characterized along a continuum of current and/or recalled childhood gender conformity and nonconformity. Indeed, recalled childhood gender-nonconforming expression has been shown to be a critical determinant of health (Calzo et al. 2014; Roberts et al. 2012, 2013). It is important to note that accurate characterizations of respondents as gender nonconforming also depend upon the availability of accurate data about assigned sex at birth. Future research is needed to identify recommended gender-expression measures for population-based surveys.

The GenIUSS Group notes that population-based research is not the only source of meaningful data about gender minorities. Diversifying sources of information that contribute to the knowledge base in gender minority health is important for future research efforts. Community-based surveys represent an important and valuable source of information about transgender and gender-nonconforming health. Research that uses community-based participatory research (CBPR) principles and that works *with* transgender and gender-nonconforming communities to identify and address their specific health-related needs (Leung, Yen, and Minkler 2004) is especially vital for gender minority health research, given that transgender and gender-nonconforming people largely represent a "hidden" population. Large samples of transgender and gender-nonconforming people are efficiently reached through social network linkages to other gender minority people and their allies. The best example of large-scale application of CBPR principles with gender minority communities to gather information about specific health-related issues affecting gender minority adults is the US NTDS (Grant et al. 2011). Between September 2008 and March 2009, more than 6,400 transgender adults were recruited using multimodal data collection methods (in person and online) to ensure a sociodemographically and geographically diverse national sample (Reisner et al. 2014a). NTDS remains the largest sample of US gender minorities to date. Data from NTDS led to widespread advocacy and policy changes that benefit the health and well-being of transgender and gender-nonconforming individuals. Surveys such as NTDS can lead to rigorous community-based research that engages communities and contributes to transgender and gender-nonconforming health, including methodological innovations (Reisner et al. 2014a).

Survey research is only one means of collecting data to assess the experiences of the gender minority population. Clinical settings and electronic health records (EHR) have been identified as important and underutilized sources of information about sexual and gender minority health disparities (Cahill and Makadon 2014; Deutsch et al. 2013). Clinical settings and EHR are particularly valuable in light of the dearth of comparative data that exist to understand the health and well-being of gender minorities relative to gender nonminorities.

Other sources include administrative data such as the data collected by government agencies to monitor compliance with civil rights laws, cohort studies that offer unique longitudinal and developmental data, and other cohort-related surveillance systems such as those maintained by the Department of Veterans Affairs. Addition of gender-related measures—along with measures related to sexual orientation—to clinical settings, EHR, and other administration data collection systems represents an important way forward to reduce health disparities and improve population health.

In coming years, the addition and refinement of questions that measure gender identity will allow researchers, policy makers, and transgender and gender-nonconforming individuals themselves to add to the science about transgender and gender-nonconforming health and, in time, to monitor and evaluate efforts to eliminate health disparities and achieve health equity. Such an endeavor also offers the opportunity to learn more about sex and gender differences that may be relevant for the health of all people—gender minority and majority alike.

Sari L. Reisner, ScD, is a postdoctoral research fellow in the Department of Epidemiology at Harvard School of Public Health and a research scientist at the Fenway Institute at Fenway Health. He is the author of more than sixty peer-reviewed publications in sexual and gender minority health.

Kerith J. Conron, ScD, MPH, is a research scientist at the Fenway Institute at Fenway Health. She is adjunct assistant professor in the Department of Health Sciences at Northeastern University, and visiting scholar at the Heller School of Social Policy at Brandeis University.

Scout, PhD, is the director of LGBT HealthLink, the health arm of the national community of LGBT centers, and an adjunct assistant professor at Boston University. He leads one of the CDC's eight national tobacco and cancer disparity networks and is a *Huffington Post* blogger.

Kellan Baker is a senior fellow with the LGBT Research and Communications Project at the Center for American Progress, where he focuses on federal policy initiatives relating to LGBT health and data collection.

Jody L. Herman, PhD, is the Peter J. Cooper Public Policy Fellow and manager of transgender research at the Williams Institute at the University of California, Los Angeles, School of Law. She holds a PhD in public policy and public administration from the George Washington University.

Emilia Lombardi, PhD, is an assistant professor in Baldwin Wallace University's Department of Public Health, School of Health Sciences. She has a PhD in sociology and has been examining health disparities among transgender populations since the mid-1990s and has authored many peer-reviewed papers on transgender health issues.

Emily A. Greytak, PhD, is the director of research at GLSEN (Gay, Lesbian and Straight Education Network), a national education organization addressing LGBT issues in K–12 schools. She regularly presents and publishes research in scholarly and practitioner outlets and has particular expertise in transgender youth issues and educator professional development.

Alison M. Gill, JD, is the senior legislative counsel at the Human Rights Campaign, where she focuses on advocacy related to state legislation, LGBT youth issues, transgender issues, and data collection.

Alicia Matthews, PhD, is nationally known for health disparities research with underserved populations, primarily focused on the development and evaluation of culturally targeted cancer risk reduction interventions. Dr. Matthews is an associate professor and clinical psychologist with more than fifteen years of experience in examining determinants of cancer-related health disparities with a particular focus on African American and LGBT populations. Recent research focuses on the use of community-based and culturally targeted health promotion interventions to reduce risk factors associated with cancer disparities, including smoking cessation treatments.

References

Bockting, W. O. 2008. "Psychotherapy and the Real-Life Experience: From Gender Dichotomy to Gender Diversity." *Sexologies* 17, no. 4: 211–24.

———. 2009. "Transforming the Paradigm of Transgender Health: A Field in Transition." *Sexual and Relationship Therapy* 24, no. 2: 103–7.

Bockting, W. O., et al. 2013. "Stigma, Mental Health, and Resilience in an Online Sample of the US Transgender Population." *American Journal of Public Health* 103, no. 5: 943–51.

Bowleg, Lisa. 2012. "The Problem with the Phrase Women and Minorities: Intersectionality—An Important Theoretical Framework for Public Health." *American Journal of Public Health* 102, no. 7: 1267–73.

Bradford, Judith, et al. 2013. "Experiences of Transgender-Related Discrimination and Implications for Health: Results from the Virginia Transgender Health Initiative Study." *American Journal of Public Health* 103, no. 10: 1820–29.

Braveman, Paula. 2006. "Health Disparities and Health Equity: Concepts and Measurement." *Annual Review of Public Health* 27: 167–94.

Budge, Stephanie L., Jill L. Adelson, and Kimberly A. S. Howard. 2013. "Anxiety and Depression in Transgender Individuals: The Roles of Transition Status, Loss, Social Support, and Coping." *Journal of Consulting and Clinical Psychology* 81, no. 3: 545–57.

Cahill, Sean, and Harvey Makadon. 2014. "Sexual Orientation and Gender Identity Data Collection in Clinical Settings and in Electronic Health Records: A Key to Ending LGBT Health Disparities." *LGBT Health* 1, no. 1: 34–41.

Calzo, Jerel P., et al. 2014. "Physical Activity Disparities in Heterosexual and Sexual Minority Youth Ages 12–22 Years Old: Roles of Childhood Gender Nonconformity and Athletic Self-Esteem." *Annals of Behavioral Medicine* 47, no. 1: 17–27.

CoE (Center of Excellence for Transgender Health). 2011. *Primary Care Protocol for Transgender Patient Care*. San Francisco: University of California, San Francisco. transhealth.ucsf .edu/trans?page=protocol-00-00.

CDC (Centers for Disease Control and Prevention). 2013a. "HIV among Transgender People." www.cdc.gov/hiv/risk/transgender.

———. 2013b. HIV/AIDS, "Statistics Overview." www.cdc.gov/hiv/statistics/basics.

———. 2014. National Health Interview Survey, "Questionnaires, Datasets, and Related Documentation 1997 to the Present." www.cdc.gov/nchs/nhis/quest_data_related_1997 _forward.htm.

Clements-Nolle, Kristen, et al. 2001. "HIV Prevalence, Risk Behaviors, Health Care Use, and Mental Health Status of Transgender Persons: Implications for Public Health Intervention." *American Journal of Public Health* 91, no. 6: 915–21.

Clements-Nolle, Kristen, Rani Marx, and Mitchell Katz. 2006. "Attempted Suicide among Transgender Persons: The Influence of Gender-Based Discrimination and Victimization." *Journal of Homosexuality* 51, no. 3: 53–69.

Conron, Kerith J., et al. 2012. "Transgender Health in Massachusetts: Results from a Household Probability Sample of Adults." *American Journal of Public Health* 102, no. 1: 118–22.

———. 2014. "Sex and Gender in the US Health Surveillance System: A Call to Action." *American Journal of Public Health* 104, no. 6: 970–76.

Conron, Kerith Jane, Scout, and S. Bryn Austin. 2008. "'Everyone Has a Right to, Like, Check Their Box': Findings on a Measure of Gender Identity from a Cognitive Testing Study with Adolescents." *Journal of LGBT Health Research* 4, no. 1: 1–9.

Corby, Brooke C., Ernest V. Hodges, and David G. Perry. 2007. "Gender Identity and Adjustment in Black, Hispanic, and White Preadolescents." *Developmental Psychology* 43, no. 1: 261–66.

Courtenay, Will H. 2000. "Constructions of Masculinity and Their Influence on Men's Well-Being: A Theory of Gender and Health." *Social Science and Medicine* 50, no. 10: 1385–401.

D'Augelli, Anthony R., Arnold H. Grossman, and Michael. T. Starks. 2006. "Childhood Gender Atypicality, Victimization, and PTSD among Lesbian, Gay, and Bisexual Youth." *Journal of Interpersonal Violence* 21, no. 11: 1462–82.

Deutsch, Madeline B., et al. 2013. "Electronic Medical Records and the Transgender Patient: Recommendations from the World Professional Association for Transgender Health EMR Working Group." *Journal of the American Medical Informatics Association* 20, no. 4: 700–703.

Doyal, Lesley. 2001. "Sex, Gender, and Health: The Need for a New Approach." *British Medical Journal* 323, no. 7320: 1061–63.

———. 2003. "Sex and Gender: The Challenges for Epidemiologists." *International Journal of Health Services* 33, no. 3: 569–79.

Egan, Susan K., and David G. Perry. 2001. "Gender Identity: A Multidimensional Analysis with Implications for Psychosocial Adjustment." *Developmental Psychology* 37, no. 4: 451–63.

Feldman, Jamie. 2007. "Preventive Care of the Transgendered Patient: An Evidence-Based Approach." In *Principles of Transgender Medicine and Surgery*, edited by Randy Ettner, Stan Monstrey, and A. Evan Eyler, 34–38. New York: Haworth.

Feldman, Jamie L., and Joshua M. Goldberg. 2006. "Transgender Primary Medical Care." *International Journal of Transgenderism* 9, nos. 3–4: 3–34.

Ferrant, Gaëlle. 2014. "The Multidimensional Gender Inequalities Index (MGII): A Descriptive Analysis of Gender Inequalities Using MCA." *Social Indicators Research* 115, no. 2: 653–90.

Field, Alison E., et al. 1999. "Overweight, Weight Concerns, and Bulimic Behaviors among Girls and Boys." *Journal of the American Academy of Child and Adolescent Psychiatry* 38, no. 6: 754–60.

Garofalo, Robert, et al. 2006. "Overlooked, Misunderstood, and At-Risk: Exploring the Lives and HIV Risk of Ethnic Minority Male-to-Female Transgender Youth." *Journal of Adolescent Health* 38, no. 3: 230–36.

Gates, Gary J. 2011. "How Many People are Lesbian, Gay, Bisexual, and Transgender?" Williams Institute. williamsinstitute.law.ucla.edu/wp-content/uploads/Gates-How-Many-People -LGBT-Apr-2011.pdf.

GenIUSS Group (Gender Identity in US Surveillance). 2013. "Gender-Related Measures Overview." Los Angeles: Williams Institute, University of California, Los Angeles, School of Law. williamsinstitute.law.ucla.edu/wp-content/uploads/GenIUSS-Gender-related -Question-Overview.pdf

———. 2014. "Best Practices for Asking Questions to Identify Transgender Respondents on Population-Based Surveys." Los Angeles: Williams Institute, University of California, Los Angeles, School of Law. williamsinstitute.law.ucla.edu/wp-content/uploads/geniuss -report-sep-2014.pdf.

Gordon, Allegra R., and Ilan H. Meyer. 2007. "Gender Nonconformity as a Target of Prejudice, Discrimination, and Violence against LGB Individuals." *Journal of LGBT Health Research* 3, no. 3: 55–71.

Gorman, Bridget K., and Jen'nan Ghazal Read. 2006. "Gender Disparities in Adult Health: An Examination of Three Measures of Morbidity." *Journal of Health and Social Behavior* 47, no. 2: 95–110.

Grant, Jaime, et al. 2011. "Injustice at Every Turn: A Report of the National Transgender Discrimination Survey." Washington, DC: National Center for Transgender Equality and National Gay and Lesbian Task Force.

Grossman, Arnold H., and Anthony R. D'Augelli. 2006. "Transgender Youth: Invisible and Vulnerable." *Journal of Homosexuality* 51, no. 1: 111–28.

Haig, David. 2004. "The Inexorable Rise of Gender and the Decline of Sex: Social Change in Academic Titles, 1945–2001." *Archives of Sexual Behavior* 33, no. 2: 87–96.

Harrison, Jack, Jaime Grant, and Jody L. Herman. 2011. "A Gender Not Listed Here: Genderqueers, Gender Rebels, and Otherwise in the National Transgender Discrimination Survey." *LGBTQ Policy Journal at the Harvard Kennedy School* 2: 13–24.

Hendricks, Michael L., and Rylan J. Testa. 2012. "A Conceptual Framework for Clinical Work with Transgender and Gender Nonconforming Clients: An Adaptation of the Minority Stress Model." *Professional Psychology: Research and Practice* 43, no. 5: 460–67.

Herbst, Jeffrey H., et al. 2008. "Estimating HIV Prevalence and Risk Behaviors of Transgender Persons in the United States: A Systematic Review." *AIDS and Behavior* 12, no. 1: 1–17.

Hwahng, Sel Julian, and Larry Nuttbrock. 2007. "Sex Workers, Fem Queens, and Cross-Dressers: Differential Marginalizations and HIV Vulnerabilities among Three Ethnocultural Male-to-Female Transgender Communities in New York City." *Sexuality Resesearch and Social Policy* 4, no. 4: 36–59.

IOM (Institute of Medicine). 2011. *The Health of Lesbian, Gay, Bisexual, and Transgender People: Building a Foundation for Better Understanding.* Washington, DC: National Academic Press.

Kenagy, Gretchen P. 2005. "Transgender Health: Findings from Two Needs Assessment Studies in Philadelphia." *Health and Social Work* 30, no. 1: 19–26.

Krieger, Nancy. 2003. "Genders, Sexes, and Health: What Are the Connections—and Why Does It Matter?" *International Journal of Epidemiology* 32, no. 4: 652–57.

Leung, Margaret W., Irene H. Yen, and Meredith Minkler. 2004. "Community-Based Participatory Research: A Promising Approach for Increasing Epidemiology's Relevance in the Twenty-First Century." *International Journal of Epidemiology* 33, no. 3: 499–506.

Lombardi, Emilia. 2009. "Varieties of Transgender/Transsexual Lives and Their Relationship with Transphobia." *Journal of Homosexuality* 56, no. 8: 977–92.

Lombardi, Emilia, et al. 2001. "Gender Violence: Transgender Experiences with Violence and Discrimination." *Journal of Homosexuality* 42, no. 1: 89–101.

———. In preparation. "Examination of Gender Identity and Expression Measures within a Midwest Sample: Results from the Population-Based Gender Identity Measurement Small Research Project."

Mayer, Kenneth H., et al. 2008. "Sexual and Gender Minority Health: What We Know and What Needs to Be Done." *American Journal of Public Health* 98, no. 6: 989–95.

McLeroy, Kenneth R., et al. 1988. "An Ecological Perspective on Health Promotion Programs." *Health Education Quarterly* 15, no. 4: 351–77.

Nieuwenhoven, Linda, and Ineke Klinge. 2010. "Scientific Excellence in Applying Sex- and Gender-Sensitive Methods in Biomedical and Health Research." *Journal of Womens Health* 19, no. 2: 313–21.

Nowatzki, Nadine, and Karen R. Grant. 2011. "Sex is Not Enough: The Need for Gender-Based Analysis in Health Research." *Health Care for Women International* 32, no. 4: 263–77.

Nuttbrock, Larry, et al. 2010. "Psychiatric Impact of Gender-Related Abuse across the Life Course of Male-to-Female Transgender Persons." *Journal of Sex Research* 47, no. 1: 12–23.

Pearlin, Leonard I., et al. 2005. "Stress, Health, and the Life Course: Some Conceptual Perspectives." *Journal of Health and Social Behavior* 46, no. 2: 205–19.

Read, Jen'nen Ghazal, and Bridget K. Gorman. 2006. "Gender Inequalities in US Adult Health: The Interplay of Race and Ethnicity." *Social Science and Medicine* 62, no. 5: 1045–65.

Reisner, Sari L. 2013. "Gender Identity as a Social Determinant of Health: Methods for Transgender Health Research." ScD diss., Harvard School of Public Health.

Reisner, Sari L., et al. 2014a. "Comparing In-Person and Online Survey Respondents in the U.S. National Transgender Discrimination Survey: Implications for Transgender Health Research." *LGBT Health* 1, no. 2: 98–106.

———. 2014b. "Dyadic Effects of Gender Minority Stressors in Substance Use Behaviors among Transgender Women and Their Non-Transgender Male Sex Partners." *Psychology of Sexual Orientation and Gender Diversity* 1, no. 1: 63–71.

———. 2014c. "Gender Minority Social Stress in Adolescence: Disparities in Adolescent Bullying and Substance Use by Gender Identity." *Journal of Sex Research.* doi:10.1080/00224499.2014.886321.

———. 2014d. "Monitoring the Health of Transgender and Other Gender Minority Populations: Validity of Natal Sex and Gender Identity Survey Items in a US National Cohort of Young Adults." *BMC Public Health* 14: 1224. doi:10.1186/1471-2458-14-1224.

———. 2014e. "Using a Two-Step Method to Measure Transgender Identity in Latin America/the Caribbean, Portugal, and Spain." *Archives of Sexual Behavior* 43, no. 8: 1503–14.

Reisner, Sari L., Zinzi Bailey, and Jae Sevelius. 2014. "Racial/Ethnic Disparities in History of Incarceration, Experiences of Victimization, and Associated Health Indicators among Transgender Women in the U.S." *Women and Health* 54, no. 8: 750–67. doi:10.1080/03630242.2014.932891.

Roberts, Andrea L., et al. 2012. "Childhood Gender Nonconformity: A Risk Indicator for Childhood Abuse and Posttraumatic Stress in Youth." *Pediatrics* 129, no. 3: 410–17.

———. 2013. "Childhood Gender Nonconformity, Bullying Victimization, and Depressive Symptoms across Adolescence and Early Adulthood: An Eleven-Year Longitudinal Study." *Journal of the American Academy of Child and Adolescent Psychiatry* 52, no. 2: 143–52.

Rosario, Margaret, Eric W. Schrimshaw, and Joyce Hunter. 2008. "Butch/Femme Differences in Substance Use and Abuse among Young Lesbian and Bisexual Women: Examination and Potential Explanations." *Substance Use and Misuse* 43, nos. 8–9: 1002–15.

Rosario, Margaret, et al. 2014. "Disparities in Depressive Distress by Sexual Orientation in Emerging Adults: The Roles of Attachment and Stress Paradigms." *Archives of Sexual Behavior* 43, no. 5: 901–16.

Sandfort, Theo G., Rita M. Melendez, and Rafael M. Diaz. 2007. "Gender Nonconformity, Homophobia, and Mental Distress in Latino Gay and Bisexual Men." *Journal of Sex Research* 44, no. 2: 181–89.

Sausa, L. A., et al. 2009. "Policy Recommendations for Inclusive Data Collection of Trans People in HIV Prevention, Care, and Services." San Francisco: Center of Excellence for Transgender HIV Prevention, University of California.

Schwartz, Sharon, and Ilan H. Meyer. 2010. "Mental Health Disparities Research: The Impact of within and between Group Analyses on Tests of Social Stress Hypotheses." *Social Science and Medicine* 70, no. 8: 1111–18.

Sevelius, Jae M. 2013. "Gender Affirmation: A Framework for Conceptualizing Risk Behavior among Transgender Women of Color." *Sex Roles* 68, nos. 11–12: 675–89.

Singer, T. Benjamin, Mary Cochran, and Rachael Adamec. 1997. *Final Report by the Transgender Health Action Coalition (THAC) to the Philadelphia Foundation Legacy Fund [for the] Needs Assessment Survey Project.* Philadelphia: Transgender Health Action Coalition.

Skidmore, W. Christopher, Joan A. Linsenmeier, and J. Michael Bailey. 2006. "Gender Nonconformity and Psychological Distress in Lesbians and Gay Men." *Archives of Sexual Behavior* 35, no. 6: 685–97.

SMART (Sexual Minority Assessment Research Team). 2009. "Best Practices for Asking Questions about Sexual Orientation on Surveys." Los Angeles: Williams Institute, University of California, Los Angeles, School of Law. williamsinstitute.law.ucla.edu/wp-content /uploads/SMART-FINAL-Nov-2009.pdf.

Tate, Charlotte Chuck, Jay N. Ledbetter, and Cris P. Youssef. 2013. "A Two-Question Method for Assessing Gender Categories in the Social and Medical Sciences." *Journal of Sex Research* 50, no. 8: 767–76.

Toomey, Russell B., et al. 2010. "Gender-Nonconforming Lesbian, Gay, Bisexual, and Transgender Youth: School Victimization and Young Adult Psychosocial Adjustment." *Developmental Psychology* 46, no. 6: 1580–89.

US Department of Health and Human Services. 2010. "Health Disparities." Office of Disease Prevention and Health Promotion. www.healthypeople.gov/2020/about/disparitiesAbout .aspx.

Valentine, David. 2007. *Imagining Transgender: An Ethnography of a Category.* Durham, NC: Duke University Press.

Vlassoff, Carol. 2007. "Gender Differences in Determinants and Consequences of Health and Illness." *Journal of Health, Population, and Nutrition* 25, no. 1: 47–61.

WHO (World Health Organization). 2008. *Closing the Gap in a Generation: Health Equity through Action on the Social Determinants of Health.* Final Report of the Commission on Social

Determinants of Health. Geneva: World Health Organization. www.who.int/social_determinants/thecommission/finalreport/en.

Wylie, Sarah A., et al. 2010. "Socially Assigned Gender Nonconformity: A Brief Measure for Use in Surveillance and Investigation of Health Disparities." *Sex Roles* 63, nos. 3–4: 264–76.

Xavier, Jessica M., et al. 2005. "A Needs Assessment of Transgendered People of Color Living in Washington, DC." *International Journal of Transgenderism* 8, nos. 2–3: 31–47.

Xavier, Jessica, Julie A. Honnold, and Judith Bradford. 2007. *The Health, Health-Related Needs, and Lifecourse Experiences of Transgender Virginians.* Richmond: Virginia Department of Health. www.vdh.virginia.gov/epidemiology/DiseasePrevention/documents/pdf/THIS FINALREPORTVol1.pdf.

Appendix. Eight recommendations from the GenIUSS Group

Recommendation 1: That standardized self-report questions about both sex and gender be included in all surveys of the US population.

Recommendation 2: That multiple aspects of gender be measured in US population-based research, including gender identity.

Recommendation 3: That questions specific to gender minorities be asked using skip patterns.

Recommendation 4: A measure of gender identity does not replace sexual orientation (identity, attraction, behaviors). Measuring both gender identity and sexual orientation is recommended for US population-based surveys.

Recommendation 5: Build on "best practices" for asking about minority groups on US population-based surveys: (1) gear questions asking about transgender and gender nonconforming status toward gender majority respondents; (2) offer response options beyond binary "female"/"male" or "woman"/"man" categories; (3) aggregate data over multiple years to ensure adequate sample sizes.

Recommendation 6: When two demographic items can be added to an adult survey (or, in most instances, a standing measure of sex replaced and a measure of current gender identity added), inclusion of measures of assigned sex at birth and current gender identity is recommended. The two-step approach appears the most likely to have high sensitivity as well as high specificity with adults (table 1, a, b).

Recommendation 7: When valid self-report measures of assigned sex at birth and current gender identity are not on a survey and cannot be added (or replace existing measures) and a valid measure of sexual orientation identity is already on a survey, then the BRFSS stand-alone demographic item is recommended (table 1, c).

Recommendation 8: When valid self-report measures of assigned sex at birth and current gender identity are not on a survey and cannot be added (or replace existing measures), and a valid measure of sexual orientation identity is not already on a survey and cannot be added, then a stand-alone demographic item is recommended (without a write-in response option) that includes sexual orientation and gender identity (table 1, d).

The Profusion of Things

The "Transgender Matrix" and Demographic Imaginaries in US Public Health

T. BENJAMIN SINGER

Abstract This article argues that activist claims about the erasure of transgender people in public health settings and research studies obscure a profusion of trans- and gender-nonconforming identities, embodiments, and terminology in public health contexts. Using the concept of a "transgender matrix," this work explains how proliferating transgender imaginaries result in differing conceptualizations of sex, gender, sexuality, race, and culture that resonate with similarly variable public health research categorization practices. Demographic categories are double-edged swords in that they are necessary for the redirection of resources toward socially marginalized people; at the same time, they often constitute the conditions of containment of these same people. Drawing on de Certeau's concept of a tactic, this article proposes a mode of evasion through the mobilization of alternate classificatory schemas based on interrelational race- and class-based categorical imaginaries. This is exemplified by an ethnographically documented account of the Trans-health Information Project (TIP), a federally funded public health program. TIP created nonstandard safer-sex outreach packets that employed classificatory mobility in an ongoing process of adaptation and change, mutating in response to specific racial, ethnic, and class-based differences through the use of local vernaculars. This tactical maneuver temporarily circumnavigated administrative capture.
Keywords transgender, trans, transgender matrix, demographic imaginary, tactic, Trans-health Information Project

> I have long been interested in classifications of people, in how they affect the people classified, and how the affects on the people in turn change the classifications.
> —Ian Hacking, "Making Up People"

The phrase "making transgender count" alludes, indirectly and ambivalently, to numerous interrelated problems. On one hand, the phrase gestures to the idea that injustices related to the invisibility, marginality, and neglect of issues pertaining to gender-nonconforming or gender-changing people can be addressed by demonstrating, through the enumeration of trans people as part of a general population, that such issues *should* matter, that they *should* "count" or be considered significant. On the other hand, the phrase implies that there is something forced, something coercive, in *making* "transgender" be a category or term through which a heterogeneous array of individuals should be grasped and in making counting be the means through which the injustices experienced by atypically gendered subjects should be addressed.

The project of "making transgender count" thus engages a host of questions. Answering the question, who is transgender? requires a decision not only on what transgender means but also on who has the power to say what counts as transgender and who is in a position to count what transgender has been determined to be. And once such preliminary questions have been answered, the technical question yet remains of *how* to count whatever has been decided regarding what transgender has been determined to be. All of which brackets a further set of questions regarding whether the counters and the counted might not have different stakes in the game and even whether transgender should be counted at all.

Transgender can denote a particular self-defined category of personhood, but it also operates as a catchall term, as in the popular conceptualization of a "transgender umbrella" that references a flexible collective of gender-nonconforming people. This concept can produce what pioneering trans theorist Sandy Stone calls a "bumptious heteroglossia" of transgender speech-acts and effects ([1991] 2006: 230). Critics have noted that by grouping together all sexual and gender-nonconforming identities and expressions under a singular rubric, the category transgender itself elides significant differences between different ways of being gender nonnormative. This is particularly true with regard to people who do not self-identify as transgender, whatever they may understand that word to mean, but are nevertheless captured within an all-encompassing "transgender imaginary" (Valentine 2007). Other theorists assert that transgender functions as a "third gender" category that subsumes non-Western forms of personhood, such as Hijra from India, through linguistic acts of colonization (Towle and Morgan 2006: 672–73). Anthropologist Megan Davidson extends these critiques to the boundaries of movement building, saying: "Different constructions of the category transgender, who it includes and excludes, are not simply negotiations of a collective identity but . . . negotiations about the boundaries of a social movement and that movement's efforts toward social change" (2007: 61). Inclusion, exclusion, and erasure all occur in and through these differing conceptualizations of the category even as such differences are "elided in public consciousness by the category transgender and the notion of a unified umbrella implied within it" (61).

Such critiques of transgender suggest that it is an evolving, flexible, and sometimes internally contradictory category and that there is thus no definitive answer to who can or could or should be counted as transgender. What *is* clear is that applying the umbrella approach—hoping to capture a class of persons already pregiven as "being transgender" in some ontological sense before having had the category applied to them—is a linguistic phantasm that produces material effects, what I call a "social imaginary." Social imaginaries are high-stakes biopolitical projects with the power to enact categories of personhood, construed as a priori material realities, that can either diminish or enhance the life chances of the people interpellated by those categories. They are apparatuses for making transgender count in all the senses suggested above.

While it is beyond the scope of this article to critique positivist social scientific methods through which populations are constructed and queried, others have cogently addressed this topic at length (Bowker and Star 1999; Willse 2008). My analysis extends the work of scholars such as Craig Willse, Geoffrey C. Bowker, and Susan Leigh Star not by focusing on data-driven classification practices that simply capture an existing object—that even "make people up" in the sense that Ian Hacking (2006) has discussed—but rather, following the reflexive process described in my epigraph, by focusing on the ways in which bodies can and do exert an insurrectionary pressure upon the enumerative practices designed to produce and define them. Seemingly subjugated bodies, including collectives of individuals, can push against universal data-gathering practices deployed by various agents of governmentality.

Twin Skins: Categorical Erasure and Proliferative Excess
This article examines the manner by which transgender is imagined and operationalized in different public health research and HIV service provision settings. I began gathering material during fieldwork by asking the simple question, what is trans-health? This query focused on the play of expertise between bodies of experts—medical and HIV/AIDS service providers—and people who modified their sexed bodies (not mutually exclusive groups). Based on previously published literature, I expected to find sex/gender-transition-related medical technologies being strictly regulated by a group of credentialed experts as well as a widespread erasure of trans-identified and gender-nonconforming people within public health systems. For example, Viviane K. Namaste's groundbreaking analysis, *Invisible Lives: The Erasure of Transsexual and Transgendered People* (2000), documents and analyzes the exclusion of trans-identified people from Canadian health care services. While health care in the United States and Canada differs structurally, Namaste's research findings are congruent with US studies such as that of sociologist Anne Bolin, who documents systemic erasures through her

observation of middle-class male-to-female transsexuals (1988). For Namaste, Bolin, and others, accessing medical care is typically predicated on administrative processes that accomplish "the erasure of transsexuals [and other gender-nonconforming individuals] from the everyday social world" (Namaste 2000: 159). During my research I did indeed document similar erasures during multi-sited fieldwork conducted in clinics located in Boston, Philadelphia, New York City, and San Francisco. Systemic exclusionary practices included binary (M/F) gender boxes on clinic intake forms, lack of medical information on exogenous hormone use, and widespread pronoun misuse by receptionists who greeted trans and gender-nonconforming people who walked through a medical provider's door. Such exclusionary practices should not be minimized, because of the ways in which they are embedded within institutions and operate on the individuals addressed by those institutions, but they do not tell the whole story.

During fieldwork, I discovered that erasure was only part of the story. I witnessed a bewildering profusion of trans-related categories, identity terms, and embodiment practices as well as an increasing number of trans-specific initiatives being developed in public health clinics and HIV prevention programs in the early 1990s. In what follows, I discuss alternate classification practices developed in one trans-specific HIV prevention public health program, which made innovative use of street slang. This program engaged its participants along a continuum of identifications not reducible to two sex/gender categories, identifying people instead through various nonbinary racialized gender categories. While the staff of the HIV program under examination routinely applied universal "top down" categories with the goal of (re)shaping individual behaviors, they also mobilized classifications that rose up from the streets, using vernacular terms rooted in counterdominant epistemologies articulated by radically specific social actors. My reading of this program's work thus suggests ways in which socially subordinated individuals can maneuver transversely through biopolitical regimes to leave marks of alterity that disrupt the state-sanctioned administrative categorization and classification of their bodies.

This particular case study exemplifies a trend I witnessed from the mid-1990s forward in urban centers such as San Francisco, New York, Boston, and Vancouver, where a variety of efforts were underway to include the *T* in LGBT by adding trans-specific programs to existing gay, lesbian, and bisexual medical services at public health clinics. Over the past two decades, especially in urban areas, it is possible to witness a flurry of efforts to include transgender in needs-assessment studies, in trans-specific HIV prevention and care services, and in model LGBT public health clinics. Even while the exclusion of trans-identified people continues to occur in medical contexts as a result of institutional practices structured by the male/female gender binary, my investigation revealed a seemingly paradoxical proliferation of bodies, genders, and categories entering public health systems—driven by the generative capacity of the category transgender itself.

In order to account for this often disorienting profusion of categories, identities, bodies, and social practices, this article conceptualizes transgender not only as an umbrella term that can operate in a reductive manner that flattens and homogenizes difference; it also functions as a productive site of struggle whereby subordinated forms of gender-variant embodied personhood can emerge into social visibility: what I conceptualize as a "transgender matrix." The transgender matrix names a phenomenon of rapidly proliferating embodiments and identities that exceed familiar sex and gender categorization, thus producing categorical excesses. Conventional sex/gender categories and systems are perceived as natural, self-evident, and ontologically given precisely because they are organized according to categorical and aesthetic ideals that remain uninterrogated; the multiplicative effect of transgender excess bursts open these normative classificatory frames. The generative dimension of transgender's excessive quality underpins the ever-expanding mutations of linguistic forms and practices of bodily modifications in trans social worlds as well as the increase of social-service programs designed to serve trans-identified people (or others who get caught in transgender's categorical net) and in the profusion of popular media images and discourses regarding trans identities and bodies. This same proliferation operates across public health research studies and HIV health programming; if we want to understand trans health practices as they have emerged in North American urban locales over the past twenty years, we cannot rely upon the paradigm of erasure alone.

Caution! "New Identity Terms Are Constantly Emerging . . . "

"I'm not supposed to be here . . . forbidden by my employer, one of the major public health divisions of the U.S. government. I'm the girl who knew too much. So today I'm going by the name Doris Dayta, after the movie *The Man Who Knew Too Much* starring Doris Day." These provocative words of introduction were spoken at the first institute on the Future of Transgender/Transsexual Health Research, convened in 2008 at the University of Pittsburgh by faculty of their newly created LGBT Health Studies Program. My longtime friend Doris and I sat next to one another among a group of invited presenters, which included both trans- and non-trans-identified health care providers and health advocates who had collaborated on research studies, health campaigns, and other projects over the span of many years. The group was asked to brainstorm a new research agenda that would advance the growing trans health movement into the next decade. Most participants understood that Doris embodied an uneasy relationship between an insurgent grassroots health movement and official government bodies that operate as institutional regulatory forces. The fact that she was "the girl who knew too much" and needed to hide her activist identity behind a fictitious name to preserve her job as a public health official simply highlighted the politically charged atmosphere in the room.

The session began with a trans-identified medical doctor who explained the use of "evidence-based medicine" for trans health advocacy. He compared the current state of medical knowledge to a Ford Pinto, saying: "While we would all like to be driving a Ferrari, what we have is the equivalent of an outdated auto-mobile." Doris followed with an epidemiological overview of research statistics on the incidence of HIV infection, substance abuse, violence, and other risk factors that adversely impacted the health status of trans-identified individuals. I closed the session by offering an account of what I called the "transgender imaginary," building upon the anthropologist David Valentine's 2007 *Imagining Transgender: An Ethnography of a Category*.

Social imaginaries can be conceptually hard to grasp. They operate at the large-scale level of nation building, colonization, and globalization while also occurring through local-level everyday practices by which people engage one another to develop a sense of self, or of belonging in the context of collective life. One way trans people have entered the US social imaginary is through public health discourses that define transgender as a "target" or "high-risk population" that can function as a disease vector, especially of HIV/AIDS, for the general population. Such a concept of transgender can suggest a greater level of group cohesiveness than exists in actual fact, and can even can work to co-opt or recruit into it "putative members" who "might *not* imagine themselves belonging to such a community" (Valentine 2007: 103). This could include, for example, fem queen youths of color from the house and ballroom scene who were assigned male at birth as well as male-identified gay men who sometimes do drag and do not think of themselves as transgender. My work extends Valentine's critique to argue that there is not one but *multiple* transgender imaginaries at work in US public health systems that correspond to race, class, gender identity, sexuality, culture, region, and other variations. These multiple imaginaries necessitate an intersectional approach instead of being read through a singular transgender axis of identity.

Structural linguistics teaches us that all acts of categorization are built upon fundamental exclusions that collapse disparate specificities into consolidated generalities. Because such distinctions are true for any type of thing or person, the categorical violences of transgender must be understood as a special case of a more general phenomenon, albeit one whose effects are intensified by its recent arrival and lack of definitional clarity as well as by how it rearticulates and reorders such existing categories as transsexual, transvestite, and drag—all of which impinge on deeply held cultural beliefs about what constitutes the reality of sexed embodiment and the naturalness of sex dichotomies. These conditions combine to make transgender unstable to the point that it stands in stark contrast to seemingly stabilized and consolidated, if illusory, categories like male and female.

The proliferative capacity of this volatile categorical instability threatens institutional systems with the problem of incoherence, which, in public health research, often results in classifying transgender data as outliers that cannot be properly coded, managed, and analyzed. When Doris presented her work on the challenges of trans-specific data collection, she showed a PowerPoint slide that visually illustrated this problem of classification and outlier status. She called her slide the "blizzard of self-identifications" and claimed that it contained "only *some* of the many types" of people grouped under the transgender label:

Ag / Androgyne / Basement Transvestite / Bigendered / Bigenderist / Boi / Boss grrrl / Boychick / Butch / Changeling / Clotheshorse / Creatively Gendered / Crossdresser / Dom / Drag King / Drag Monarch / Drag Queen / Fairy / Female Crossdresser / Femme / Femme Queen / Flaming / Former transsexual / Fribble / FTM, F2M, Female-to-Male / Gender Bender, gender-bending / Gender Blender, gender-blending / Gender Breaker / Gender Dysphoric / Gender Euphoric / Gender-fluid / Gender Free / Gender Fuck, Gender Fucker / Gender Illusionist / Gender Outlaw / Gender Queer / Gender Refusenik / Gender Transgressor / Gender Trash / Gender Variant / Grrl / Gynander / Gynadroid / Gynandromorph / Hermaphrodite / Heesh / Hem / He-she / Heterogendered / Heterovestite / Humangendered / Intersex, Intersexed / Invert / Man of transsexual experience / Maricón / Mariposa / Metagendered / MTF, M2F, Male-to-Female / Multigendered / Nelly / Neutrois / No-Ho / No-Op / Nongendered / Non-op / Pangender, Pan-gendered / Polygendered / Post-op / Pre-op / Queen / Queerer / Recast / Shape-shifter / S/he / Shim / Stealth FTM / Stealth MTF / Stone Butch / T* / *T / *TG / Third Sex / Tomboy / Tranny / Trannyboy / Trannyfag / Trannydyke / Trannygirl / Trans / Transfag / Transcendent / Transgender / Transgenderist / Transman / Transsexual / Transsexual Man / Transsexual Woman / Transvestite / Transwoman / Travesti / Tryke / Two-spirit / Woman of transsexual experience (Dayta 2008: slide 4)

At the bottom of this visually overwhelming slide, Doris included a caveat: "This list is *not* exhaustive! New identity terms are constantly emerging. No offense is implied or intended if your term of self-identification is not listed above."

Doris's slide provides vivid evidence of the cognitively disorienting and unruly profusion of identities produced by the transgender matrix. While qualitative researchers would see in it a rich data set, quantitative researchers find themselves confronting chaotic data in need of ordering and systematization through epidemiological techniques. The fact that "new identity terms are constantly emerging" complicates quantitative data analysis in what Doris claims are "otherwise well-structured" research studies. This is in fact what had happened when Doris tried to include an extensive array of self-reported identity terms in her first trans-specific needs-assessment study. This example of "data gone wild" points toward the inevitable uncontainability of categorical excess and the unresolved, perhaps unresolvable, problem of trans-specific data collection.

Documenting Trans Identities: Analysis of Four Needs-Assessment Studies

During fieldwork in community health settings, I too encountered a dizzying array of gender expressions and bodily modifications as well as new terminology that animated the proliferative effect of the category transgender. Additional analysis of trans-specific health care needs-assessment studies revealed a similar profusion of attempts to categorize these emerging transgender phenomena, which resulted in a great deal of methodological variation. Because needs-assessment studies operate as an interface among communities, on-the-ground social action, and administrative governmental bodies, they have provided a good window onto the impact of transgender categorical proliferation in public health worlds. They are where the research rubber hits the road of direct service provision, where top-down and bottom-up institutional operations palpably and legibly collide.

In this section, I analyze four needs-assessment studies ranging from 1996 to 2007, described below. The demographic sections from three of these survey instruments along with a fourth (to be discussed in the next section) are provided at the end of this article as appendixes 1–4. Because the juncture between community mobilization and governmental operations is my main concern in this article, I will not analyze the statistical results of these studies—the ways in which data are conventionally interpreted in public health research—but will instead read the survey instruments deconstructively to expose the hidden and contradictory demographic imaginaries that undergird the categories of things counted, through which the statistical analyses operate.

One common problem encountered in survey instruments that seek to capture information about transgender people involves the conceptual segregation of sexual orientation from gender identity, a distinction that enables the contemporary alignments of homosexuality with sexual orientation and transgender with gender. Historian Joanne Meyerowitz notes that this distinction simply did not exist before the mid-twentieth century, when the concept of a core psychological gender identity, understood to be distinct from sex and sexual orientation, was first posited (2002). Anthropologists Evan B. Towle and Lynne M. Morgan (2006) and other cross-cultural researchers similarly demonstrate that the sex(uality)/gender-identity dichotomy is not universal in human culture but is rather specific to Eurocentric modernity. The seemingly commonsensical separation of sexual orientation from gender identity is thus not a simple onto-logical given so much as it is a recent, and localized, historical and cultural development. Survey instruments organized according to the sex(uality)/gender-identity dichotomy are therefore often at a loss as to how to classify transgender phenomena. On one hand, they routinely conflate and confuse transgender as a gender category comparable with male or female; or else, on the other hand, they problematically list it with sexual identity categories such as heterosexual or homosexual (City of Minneapolis 2002). Such surveys are destined to undercount trans-identified respondents, who are required to choose between legibility as transgender and eliding other aspects of themselves, and who may well privilege a descriptor other than transgender. A transsexual lesbian, for example, might have to choose between checking the gender box—for either woman *or* transgender—or, alternatively, checking the sexual orientation box for either transgender *or* lesbian.

One strategy for negotiating the relatively recent and culturally specific separation of sex (and by extension sexuality) and gender is found in a data-gathering method first developed for a Philadelphia needs-assessment study in the mid-1990s (Singer 1996), which subsequently came to be called the two-step method. This method separates sex assigned at birth from current gender identity in order to detect a discordance between physical embodiment and gender identity that signals the possibility of someone's being trans-identified. This method requires separating sex (as proxy for embodiment) from gender (as a social construct), positing sexuality as yet another dimension by asking a third question about sexual orientation. While the detection of sex and gender dis-cordance can be methodologically useful, this distinction reinforces the suppo-sition that sex (and sexuality) is wholly separable from gender. Feminist theorists have critiqued this false binary, saying that sex and gender operate more like a Möbius strip—an image that figures sex and gender as semiseparable but inex-tricably bound and mutually created (Fausto-Sterling 2000). Another study using the two-step method, the first of the four I discuss in this section, is the trans-gender survey project funded by the New York City Department of Public Health HIV Planning Unit (appendix 1). The Executive Summary reads:

> 39 (of 111) participants were assigned male at birth by medical professionals and reported a male primary gender role at the time of the study. They were included

in this study under the "*transgender umbrella*" because they participated in gender variant activities such as wearing feminine clothing for performance or personal expression. Participants in this group, while indicating their primary gender role was male, also self-selected the gender identity categories of drag queen (47%), transgender/transsexual (34%), cross-dresser (32%), transvestite (29%), and bi-gendered (5%). (McGowan 1999: 8; emphasis added)

Despite this survey's methodological division of sex assigned at birth from current gender identity, the principal investigator's explanatory note states that this separation of sex and gender became problematic when counting research participants. Comparing this 1999 study with the second one considered here, conducted in 2005—New York City MTF Transgender Survey Project (Anonymous 2005) (appendix 2)—highlights contradictions between the two methodologies employed. The 2005 survey used participant eligibility questions that disqualified people from the study whose sex assigned at birth and current gender identity were both identified as male. This method would have *excluded* the 39 of 111 participants from the 1999 study who answered yes to the second question, because they did not register a discordance between their birth-sex assignment and current gender identity.

It is possible that the 2005 survey was designed to exclude respondents who did not fit the researcher's imaginary of transgender—for example, people who medically transition versus people who occasionally dress in drag. Having consulted on a draft of this survey, I know that the researchers did not intend to eliminate individuals from their study by way of built-in exclusions. Instead, they wanted to include individuals who did not identify as transgender yet experienced similar health disparities. Research participants were unintentionally excluded because the screening criteria relied on a data-detected discordance between assigned birth-sex and current gender identity. That this survey design resulted in unintended exclusions reveals how social imaginaries and classificatory systems operate most powerfully when they are rendered invisible.

From a quantitative methods perspective, the data derived from these studies are not comparable due to inconsistent classificatory methods: data concordance cannot be achieved because the study questions are not standardized. Whereas comparability of data is a legitimate epidemiological concern, the standardization of survey questions, of identity categories, and of data collection techniques is not central to my research, because data-gathering inconsistencies indicate a more complex and (to me) more interesting phenomenon. Methodological variability symptomatically indexes the category-defying aspect of the transgender matrix that proliferates different, competing social imaginaries.

Indeed, contradictory methods across these studies reveal how individuals, both included and excluded, get caught in the crosshairs of what Mary Douglas calls a "system at war with itself" (1996).

If we focus on the 2005 survey that excluded people for whom sex assigned at birth and current gender identity match, we see that "transgender" operates insidiously to obscure race and class differences. My ethnographic research identifies the disqualified research participants to be gender-nonconforming racial minorities who occupy the bottom rungs of the socioeconomic ladder—people who are less likely to have adopted the sex(uality)/gender-identity dichotomy popularized by mid-twentieth-century social-scientific elites. This unintended exclusion results from the disarticulation of gender identity from sex and sexual orientation, which Valentine identifies as most characteristic of the transgender imaginary of a largely white, middle-class US activist and social-service provider (2007: 103). Whereas separating sex, gender, and sexuality in the search for noncongruence might make some trans-identified and gender-nonconforming people legible, it perniciously obscures the existence of others. From an intersectional perspective, research methods that seek sex(uality)/gender discordance elide the ways in which categories can be constructed otherwise, in ways that better represent the social formation of sex, sexuality, and gender expression as interdependent in the lives of low-income people of color. Research outcomes that result in unintended exclusions thus demonstrate the pervasiveness of a dominant US transgender imaginary that disqualifies racial minorities and economically marginalized gender-nonconforming individuals from health disparity studies. And yet such individuals experience violence, discrimination, and other forms of social exclusion that are at least consistent with, if not more pronounced than, those of trans-identified study participants for whom sex(uality)/gender discordance is detectable. This observation should compel researchers to consider the unintended effects of their research methods and instead conduct critical demography as an alternative practice.

I turn to one final study, conducted by George Washington University's YES Center on "young men who have sex with men—youth of color" (Magnus 2007: 1) (appendix 3). This survey instrument presents an expanded array of demographic choices derived from the transgender umbrella model but with an ironic twist: it is from a survey of young men who have sex with men (YMSM). Non-trans-identified men and broadly defined gender-nonconforming individuals were explicitly included in this study. The demographic imaginary informing this study differs from the previous two by placing "transgender" or "transsexual" among demographic choices that pertain to male-birth-assigned nontrans individuals. This observation is significant because the US Centers for Disease Control and Prevention has categorized male-born and feminine-presenting individuals (a spectrum that includes nontrans gay and trans-identified people) under the category of men who have sex with men (MSM). The sorting together of transgender women and feminine people who are assigned male at birth confirms what advocates and activists already know, that the primary avenue through which transgender has entered US public health systems is through the back door of the MSM category—a category significantly more heterogeneous and capaciously operational than its name suggests.

Like the previous studies, YES separates sex assigned at birth from current gender identity. This distinction is not made in survey instruments unless it has been informed by the trans-derived methodology that I have been critiquing in this article. The YES survey evinces mixed vernaculars; for example, "femme queen"—a category exclusive to gay or queer communities of color—is placed alongside terms that are often, though not always, associated with a largely white US transgender political movement and demographic. While not a trans-specific survey, this format appears to be influenced by the logic of the transgender umbrella, based on the observation that it offers so many choices of current gender identity, including transgender and transsexual. Categorical imaginaries in research paradigms arrive full circle here in a survey that *includes* those who self-identify as femme queens among the umbrella-like list of identity choices. In this case, however, identity-term choices arise in a study that does not primarily circulate within trans-specific research contexts and social worlds.

YES's demographic imaginary indicates racial and socioeconomic differences regarding classification practices that can only be understood through an interrelational social lens. Specifically, femme queens often, though not always, identify as male-birth-assigned and as currently male-identified individuals. Some may even alternate, depending on the context and/or the audience, between self-identifying as gay and as transgender. Identificatory variability is attributed to the fact that if transgender exists at all in low-income communities of color, it is formed from the inextricable relation of sexuality and gender identity. This makes "femme queen" an identifier of sexuality as much as a gender descriptor. In this context, femme queen literally means: "I am a *different* kind of gay." The separation of sexual orientation from gender identity is subverted here, because transgender signifies a specific type of sexuality, indicating the co-constitutive nature of sexuality and gender for YES Center research participants. The study's focus on "men who have sex with men" further subsumes gender identity and/or trans-specific identity under a sexuality-centered rubric. Notably, individuals who would otherwise have been folded back into the research findings of the 1999 NYC DPH study, or who would have been determined to be ineligible to participate in the 2005 NYC study, are explicitly *included* on their own terms through the category of femme queen. According to the YES Center's principal investigator, whom I interviewed, their method represents the input of gay youth of color who were engaged in participatory research design. The inclusion of femme queens came about because they were part of these youth's social networks.

While not a trans-specific survey, the YES Center's methodological approach demonstrates the proliferative power of transgender that responds to current sociopolitical demands by spilling over into a study that is not exclusive to trans-identified people. The YES Center's study design arguably thus reaffirms the ever-expanding phenomenon of transgender categorical multiplicity and transmogrification.

TIP Tactics: A Politics of Mobility

While voicing concern over the colonizing effect of transgender-umbrella logic and the data-collection practices derived from it, thus far I have only touched lightly on potential mobilization of the destabilizing categorical excess of transgender toward political ends. To demonstrate that the categorical excessiveness of transgender can be leveraged for antihegemonic work within biopolitical systems, I conclude with an example drawn from my time as director of Philadelphia's Trans-health Information Project (TIP).[1] TIP is a peer-driven harm-reduction program designed to decrease health risks among individuals self-identifying as transgender (or trans) or anyone else who is gender nonconforming. Simplistic notions of umbrella-like inclusion were eschewed at TIP in favor of a tactical, local, and shifting outreach approach.

The first programmatic challenge arose as staff gathered around an office conference table littered with safer-sex street outreach packets borrowed from the Midnight Cowboy Project, a program for men who have sex with men. We faced a pile of "male" and "female" latex barrier packs, coded pink and blue, with gendered images on the labels, including a muscled man wearing a cowboy hat. How could the vast range of identities and bodies engaged by our outreach activities ever be recognized by or orient themselves toward such objects? How could our staff identify risky sexual and injecting practices and then create effectively targeted harm-reduction messages? In response to our conundrum, Rick, a program outreach worker, came to our second staff meeting bearing six color-coded and individually named safer-sex packets. Ideally, we would have placed all the latex barriers (e.g., condoms, dental dams, finger cots) in each packet, but budgetary constraints limited our options, and necessity became the mother of invention. Rick's solution was a customized set of materials he called the "TIP Menu"—suggesting we could order up whatever was needed on a particular outreach excursion and customize the packs for the venue. He explained the TIP Menu (appendix 4) as follows:

> Because the sexual health needs of our population vary on an individual basis, I have devised 6 different color-coded packs we can make and choose from, depending on where we are doing outreach and who we are doing outreach to. *We all know it's more complex than this, but it's a start.*
>
> We can pack in advance, so we'll have an idea of what we may need. For example, if doing outreach on 13th Street [a popular sex work stroll], I might need 20 Flygirls, 20 Divas, 5 Daddies, and 5 Stallions. If doing outreach at an event like Transpyre [a local trans-specific nightclub], I might need 10 Divas, 20 BoiScouts, 10 Daddies, 5 Stallions and 5 Sisters. (TIP 2002; emphasis added).

Under a subheading "MtF Menu," for example, could be found the Diva pack, with a purple colored label that read "For ladies who turn it." Meaning, to turn a trick: sex work. Instructions for packing indicated a specific set of latex barriers and their proper labeling.

In the context of public health systems that rely on standardized categories and binary-gendered outreach practices, this recoding tactic was really rather brilliant. The classifications emerging from Rick's social imaginary, derived from direct contact with specific gender-nonconforming people, echo queer studies critic Eve Kosofsky Sedgwick's concept of a "nonce taxonomy": an inventive system of concepts and terms fashioned against social norms for a particular purpose, which are to be discarded or redesigned as utility dictates (1990: 23). They follow a transitive trajectory of intentional impermanence. Sedgwick emphasizes the proliferative and transfigurative aspect of nonce taxonomies, which enact "the making and unmaking and *re*making and redissolution of hundreds of old and new categorical imaginings concerning all the kinds it may take to make up a world" (23).

The TIP Menu is just such a nonce taxonomy. Employing subjugated knowledge derived from peer-based expertise, program staff mobilized street vernaculars in order to nimbly navigate incoherence as an effect of transgender proliferative excess. Theorizing the impact of TIP outreach work necessitates a concession; because public health systems function in normative ways through the use of standardized classification, the Menu relies on categories that it temporarily and provisionally breaks, reframing bodies in nonbinary code akin to a street poetry that riffs on and with standardized public health practices. Faced with the chaos of classificatory proliferation, TIP packs employed a classificatory mobility in an ongoing process of adaptation and change, mutating in response to specific racial, ethnic, and class-based differences through the use of shifting vernaculars.

TIP is not a radical political enterprise operating stealthily within the world of public health like a spy in the house of biopolitical regulation. Rather, the program functions simultaneously as a part of and apart from the system, paralleling Michel de Certeau's assertion in *The Practice of Everyday Life* (1988) that consumers can navigate a capitalist system of exchange by reusing its materials in counterhegemonic ways. De Certeau's distinction between a strategy and a tactic is crucial for my understanding of what TIP was able to accomplish. Whereas strategies are aligned with dominant systems and seek their self-perpetuation, they are relatively uniform, stable, and engaged in the work of imposing order; strategies operating within US public health systems include epidemiological classification practices designed to enforce order in accord with biopolitical imperatives. A tactic, on the other hand, is fragmentary and used by individuals who are incapable of grasping and controlling the whole. Tactics lack a fixed location, thus enabling adjustment and swift travel according to immediate necessity. In this way, a tactic responds to conditions that are not of its own making. For de Certeau, tactics "play on and with a terrain imposed on [them] and organized by the law of a foreign power" (37) and "select fragments taken from vast ensembles of production in order to compose new stories with them" (35). The TIP Menu did precisely this: it took fragments from a vast ensemble, including public health and gender systems, and recombined their elements to compose new stories. TIP re-narrated the origins of sex and gender as a multicolored tale of "Divas," "Daddies," "Girlfriends," and "Boiscouts" that was far more interesting than the blue and pink myth of Adam and Eve, thereby reshaping both concrete institutions and larger social worlds.

Given the practical necessity to support precarious lives, working tactically from within public health systems is just as urgent as revolution from outside. This is tricky business. Performing advocacy in public health contexts necessitates consolidating identity formations like transgender. This is because, advocates argue, categories create places for resources to accrue and enable the redirection of social services toward marginalized people in ways that increase their life chances. This work simultaneously demands that we resist categorizing and classifying operations that advance seemingly benign yet insidious state strategies harmful to the lives of those very people. Programs like TIP demonstrate that state-driven adjurations can and will be circumnavigated. People resist the standardized categories that hail and ensnare them, erupting in unanticipated excesses instead. In charting the treacherous terrain toward making transgender count, our research practices and programmatic responses must focus on the *trans* in transgender rather than the *gender*. Ever in transit, the imperative is to always keep moving and eluding.

T. Benjamin Singer is a Mellon Visiting Assistant Professor of Women's and Gender Studies at Vanderbilt University. His work has appeared in *The Transgender Studies Reader*, the *Journal of Medical Humanities*, *TSQ*, and *Discourse*.

Note

1.   The project began in 2002 as a collaboration between the Prevention Point Philadelphia needle exchange and the Gay and Lesbian Latino AIDS Education Initiative (GALAEI), with funding from the US Centers for Disease Control and Prevention, managed through the Philadelphia Department of Public Health.

References

Anonymous. 2005. "New York City MTF Transgender Survey Project." In the author's possession.

Bolin, Anne. 1988. *In Search of Eve: Transsexual Rites of Passage*. New York: Bergin and Garvey.

Bowker, Geoffrey C., and Susan Leigh Star. 1999. *Sorting Things Out: Classification and Its Consequences*. Cambridge, MA: MIT Press.

City of Minneapolis, Health and Family Support Division, Department of Public Health. 2002. "Lesbian, Gay, and Bisexual Adults in Minnesota: Needs Assessment Study." Poster displayed at 130th Annual Meeting of the American Public Health Association, Philadelphia, November 10.

Davidson, Megan. 2007. "Seeking Refuge under the Umbrella: Inclusion, Exclusion, and Organizing within the Category Transgender." *Sexuality Research and Social Policy* 4, no. 4: 60–80.

Dayta, Doris [pseud.]. 2008. "A Survey of U.S. Transgender Epidemiology." Paper presented at the Future of Transgender/Transsexual Health Research Institute, University of Pittsburgh Graduate School of Public Health, July 24.

de Certeau, Michel. (1984) 1988. *The Practice of Everyday Life*. Berkeley: University of California Press.

Douglas, Mary. 1966. "The System at War with Itself." In *Purity and Danger*, 173–95. New York: Routledge.

Fausto-Sterling, Anne. 2000. *Sexing the Body: Gender Politics and the Construction of Sexuality*. New York: Basic.

Hacking, Ian. 2006. "Making Up People." *London Review of Books*, August 17.

Magnus, Manya. 2007. "Young Men Who Have Sex with Men (YMSM) Study." Washington, DC: YES Center, George Washington University.

McGowan, C. Kelly, 1999. *Final Report of the Transgender Needs Assessment*. New York: HIV Prevention Planning Unit of the New York City Department of Public Health.

Meyerowitz, Joanne. (2002) 2004. *How Sex Changed: A History of Transsexuality in the United States*. Cambridge, MA: Harvard University Press.

Namaste, Viviane K. 2000. *Invisible Lives: The Erasure of Transsexual and Transgendered People*. Chicago: University of Chicago Press.

Sedgwick, Eve Kosofsky. 1990. *Epistemology of the Closet*. Berkeley: University of California Press.

Singer, T. Benjamin, Mary Cochran, and Rachael Adamec. 2006. *Final Report by the Transgender Health Action Coalition (THAC) to the Philadelphia Foundation Legacy Fund (a.k.a. The Delaware Valley Transgender Survey)*. Philadelphia: Transgender Health Action Coalition.

Stone, Sandy. (1991) 2006. "The *Empire* Strikes Back: A Posttranssexual Manifesto." In *The Transgender Studies Reader*, edited by Susan Stryker and Stephen Whittle, 221–35. New York: Routledge.

TIP (Trans-health Information Project). 2002. "TIP Menu." Volunteer handout. Philadelphia: TIP.

Towle, Evan B., and Lynne M. Morgan. 2006. "Romancing the Transgender Native." In *The Transgender Studies Reader*, edited by Susan Stryker Susan and Stephen Whittle, 666–84. New York: Routledge.

Valentine, David. 2007. *Imagining Transgender: An Ethnography of a Category*. Durham, NC: Duke University Press.

Willse, Craig. 2008. "'Universal Data Elements,' or The Biopolitical Life of Homeless Populations." *Surveillance and Society* 5, no. 3: 227–51.

Appendix 1A. New York City Department of Public Health HIV Planning Unit—1999 (McGowan 1999)

Identity: The following section asks questions about your gender and sexual identity:

18. How did medical professionals assign your sex at birth?
Male _____ Female _____ Intersex/hermaphrodite _____ Don't know _____

19. What gender role did your guardians raise you?
Male _____ Female _____ Intersex _____

20. What word best describes your primary gender role?
Male _____ Female _____ Intersex _____ None of these _____

21. What is your legal sex today?
Male _____ Female _____

Appendix 1B. New York City Department of Public Health HIV Planning Unit—1999 (McGowan 1999)

22. Please circle the number(s) of terms that describe your gender identity:
1. Transgender
1.a. non-operative (I choose not to have surgery)
1.b. pre-operative (I have plans to have surgery, but haven't yet)
1.c. partial-operative (I have had some surgery)
1.d. post-operative (I have completed "SRS" surgery)

2. Transexual
2.a. non-operative (I choose not to have surgery)
2.b. pre-operative (I have plans to have surgery, but haven't yet)
2.c. partial-operative (I have had some surgery)
2.d. post-operative (I have completed "SRS" surgery)

3. Drag King
4. Transvestite
5. Cross-Dresser
6. Male
7. FTM (female-to-male)

8. Bi-gendered/Third gender
9. Intersex
10. Drag Queen
11. Female
12. MTF (male-to-female)
13. Other _____

(If you choose more than one number, please put a check next to your primary choice)

Appendix 2. New York City MTF Transgender Survey Project (draft)—2005 (Anonymous 2005)

How did medical professionals assign your sex at birth?
1. Male
2. Female
3. Intersex/hermaphrodite
4. Don't know
[IF NOT MALE, R IS NOT ELIGIBLE FOR STUDY]

Do you currently see yourself as "male" in most situations?
1. No
2. Yes
[IF YES, R IS NOT ELIGIBLE FOR THE STUDY]

Appendix 3. George Washington University YES Center—Young Men Who Have Sex with Men—Youth of Color (YMSM) Study—2007 (Magnus 2007)

What sex were you at birth?
1. Female
2. Male
3. Other, specify
4. Don't know
5. Declined

What is your current gender identity . . . (Circle all that apply)?
1. Male
2. Female
3. Transgender
4. Transsexual
5. Genderqueer
6. Realness
7. Butch queen
8. Femme queen
9. Trannie
10. Intersex, specify
11. Crossdresser
12. Other, specify_____
13. Don't know
14. Declined

Appendix 4A. Trans-health Information Project: MTF Menu (packing instructions)

#1. The Flygirl: *An outreach classic.*
Face out with a hot pink MTF resource guide, backed up by a lime green TIP card. Follow up with 2 regular condoms, 1 flavored condom, and 1 lube.

#2. The Diva: *For ladies who turn it.*
Face out with a purple MTF resource guide, backed up by a yellow TIP card. Follow up with 1 "female" condom, 2 regular condoms, 1 flavored condom, and 1 lube.

#3. The Sister: *She's got everything she needs.*
Face out with a baby pink MTF resource guide backed up by a sea green TIP card. Follow up with 1 dental dam, 1 glove, 1 condom, and 1 lube.

Appendix 4B. Trans-health Information Project: FTM Menu (packing instructions)

#4. The Daddy: *He knows how to treat 'em right.*
Face out with a hunter green FTM resource guide, backed up by a lime green TIP card. Follow up with 1 dental dam, 1 glove, and 1 lube.

#5. The Stallion: *For guys who want to take 'em for a ride.*
Face out with a red FTM resource guide, backed up by a lime green TIP card. Follow up with 1 "female" condom, 2 regular condoms, 1 flavored condom, and 1 lube.

#6. The BoiScout: *Be prepared (for anything!).*
Face out with a blue FTM resource guide, backed up by a yellow TIP card. Follow up with 1 dental dam, 1 glove, 1 condom, 1 flavored condom, and 1 lube.

From Multiracial to Transgender?

Assessing Attitudes toward Expanding Gender Options on the US Census

KRISTEN SCHILT and JENIFER BRATTER

Abstract In 2000, the US Census Bureau acknowledged multiracial Americans on the decennial census in an attempt to better capture racial heterogeneity and to more closely align what is publicly collected on forms with people's personal understandings of their racial identity. In this article, we start a discussion of how the census—a major source of political identity recognition and legitimation—could be more inclusive of gender variance. We ask: (1) Is there support for a transgender category on the US census? (2) Who might select a transgender option if it were provided? To answer these questions, we conducted questionnaire research at three transgender and genderqueer conferences and found strong support for the inclusion of a transgender category. Conversely, we found that many people did not currently check "transgender" on forms when given the opportunity. As we show, the decision to check "transgender" varies by what we term *gender identity validation*. In other words, people who identified as male or female and who felt others viewed them as unequivocally male or female, respectively, were less likely to check "transgender" than people who identified as transgender or who experienced a discrepancy between their self-perceived and other-perceived gender identity. These differences suggest that—similar to the push for adding a multiracial category to the census—the expansion of sex/gender categories is most likely to come from individuals who experience themselves as constrained by the existing possibilities and/or who are stigmatized by others' conceptions of the appropriate alignment of bodies and genders.
Keywords trans, transgender, census, population statistics, gender identity measurements

I n April 2010 a media frenzy surrounded President Barack Obama's public acknowledgment that he had checked only the "Black, African-American, Negro" box on his decennial US Census Bureau survey. One pundit expressed surprise that Obama, the son of a white mother and African father, would choose to represent himself as "unequivocally part of black America," a choice she viewed as "a holdover from racially ugly times" (Thernstrom 2010). Others supported him, arguing that racial identity is a personal decision that should not be open to criticism (Avila 2010). Yet what is notable about Obama's decision from a social

TSQ: Transgender Studies Quarterly ★ Volume 2, Number 1 ★ February 2015   **77**
DOI 10.1215/23289252-2848895   © 2015 Duke University Press

science perspective is that he, and all other Americans, even had the opportunity to select multiple races (Thompson 2012; Perlman and Waters 2002). Prior to the 2000 census, respondents could only select one racial category from a set list, just as they can make—as of the 2010 census—only a singular response of "Male" or "Female" for sex/gender categories.[1]

Expanding the categories for sex/gender on the US decennial census would not be without precedent. In 2011, Nepal included a "third gender" category on their national census, and in 2014, the Australian High Court recognized a citizen's right to identify as neither male nor female on government documents.[2] And the many shifts in race options since the 1790 inception of the decennial US census demonstrates that the US Census Bureau has responded to transformations in political ideologies and identity-based activism—such as those that occurred around race in the civil rights era (Nobles 2000). The shift toward a "check all that apply" race option on the 2000 US census was an attempt on the part of this government agency to better capture racial heterogeneity and to more closely align what is publicly collected on forms with people's personal understandings of their racial identity (Brunsma 2006). Since many people conceive of sex/gender as more complex than a binary, we start a discussion in this article of how the US decennial census—a major source of political identity recognition and legitimation (Baumle and Compton 2013; Thompson 2012)—could be more inclusive of gender variance. While the comparison between the categorization of sex/gender and that of race on official documents has limitations—limitations we address in this article—we use empirical data on the development and use of the multiracial census option as a starting point for our research questions: (1) Is there support for adding a transgender category to the US census? (2) Who might select a transgender option if it were provided?

In this article, we explore how complexities of gender identity could be expressed in an official classification system in more inclusive ways. We acknowledge that surveys are problematic for locating personal identity, an unbounded concept that is a reflection of the self (Owens 2003) and wholly distinct from *identification* or classification, which is a more public, bounded, and specific approach to classifying selves (see Brunsma 2006). Additionally, we recognize that the term *transgender* has a fraught history (Meyerowitz 2002) and fails to capture many people's lived experiences of gender. However, such classification on official forms carries important outcomes, as it is used to set funding priorities and to measure discrimination faced by demographic subgroups (Anderson and Fineburg 2001). Our goal is to capture how new forms of identification could apply to a previously unmeasured population and to discuss how such identification may generate greater gender protections.

The Census and Statistical Representation

The Multiracial Case

Since 1790, the US decennial census has reported the race of American residents from a list of predetermined categories. The organization of the early classification schemes reflected the ways in which racial ideology intertwined with evolving political priorities of denoting civil status (slave vs. free), presumptions of biologically based differences, and upholding systems of formal segregation to enshrine privileges associated with race-specific access to political, social, and economic resources (Davis 1991; Nobles 2000). While "white" was defined as the absence of non-European origins, the categories "black" and "American Indian" included people of partial ancestry and even allocated, in some censuses, particular categories denoting the idea of blood quantum (e.g., "octoroon," "quadroon," or "mulatto"). With the Civil Rights Act of 1965, the aims of the census shifted toward providing a means to track and measure adherence to policies aimed at ending discrimination. The Office of Management and Budget (OMB) began to prioritize racial self-identification (Perez and Hirschman 2009) and set forth standards of racial classification by which residents could choose one response from a list of categories or select "some other race" and write in an open-ended response (J. Spencer 1997; Morning 2003; Saperstein 2006). In the 2000s, the census again changed to reflect notions of multiracial—rather than monoracial—identification.

The change from single to multiple race options came from activists in the 1990s who lobbied the OMB to revise its standards of racial and ethnic classification. People's early attempts to check multiple categories in this singular system were allocated by census officials to a single race category or the "some other race" category (R. Spencer 2003; Saperstein 2006), which effectively erased the official existence of multiracial-identified Americans. While the US Census Bureau held up "other" as an option, many people who identified as multiracial saw it as an empty category that signified a racially nonspecific second-class citizenship. Activists initially sought the addition of a specific "multiracial" category that would be listed alongside black and white, arguing that such a lack ignored the changed cultural landscape of the United States, where interracial marriage was both legal and increasingly prevalent (Nobles 2000). Opponents viewed a multiracial category as a detriment to the larger goals of using racial enumeration as a means to remedy discrimination and track inequality. Many civil rights activists feared the demographic impact of the exit of large numbers of people from the category "black" to the category "multiracial," particularly as census-based group size played a key role in the allocation of resources in public policies (J. Spencer 1997; Farley 2004).

The OMB opted for a compromise wherein individuals could "mark one or more" racial categories from a preset list (Nobles 2000). Respondents could declare a complex racial identity, and the Census Bureau could allocate them to single-race categories for compliance monitoring and resource allocation purposes (Goldstein and Morning 2002). Yet Barack Obama's public declaration that he selected only one race category underscores research findings that people's racial identification decisions on surveys are driven by many factors. Estimates based on the 2000 census showed that only 33 percent of families involving a husband and wife who selected two distinctive races had children who were reported as two or more races (Lee and Edmonston 2005), echoing findings in other studies (Brunsma 2005; Roth 2005; Bratter 2007; Gullickson and Morning 2011). These patterns are framed by historical legacies of racial discrimination that continue to drive many persons who identify as having mixed-race ancestry toward single race categories on governmental forms (Gullickson and Morning 2011).

A person's decision to select multiple race categories on the census is dependent on many factors, such as generation, region, individual background, and social interactions with others. Cohorts born after the civil rights era of the 1960s with parents who report a high SES (usually college-educated) and who lived outside the South are more likely to select multiple race categories on the census (Tafoya, Johnson, and Hill 2004; Brunsma 2005). In addition, people are more likely to select multiple race categories when they report that their self-identity as multiracial or biracial is "validated" or legitimated by other people in their lives (Khanna 2004, 2010; Rockquemore and Brunsma 2008). In contrast, people who identify as multiracial or biracial but feel that other people do not recognize this identity (in other words, that they are seen as black *or* as white) are more likely to select only one race category even when they have the option to select multiple categories (Brunsma 2006). These findings suggest that a person's decisions about racial identification on survey instruments is influenced by *personal identity*—how one thinks about one's own racial identity—and *social identity*—how one thinks one is viewed and treated by others in regard to racial identity.

A sense of connection to a community also can be what sociologists call a "push" factor in people's self-reporting of race identification. Finding a collective of strongly identified multiracial individuals can push people who identify as having mixed-race ancestry toward claiming such an identity (Bernstein and De la Cruz 2009). Yet people with the same idea of their race ancestry may choose to select only one race in order to politically align themselves with a historically marginalized group, such as Native Americans or blacks (Khanna 2010). This political alignment reflects in part how negative interactions such as race-based harassment and discrimination can push individuals toward collective organizing, as such treatment often follows being perceived by others as a member of a historically marginalized racial group (Herman 2004; Lee and Bean 2012). By contrast, people who identify as having mixed-race ancestry but who do not face such experiences may perceive themselves as having different options for racial identification (Lee and Bean 2012).

For activists, the move toward "check all that apply" in race categories on the census legitimized the existence of Americans who identify as multiracial. This official recognition is important, as "the act of naming helps to establish the structure of the world, and does so all the more significantly the more widely it is . . . authorized" (Bourdieu 1999: 105). While categorization has the power to both create and reify particular identities, the refusal to name a category erases and hides the existence of particular groups (Kertzer and Arel 2002; Baumle and Compton 2013).

A Transgender Option on the Census: Potential Parallels?

Expansion of the sex/gender options on governmental surveys such as the census has yet to emerge as an OMB agenda item at the time of this writing. However, the current public attention on LGBTQ rights in a variety of spheres (e.g., marriage equality, employment discrimination) has brought issues facing transgender people into wider public conversation. Advocates' push for enumeration is well under way, and success could signify greater legitimization of transgender Americans and generate more reliable estimators of the size of the population. Attempts at such enumeration have been historically fraught (see De Cuypere et al. 2007; Meyerowitz 2002; Olyslager and Conway 2007). Drawing on an analysis of large, population-based surveys that "include questions to identify the transgender population" (Gates 2011: 5), demographer Gary Gates has estimated the size of the US transgender population as 0.3 percent. Yet it is difficult to assess the reliability of this estimate, as it is not known how well such surveys capture this diverse population or how many people who identify as transgender choose not to do so on surveys for a variety of reasons. Further, we have little information on whether this push for enumeration on the part of advocates aligns with the desires of transgender people more broadly.

A more accurate estimation of the transgender population could have important impacts. People who can be conceived of as gender variant, whether this is an internal conception or an identity imposed on them by others, have been subject to discrimination in many social arenas (Currah, Juang, and Minter 2006; Stryker 2008). While transgender lives and experiences have increased in public visibility over the last thirty years (Stryker 2008; Schilt 2010), the lack of reliable statistics on the percentage of transgender people in the US population can be an impediment to policy changes. It is population statistics that separate groups seen as legitimate minorities from "fringe" anomalies. In other words, transgender people's experiences with discrimination carry more weight at the level of policy when they are a "counted" group who can demand federal and state protections. Inclusion on the US decennial census could demonstrate a kind of "statistical citizenship" or new form of institutional legitimization for transgender people, as it did for multiracial Americans, even if the population is small.[3]

Yet there are several ways in which including a transgender category on the census differs from the multiracial case. While people who identify as multiracial may choose to identify as a single race on their census form, they do not typically report a fear of potential repercussions of making their identity as multiracial public.[4] The long history of discrimination and persecution of transgender people (Meyerowitz 2002; Stryker 2008)—particularly by police and other state-sponsored actors—and the lack of federal protections for gender identity and gender expression could create fear over identifying as transgender on an official document (particularly as the census survey arrives through the US mail, signifying that respondents' locations are known). It may be difficult to allay the fears of repercussions, particularly for people whose gender transitions are largely unknown by others in their lives.

Second, race is no longer legally defined (Haney-Lopez 1995) in the United States, meaning that anyone can select multiple racial identities on the census without penalty and without external verification of their "true" race (see Yang 2005). In contrast, the US government continues legal regulation of sex/gender, as people are tied to the "M" or "F" listed on their birth certificates. This sex/gender mark is listed on many government-issued documents, such as Social Security cards, driver's licenses, and marriage licenses (Meadow 2010). While changing legal sex/gender is possible in many states, it is not an easy, expedient, or inexpensive process. People who self-identify as transgender but who have not legally changed their sex marker, then, could feel bound to report their legal sex/gender for fear of "misrepresenting" themselves on a government document.

While the sex/gender and race parallel is not perfect, there are enough similarities to suggest that the characteristics that lead people to select one or multiple race categories might predict (a) support for a transgender category on the census sex/gender question and (b) reporting one's gender when given a transgender option. In what remains of this article, we explore these demographic, experiential, and relational factors.

Research Questions and Hypotheses

We constructed an original questionnaire that drew on biracial identity research (Rockquemore and Brunsma 2008; Khanna 2010). We tapped respondents' experiences of identity validation—a social science term typically applied to racial identity that signifies the relationship between a person's personal identity (the identity that speaks to how one understands oneself) and success in having this identity validated by outsiders, what sociologists imagine as a social identity (Goffman 1963). We asked respondents to identify their personal gender identity, both from a list of possible options (check all that apply) and in their own words in an open-ended response. For social identity, we asked for respondents' best estimate of how other people read their gender expression in a variety of settings. Such responses do not necessarily reflect the "truth" of how someone is being read by others in social situations, but they do reflect people's feelings about how they are being read—and it is these feelings (rather than verified facts) that typically motivate social action (Goffman 1963). When respondents reported that their personal identity and social identity aligned, we describe them as having a *validated gender identity*. Respondents could be validated as men, women, or transgender. When such identities did not align, we described respondents as having an *unvalidated gender identity*.

We anticipated that interest in a transgender census category and current usage of such a survey category would be most common among respondents with validated transgender identities and those with any unvalidated gender identity. Both groups might be the most likely to experience hostility in regard to their gender and thus be invested in utilizing the state-sponsored instrument of the census to mobilize antidiscrimination advocacy. We also theorized that respondents' support or usage of a transgender option would overlap with close ties or associations with various LGBTQ groups. Additionally, we anticipated that respondents who felt close to people who had experienced gender-based violence and harassment and/or who had experienced such behaviors personally would exhibit more support for a transgender option on the census as a potential avenue for addressing such treatment as discrimination.

Overview of Data Collection

We applied and received approval for our questionnaire study from the Rice University Institutional Review Board. The first section of the questionnaire focused on background characteristics (see table 1). We then asked respondents how they publicly identified their sex/gender on forms when they could choose only one option from the list of "Male, Female, Transgender." Then we proposed a scenario in which the decennial census offered the following options: "Male, Female, Transgender." We selected this particular scenario for two reasons: (1) it mirrors the current practices of some official surveys; (2) it mirrors the original demands of multiracial activists for a singular category (as the "check all that apply" option was a compromise offered by the Census Bureau).[5] To gauge respondents' attitudes, we presented a set of statements that described why this approach might be a "good" or "bad" idea. Next, we asked a series of social distance questions, to gauge how "close" respondents felt to particular communities, as well as a set of questions about personal identity and social identity.

We collected data at three conferences aimed at transgender, genderqueer, and gender-variant people that took place in 2007 and 2008. We sought out conferences that had regional variation, variation in gender, race, and age of attendees, and variation in cost. Our conference cities were Seattle, Los Angeles, and Philadelphia. The Seattle conference was predominantly attended by transmasculine participants and drew a younger (18–34), racially diverse crowd. The Philadelphia conference was attended by older (35–65), predominantly white transfeminine participants. The Los Angeles conference had a great deal of age, gender, and racial diversity. The Seattle and Philadelphia conferences were both pay-to-register events (between $100 and $300) that took place at hotels and conference centers, while the Los Angeles conference was free and took place at an LGBTQ community center readily accessible by public transportation.

The first author attended each conference to collect questionnaires. Any person who asked for a questionnaire was eligible for participation. Each questionnaire contained a consent form and an informational tear-off sheet for respondents to keep. Respondents were not compensated for their participation. This data collection strategy did not generate a random sample from which to generalize; it did, however, provide variation in response to show where the extremes of positive and negative attitudes toward a potential census question might lie.

Data and Sample
A total of 167 questionnaires were collected and coded. We constrained our sample to those reporting a gender identity that differed from their response to the question, "What gender were you assigned at birth?" with responses for (1) male and (2) female. The next question asked how they currently defined their gender identity, with the responses (1) male, (2) female, (3) transgender (either transman or transwoman), (4) genderqueer, and (5) other (with space for a written response). Respondents whose current gender identity aligned with how they were assigned at birth (e.g., those assigned male at birth who currently identified as men) were omitted from the analysis (15 cases removed).[6] We then omitted an additional 18 cases that provided incomplete information on a census classification question or how they currently report their gender on forms. Our analytic sample for this analysis consists of 134 respondents.

Dependent Variables Our key dependent variables are those that address support for a transgender category in relation to a hypothetical census option and declaration of whether respondents do/would use the category of transgender on forms when provided with the option. To assess support for this option, we asked respondents to indicate on a five-point Likert scale (1 = strongly agree, 2 = agree, 3 = neutral, 4 = disagree, and 5 = strongly disagree) their agreement with the following statements:

1   Adding a transgender category is extremely important because knowing the size of the group will allow for policies to address the needs of the transgender population.

2   The Census Bureau should add a category because two gender categories are not adequate to describe people's gender identity.

3   Adding a transgender category on the census is a bad idea because it could identify transsexual and transgender people and expose them to discrimination.

4   Adding a transgender category on the census is a bad idea because the goal of transsexual and transgender people should be to be seen as male or female, not as a separate group.

Based on responses to these questions, we constructed a dichotomous measure indicating "1" if respondents agree/strongly agree with the affirmative statements on the transgender option or disagree/strongly disagree with the negative statements. We then created a summative scale, as responses to these questions were found to be highly correlated (Cronbach's α = .778) when entered into a reliability analysis, and thus appropriate to combine into one measure.

Our second variable indicated respondents' current practices of reporting their gender on forms. Respondents were asked, "On forms asking my sex or gender, I usually identify myself as _____ (if I have to check one box)." The response categories were (1) male, (2) female, and (3) transgender. This question allows us to see who is currently employing, or feels they will likely employ, a transgender option when that choice is provided. We recoded these responses to a dichotomous variable indicating (1) transgender and (0) male or female.

Independent Variables Our independent variables tap the forces most prominent in the discussion of the multiracial census question. We control for age with a dichotomous variable indicating birth after the Stonewall riots (1 = birth year is post-1969),[7] race (1 = nonwhite), education (1 = college educated or more, 0 = otherwise), childhood family structure (1 = grew up not living with both mother and father, 0 = grew up with both mother and father), and parent's education (1 = at least one parent is college educated, 0 = otherwise). Finally, we control for gender assigned at birth (1 = female, 0 = male).

The next set of variables adjusts for gender identity. We asked respondents to select an option that indicated their current gender identity. We recoded this response for those who identified as either transmen or transwomen to test whether endorsement of a transgender census option or reporting a transgender identity on forms was simply a function of stating one's identity. In other words, does everyone who identifies as transgender report as such on forms when given the option? Second, we constructed a variable that indicates how much respondents' personal gender identity aligned with their social gender identity and another that captured when respondents reported that they felt their personal identity was out of step with their social identity, a situation we classified as "unvalidated." We categorized those who reported that all of their identities aligned in the way they desired as "validated."

We then gauged dynamics of social distance. First, we asked, "How close do you feel to . . . ," and provided a list of groups that can fall under the LGBTQ rubric. We also asked about closeness to cisgender men and women. The original options were "Very close," "Close," and "Not close at all," which we collapsed to "Close" and "Not close." Second, we asked if respondents had experienced gender-based harassment or violence. Respondents were presented with two questions, one that asked if they had experienced any hostility from cisgender men or women.[8] The responses were "Frequently," "Occasionally," "Rarely," and "Never." We recoded these responses to dichotomous measures, indicating (1) for frequently/occasionally and (0) for rarely/never.

Results

Table 1 displays the distributions of the dependent and independent variables ($N = 134$). Beginning with our dependent variable, there is a high degree of support for a transgender census option, but there is relatively weak evidence that respondents currently use this category when the option is available. Nearly half (41 percent) of our sample solidly endorse a transgender census option. Yet only a quarter of the sample currently report themselves as transgender on forms when given the option. In contrast, more than 70 percent of respondents currently report their gender as either male or female. In some cases, this monogender choice reflects how a respondent was assigned at birth. In other cases, it reflects their personal gender identity.

The demographics of the sample indicate that, on average, our respondents are forty-one years of age, and 45 percent were born after the Stonewall riots of 1969. Respondents are predominantly white (79 percent), mostly educated beyond a college level (61.9 percent). Further, most respondents grew up in a two-parent household (77.6 percent) and have either a mother or father who has

Table 1. Descriptive statistics of independent and dependent variables ($N = 134$)

	Percent/Mean	Freq.
Dependent Variable		
Endorsement of census category	41.7	56
Identified as transgender on forms	25.4	34
Demographic characteristics		
Age (SD)[a]	41.1 (13.6)	
Born after 1969	45.5	61
Race (%)		
White	79.1	106
Black/Asian/American Indian	3.7	5
Hispanic	3.7	5
Some other race	3.7	5
Multiracial	9	12
Missing	0.8	1
Education (%)		
Less than high school	5.2	7
HS/trade school/some college	22.4	30
Associate's degree	9.7	13
Bachelor's degree	61.9	83
Missing	0.8	1
Family structure while growing up (%)		
Both mother and father	77.6	104
Other	22.4	30
Parent's education (%)		
At least one parent college educated	53.7	72
Other	46.3	62
Gender assigned at birth (%)		
Male	55.2	74
Female	44.8	60
Gender Identity (%)		
Male	9.7	13
Female	11.9	16
Transgender (transman/transwoman)	43.3	58
Genderqueer	20.1	27
Other	14.9	20
Validation of gender identity (%)		
Unvalidated	57.5	77
Validated male/female	23.1	31
Validated transgender	19.4	26
How close do you feel to . . . (% close)[b]		
Transwomen	74.6	100
Transmen	78.6	105
Bio women	85.1	114
Bio men	61.9	83

(*Continued*)

Table 1. (*Continued*)

	Percent/Mean	Freq.
How close do you feel to . . . (% close)[b]		
Trans people who "blend genders" w/o hormones/Surgery	74.6	100
Trans people who are stealth	70.9	95
Transsexuals on talk shows	70.9	95
Transgender activist organizations	79.9	107
People who perform gender (e.g., drag queens)	51.5	69
Transsexual people who are victims of violence/murder	76.9	103
Experienced hostility frequently/occasionally from . . . (%)		
Bio men	71.6	96
Bio women	58.2	78

[a]One respondent is missing on this information.
[b]Reference categories for these groups are "Not close." Please see table 2.

earned a college education (53.7 percent). In terms of gender, our sample is almost evenly split between those assigned male or female at birth (55.2 percent vs. 44.8 percent). We find considerable variation in gender identity, as 43 percent identify as transgender, 20 percent indicate they are genderqueer, and another 20 percent indicate a monogender identity as either male or female. The remaining 15 percent chose multiple boxes on the gender question (such as transman and male) or wrote in answers for the "other" option. Despite this variation, the majority of respondents (57 percent) report a personal gender identity that they feel is unvalidated by outsiders. In contrast, a substantial segment reports being validated as male or female (23.1 percent) or as transgender (19.4 percent).

Next, we gauge their feelings of closeness to a variety of communities and any experiences of gender-based hostility and harassment. The majority report feeling close to nearly all the communities we identified, with the highest level of reported closeness being to cisgender women, the least closeness to cisgender men (61.9 percent) and to people who playfully perform gender, such as drag queens and drag kings (51.5 percent). Finally, the majority reported frequently or occasionally experiencing some hostility about their gender expression from cisgender men or cisgender women.

Bivariate Distributions

In table 2, we show the bivariate relationships between our independent variables and our two key dependent variables: percent supporting a transgender census option and percent selecting a transgender category (if offered) on forms. In the first column, we show the percent support for the census option by each category of our independent variables and indicate significant differences (with +), according to two-way chi-square test ($\alpha < .10$, two tailed) in light of the small size of our sample. In the second column, we show the percent selecting transgender

Table 2. Distribution of endorsement of a transgender census category on forms and usage of transgender category, by independent variables

	% endorse transgender on census	% mark transgender on forms	N
Total sample	41.7	29.0	134
Generation			
Born after 1969	39.9	34.4	73
Born in 1969 or before	43.8	24.7	61
Race			
Nonwhite	29.6	22.2	27
White	44.9	30.8	62
Parent's education			
College educated	45.8	29.2	83
Neither parent college educated	37.1	29.0	51
Gender assigned at birth			
Male	39.2	25.7	74
Female	45.0	33.3	60
Gender identity			
Transgender (transman/transwoman)	39.7	29.3	58
Male/female/genderqueer/other	43.4	28.9	78
Validation of gender identity[a]			
Unvalidated	45.5	31.2	77
Validated male/female	25.8+	6.5+	31
Validated transgender	50.0	50.0	26
Closeness to Transwomen (male to female)			
Close	46.0+	28.0	100
Not close	29.4	32.4	34
Transmen (female to male)			
Close	40.0	33.0+	105
Not close	48.3	13.8	29
Bio women			
Close	45.6+	28.9	114
Not close	20.0	30.0	20
Bio men			
Close	43.4	31.4	51
Not close	39.2	27.7	83
Trans people who "blend genders"			
Close	43.0	27.7	100
Not close	38.2	31.4	34
Trans people who are stealth			
Close	38.9	34.0+	95
Not close	48.7	14.7	39

(Continued)

Table 2. *(Continued)*

	% endorse transgender on census	% mark transgender on forms	N
Transsexuals on talk shows			
Close	42.4	26.3	95
Not close	41.6	35.9	39
Transgender activist organizations			
Close	38.3	29.9	103
Not close	55.6	25.9	31
People who perform gender (e.g., drag queens)			
Close	37.7	39.1	69
Not close	46.2	18.5	65
Transsexual people who are victims of violence/murder			
Close	43.7	31.1	103
Not close	35.5	22.6	31
Experiencing Hostility			
Hostility from bio men			
Frequently/occasionally	42.1	33.3+	96
Rarely/never	42.1	18.4	38
Hostility from bio women			
Frequently/occasionally	38.5	37.2+	56
Rarely/never	46.4	17.9	78

*p < .05, +p < .10, two-tailed test.
[a]Statistical difference reflects comparison with "unvalidated" category.

on forms by each independent variable and indicate significant differences between these percentages, according to a two-way chi-square test.

Although none of our background characteristics are significantly related to our outcomes, we highlight several findings of substantive interest that might have been statistically significant with a larger sample. We find greater approval for the transgender census option among those born in 1969 or before (43.8 percent), white respondents (44.9 percent), and those whose parents are college educated (45.8 percent). We also find somewhat more approval among those respondents assigned female at birth compared to those assigned male (45.0 percent vs. 39.2 percent).

Endorsing the transgender option was significantly associated with respondents' being validated as transgender or being unvalidated in their gender identities in some way. In addition, closeness to transwomen and cisgender women was associated with support for adding a transgender category. Counter to our expectations, closeness to transgender advocacy organizations corresponded to *less support* for the transgender census option compared to those who reported not being close to these organizations (38 percent vs. 55.6 percent—a difference that barely misses significance with $p = .105$). There was a null relationship between experiencing gender-based hostility and endorsing the transgender option.

In the next column, we report the patterns for marking transgender on forms and find similar correlates. Only 29 percent of the sample used transgender when given the option on a form. Such reporting is not a simple reflection of a personal identification as transgender; respondents who identify as transgender are equally likely to report themselves as such on forms as those respondents who do not identify as transgender (29.3 percent vs. 28.9 percent). As with endorsing the transgender census option, respondents who identify and are validated as either male or female are less likely to report transgender on forms than respondents with unvalidated gender identities of any kind (6.5 percent vs. 31.2 percent). And underscoring that personal identification alone does not drive identity reporting on forms, only half of respondents (50 percent) who report a validated transgender identity also report using the transgender category on forms when presented with the option.

Closeness to transmen is positively related to using a transgender category but not to supporting a census category. Closeness to transwomen shows an opposite trend: it is associated with endorsing a transgender option on the census but not with identifying as transgender on forms. Also, closeness to transgender people who go stealth and people who playfully perform gender (e.g., drag queens) is also associated with marking transgender on forms but not to endorsing the census option. Confirming our expectations, experiencing gender-based hostility and harassment is related to reporting as transgender on forms even though it is not related to endorsing a transgender option on the census.

The Multivariate Scenario
In the next set of analyses, we evaluate predictors of attitudes and behaviors around a transgender census option within a multivariate framework. Table 3 displays the results of the multivariate logistic regression models with the likelihood of endorsing the inclusion of a transgender category on the census as the outcome. We begin with a baseline model that adjusts for background characteristics and consistency between personal gender and social gender, with those who report being unvalidated in their gender identity in the reference category. We introduce covariates indicating each type of closeness to gender and sexual communities, and three emerge as significant; the results are shown in the remaining models (see table 2 for a list of all communities). In the final model, we adjust for experiences of gender-based hostility.

Table 3. Odds ratios (OR) of endorsing the addition of a transgender category on the US Census gender question

	Model 1 OR	Model 2 OR	Model 3 OR	Model 4 OR
Background/demographic characteristics				
Born after 1969	0.73	0.88	0.77	0.71
Has college education or more	0.84	0.74	0.80	0.84
Not lived with both parents	0.83	0.82	0.77	0.81
Gender at birth (born female = 1)	1.35	1.80	1.60	1.68
Race (nonwhite = 1)	0.53	0.62	0.52	0.61
Validation of gender identity (ref = unvalidated)				
Identifies as M/F / seen as M/F	0.37+	0.37*	0.36*	0.38*
Identifies as transgender / seen as transgender	1.09	1.15	1.22	1.14
Close to . . .				
Transwomen		2.61+		
Transmen			0.52	
Bio women				3.67*
Nagelkerke R square	0.08	0.113	0.097	0.127
Chi-square, df	8.195, 7	11.739	10.030, 8	13.323, 8
Sample size	134	134	134	134

*p < .05, +p < .10, two-tailed test.

Similar to the patterns in the bivariate analyses, we find that reporting a validated gender identity, particularly a monogender identity, is strongly associated with endorsing a transgender census option independent of background characteristics. According to model 1, individuals with a validated, monogender identity (male or female) are far *less likely* to endorse the transgender census option (OR = 0.37) compared to respondents with unvalidated gender identities of any kind (e.g., whose personal gender identity is not validated by outsiders). Respondents with validated identities as transgender (e.g., they identify as transgender and other people see them as transgender) are not significantly different from the reference group (OR = 1.09). This pattern holds across all of the following models, demonstrating that is it not a function of associations with specific communities or with experiences of gender-based hostility.

Models 2, 3, and 4 reveal that ties to certain communities increase the likelihood of endorsing a transgender census option. Closeness to transwomen is associated with a doubling of the odds of endorsing the census category (OR = 2.61) and closeness to cisgender women triples these odds (OR = 3.67). Personally experiencing hostility on the basis of gender expression is not significant (analysis not shown but available from the author by request); however, the direction of the effects depended on the gender of the hostile party. Hostility from cisgender men

Table 4. Odds ratios (OR) of reporting gender as transgender on a hypothetical gender question

	Model 1 OR	Model 2 OR	Model 3 OR	Model 4 OR
Background/demographic characteristics				
Born after 1969	1.72	1.63	1.79	1.76
Has college education or more	1.21	1.19	1.09	1.11
Not lived with both parents	0.52	0.48	0.42	0.58
Gender at birth (born female = 1)	1.34	1.34	1.50	1.19
Race (nonwhite = 1)	0.67	0.74	0.69	0.65
Validation of gender identity (ref = unvalidated)				
Identifies as M/F/seen as M/F	0.15*	0.17*	0.13*	0.13
Identified as transgender/seen as transgender	2.12	1.986	2.19	2.15
Close to . . .				
People who perform gender		2.42*		
Transgender victims of violence/murder			2.431	
Experienced hostility from				
Bio men				1.71
Bio women				2.316
Nagelkerke R square	0.197	0.236	0.223	0.255
Chi-square, df	19.880*, 7	24.191*, 8	22.810*, 8	26.372*, 9
Sample size	134	134	134	134

*p < .05, +p < .10, two-tailed test.

was positively correlated with endorsing a transgender census option, while hostility from cisgender women was negatively related to endorsing this option.

Next, as shown in table 4, we moved from predictors of attitudes to predictors of behaviors. Similar to the previous analysis, we find that respondents with validated monogender identities (male or female) that differ from how they were assigned at birth are far *less likely* to report their gender as transgender relative to those with unvalidated gender identities of any kind (OR = 0.15). This pattern sustains across all models and again is the most consistent predictor of reporting the use of a transgender option on forms when the option is provided. We highlight the following associations, though all findings are available from the authors by request. People who express closeness to those who perform gender are significantly more likely to use transgender on forms (OR = 2.42). Closeness to several other communities, including transgender activists and victims of violence, were positively, though not significantly, associated with the usage of transgender on forms. Additionally, experiences of gender-based hostility, specifically hostility from cisgender women, were positively related to usage of a transgender category.

Discussion

Utilizing questionnaire data from a gender-diverse sample, we ask two questions in this research: (1) What is the degree of support for the addition of a transgender category on the US census? (2) To what degree is such a category currently used? We find nearly half of our respondents support the addition of a transgender category, while fewer than 30 percent mark themselves as transgender. We also find that experiences with gender validation (e.g., the degree to which one's personal identity aligns with how they feel others see them) strongly shape patterns of endorsement and usage of a transgender category. Transgender individuals who identify solely as male or female and experience validation in these identities are far *less* likely to endorse adding a category to the US census or to use such a category on official forms compared to those whose gender identities are not validated by others or those with a validated transgender identity. It may be that those individuals on the borders will drive the expansion of gender categories. Meanwhile, those who feel like they fit within the sex/gender binary may see less to gain (or even something to lose) from an institutionalizing of transgender identity.

We also find that feeling close to specific communities patterns support for a census category. Closeness to gender communities that are highly visible as targets of gender-based violence, such as trans and cis women (Schilt and Westbrook 2009) is strongly associated with endorsement of the transgender category. Personally experiencing hostility does not differentiate support for the category, but it does elevate the likelihood of currently reporting one's identity as transgender, as does a sense of closeness to victims of violence and murder. This sense of closeness with transgender and cisgender women may bring a greater awareness of gender-based discrimination and more support for using governmental data to track such issues.

The importance of being on the borders of singular, fixed sex/gender categories shows some parallels with the experience of activists who advocated for a multiracial category on the census. In both cases, the underlying principle is making a challenge to a binary (male/female, white/nonwhite) that does not fully represent the complexity of many people's lived experiences. Within the multiracial situation, people who were unvalidated in their racial identity and/or who felt that their children's identities were not accurately represented by singular race categories pushed for the multiracial category on the census (Khanna 2010; R. Spencer 2003). Yet our data suggest new avenues of research, as the correlates for support of a transgender option did not always align with the predictors for a multiracial category. For example, closeness to transgender advocacy organizations was not a predictor of support (in fact, it was negatively correlated).

These data do have limitations. First, our small sample limits our ability to identify statistically significant differences. Second, as we collected our data at conferences organized around transgender-related issues and themes, our pool of respondents is highly selective of people who have some attachment to a transgender identity. While those attending such conferences have very diverse understandings of gender (as evidenced by our open-ended gender identity question), our data may be biased toward greater support for a transgender census option than we might have found from a random sample of transgender individuals. Finally, the more affluent and educated may be overrepresented in our sample, as two of our three conferences had registration fees.

Conclusion

Adding a transgender option to the sex/gender question on the US decennial census would be one way to make more solid estimates of the size of the transgender population, which can have a major impact on policy. This addition would also provide recognition of transgender people by a government instrument imbued with the power of determining "who counts" in America, as the census "plays a key role in reflecting . . . reality" (Kertzer and Arel 2002: 2). As this type of recognition is intimately tied to discourses and ideologies of citizenship (Nobles 2000), such a move could, like the enumeration of multiracial identity, signify a shift away from "top-down" structuring of identity categories, allowing new ways for individuals to organize their identities to guide policies of enumeration.

However, if such enumeration were possible, how reliable would this estimate be? Our data suggest that those who are supportive of a transgender census option and who would mark themselves as transgender are a selective slice of this community—specifically, those who feel unvalidated in their gender identities, those who have a validated transgender identity, and/or those who feel close to victims of gender-based harassment and violence. The size of the transgender population would likely be underestimated on population surveys, as those who have validated monogender identities or who do not encounter harassment may opt out. This potential underestimation runs parallel to multiracial enumeration, as selection of multiple race categories is highly unstable within individuals (Harris and Sim 2002; Harris 2002; Doyle and Kao 2007) and overlaps only to a limited degree with identifying as having interracial parentage (Campbell and Eggerling-Boeck 2006). Moreover, transgender as a category may be insufficient to capture the complexity of gender identity. Adopting a fixed choice (male, female, or transgender) would only replace the binary with a trichotomy and could alienate individuals who view gender identity as fluid, particularly people who identify as genderqueer, agender, or dual/multigendered.

Beyond accurate enumeration, is the addition of a transgender option on the census a possibility? Certainly it would necessitate a major shift in the popular (and statistical) understanding of sex/gender away from this notion that it is a static, "objective marker" (Kertzer and Arel 2002: 6) located in a binary. But such transformations are not unprecedented, as the shift from understanding race as based in biology to positioning it as inscribed in social experiences shows (Saperstein 2012). With this ideological shift, the biological basis of race for regulating rights and thus for having a "legal race" was eliminated in the United States. Illustrative of this point is the fact that race is not listed on governmental identification documents such as driver's licenses, passports, Social Security cards, or marriage licenses. While the eradication of a legally binding sex/gender may come in time, we see the expansion of sex/gender categorization as a more likely first step toward legitimizing, and addressing discrimination toward, gender-variant people at the federal level—particularly as some government surveys and many large-scale health surveys have begun to include transgender as a sex/gender option. And, similar to the multiracial case, the push for such an expansion may come from the growth of advocacy groups headed by the parents of transgender and gender-variant children who seek to see their children officially counted.

Kristen Schilt is an associate professor of sociology at the University of Chicago. Her research focuses on gender inequality and the workplace. She is the author of the book *Just One of the Guys: Transgender Men and the Persistence of Gender Inequality* (2010).

Jenifer Bratter is an associate professor of sociology at Rice University. Her research centers on population studies, health, and multiracial identities. She has published in *Social Forces*, *Demography*, and the *Journal of Health and Social Behavior*.

Acknowledgments
We wish to acknowledge the invaluable undergraduate research assistance of Megan Alley and Noah Tian, who aided in the initial setup of the data used for this analysis. The second author would like to acknowledge the Woodrow Wilson Fellowship Foundation, which provided time and support for this project.

Notes

1. On the census survey, the sex/gender question asks, "What is the *sex* of Person One?" However, in the summaries provided by the US Census Bureau, the data from this question are reported as "gender." In this article, we use "sex/gender" to reference the fuzziness of these terms on official forms.
2. For an evaluation of the impact of this addition in Nepal, see Knight, Flores, and Nezhad 2015 (this issue).

3. We look to census statistics on American Indians/Alaskan native populations as a reference for this point. This group encompasses a little more than 1 percent of the US population, is highly unstable in terms of who identifies as "American Indian," and includes a wide degree of racial mixture (Liebler 2010). While these facts point to a large degree of fluidity and a lack of demographic presence, they have not diminished the importance of American Indian community politically or historically, and as such this community has been enumerated on nearly every census.

4. Historically there have been repercussions for selecting a "white" race when an individual had any black ancestry. While these repercussions can still exist today, they are no longer legally sanctioned (see Yang 2005 for recent discussion of how these issues apply to cases of "racial fraud").

5. Our research goal was to determine support among a gender-diverse population for a transgender option on the census and to understand how people in this population were currently reporting their gender identity when given different options. For best practices on collecting gender identity on surveys, see the work of the GenIUSS group (2014).

6. Typically, these respondents returned the questionnaire and noted that they identified as cisgender. They also rarely filled out the entire survey, making their responses unusable.

7. We selected Stonewall because it represents the emergence of the modern LGBTQ activist movements. Coming of age in the 1990s, this post-Stonewall cohort would see more options for openly identifying as transgender. We theorized that fears about identifying as transgender on a government document might be less prevalent in this cohort.

8. In our piloting of the questionnaire, we discovered that "bio men" was a clearer term for respondents than "cisgender men," therefore we use the term *cisgender* in the text but *bio men/women* in our tables.

References

Anderson, Margo, and Stephen E. Fineburg. 2001. *Who Counts: The Politics of Census Taking in Contemporary America*. New York: Russell Sage Foundation.

Avila, Oscar. 2010. "Obama's Census Form Choice: Black." *Los Angeles Times*, April 4. articles .latimes.com/2010/apr/04/nation/la-na-obama-census4-2010apr04.

Baumle, Amanda, and D'Lane R. Compton. 2013. "Identity versus Identification: How LGBTQ Parents Identify Their Children on Census Surveys." *Journal of Marriage and Family* 76, no. 1: 94–104.

Bernstein, Mary, and Marcie De la Cruz. 2009. "What Are You? Explaining Identity as a Goal of the Multiracial Hapa Movement." *Social Problems* 56, no. 4: 722–45.

Bourdieu, Pierre. 1999. *Language and Symbolic Power*. Cambridge, MA: Harvard University Press.

Bratter, Jenifer. 2007. "Will Multiracial Survive to the Next Generation? The Racial Classification of Children of Multiracial Parents." *Social Forces* 86, no. 2: 821–49.

Brunsma, David L. 2005. "Interracial Families and the Racial Identification of Mixed Race Children: Evidence from the Early Childhood Longitudinal Study." *Social Forces* 84, no. 2: 1129–55.

———. 2006. "Public Categories, Private Identities: Exploring Regional Differences in the Biracial Experience." *Social Science Research* 35, no. 3: 555–76.

Campbell, Mary. 2007. "Thinking Outside of the (Black) Box: Measuring Black and Multiracial Identification on Surveys." *Social Science Research* 36, no. 3: 921–44.

Campbell, Mary, and Jennifer Eggerling-Boeck. 2006. "What about the Children? The Psychology and Social Well-Being of Multiracial Adolescents." *Sociological Quarterly* 47, no. 1: 147–73.

Currah, Paisley, Richard Juang, and Shannon Price Minter. 2006. *Transgender Rights*. Minneapolis: University of Minnesota Press.

Davis, F. James. 1991. *Who Is Black? One Nation's Definition*. University Park: Pennsylvania State University Press.

De Cuypere, Griet, et al. 2007. "Prevalence and Demography of Transsexualism in Belgium." *European Psychiatry* 22, no. 3: 137–41.

Doyle, Jamie, and Grace Kao. 2007. "Are Racial Identities of Multiracials Stable? Changing Self-Identification among Single and Multiple Race Individuals." *Social Psychology Quarterly* 70, no. 4: 405–23.

Farley, Reynolds. 2004. "Identifying with Multiple Races: A Social Movement That Succeeded but Failed?" In *The Changing Terrain of Race and Ethnicity*, edited by Maria Krysan and Amanda E. Lewis, 123–48. New York: Russell Sage Foundation.

Gates, Gary. 2011. "How Many People Are Lesbian, Gay, Bisexual, and Transgender?" Williams Institute, April. williamsinstitute.law.ucla.edu/research/census-lgbt-demographics-studies /how-many-people-are-lesbian-gay-bisexual-and-transgender.

GenIUSS Group. 2014. "Best Practices for Asking Questions to Identify Transgender and Gender Minority Respondents on Population-Based Surveys." Los Angeles: Williams Institute.

Goffman, Erving. 1963. *Stigma*. New York: Simon and Schuster.

Goldstein, Joshua, and Ann Morning. 2002. "Back in the Box: The Dilemma of Using Multiple-Race Data for Single-Race Laws." In *The New Race Question: How the Census Counts Multiracial Individuals*, edited by Joel Perlman and Mary C. Waters, 119–36. New York: Russell Sage Foundation and Levy Economics Institute.

Gullickson, Aaron, and Ann Morning. 2011. "Choosing Race: Multiracial Ancestry and Identification." *Social Science Research* 40, no. 2: 498–512.

Haney-Lopez, Ian. *White by Law: The Legal Construction of Race*. New York: New York University Press.

Harris, David. 2002. "Does It Matter How We Measure? Racial Classification and the Characteristics of Multiracial Youth." In *How the Census Counts Multiracial Individuals*, edited by Joel Perlman and Mary C. Waters, 62–101. New York: Russell Sage Foundation and Levy Economics Institute.

Harris, David R., and Jeremiah Joseph Sim. 2002. "Who Is Multiracial? Assessing the Complexity of Lived Race." *American Sociological Review* 67, no. 4: 614–27.

Herman, Melissa. 2004. "Forced to Choose: Some Determinants of Racial Identification in Multi-Racial Adolescents." *Child Development* 75, no. 3: 730–48.

Kertzer, David, and Dominique Arel. 2002. "Censuses, Identity Formation, and the Struggle for Political Power." In *Census and Identity: The Politics of Race, Ethnicity, and Language in National Censuses*, edited by David Kertzer and Dominique Arel, 1–42. Cambridge, MA: Harvard University Press.

Khanna, Nikki. 2004. "The Role of Reflected Appraisals in Racial Identity: The Case of Multiracial Asians." *Social Psychology Quarterly* 67, no. 2: 115–31.

———. 2010. "'If You're Half Black, You're Just Black': Reflected Appraisals and the Persistence of the One Drop Rule." *Sociological Quarterly* 51, no. 1: 96–121.

Knight, Kyle G., Andrew R. Flores, and Sheila J. Nezhad. 2015. "Surveying Nepal's Third Gender: Development, Implementation, and Analysis." *TSQ* 2, no. 1: 101–22.

Lee, Jennifer, and Frank. D. Bean. 2012. *The Diversity Paradox: Immigration and the Color Line in Twenty-First Century America*. New York: Russell Sage Foundation.

Lee, Sharon, and Barry Edmonston. 2005. "New Marriages, New Families: U.S. Racial and Hispanic Intermarriage." *Population Reference Bureau* 60, no. 2: 3–36.

Liebler, Carolyn. 2010. "A Group in Flux: Multiracial American Indians and the Social Construction of Race." In *Multiracial Americans and Social Class: The Influence of Social Class on Racial Identity*, edited by Kathleen Odell Korgen, 131–44. New York: Routledge.

Meadow, Tey. 2010. "A Rose Is a Rose: On Producing Legal Gender Classifications." *Gender and Society* 24, no. 6: 814–37.

Meyerowitz, Joanne. 2002. *How Sex Changed: A History of Transsexuality in the United States*. Cambridge, MA: Harvard University Press.

Morning, Ann. 2003. "New Faces, Old Faces: Counting the Multiracial Population Past and Present." In *New Faces in a Changing America: Multiracial Identity in the Twenty-First Century*, edited by Loretta I. Winters and Herman L. DeBose, 41–67. Thousand Oaks, CA: Sage.

Nobles, Melissa. 2000. *Shades of Citizenship: Race and the Census in Modern Politics*. Palo Alto, CA: Stanford University Press.

Olyslager, Femke, and Lynn Conway. 2007. "On the Calculation of the Prevalence of Transsexualism." Paper presented at the World Professional Association for Transgender Health 20th International Symposium, Chicago, September 5–8. ai.eecs.umich.edu /people/conway/TS/Prevalence/Reports/Prevalence%20of%20Transsexualism.pdf.

Owens, Timothy J. 2003. "Self and Identity." In *The Handbook of Social Psychology*, edited by John D. DeLamater, 205–32. New York: Kluwer/Plenum.

Perez, Anthony Daniel, and Charles Hirschman. 2009. "The Changing Racial and Ethnic Composition of the US Population: Emerging American Identities." *Population and Development Review* 35, no. 1: 1–51.

Perlman, Joel, and Mary C. Waters. 2002. Introduction to *The New Race Question*, edited by Joel Perlman and Mary C. Waters, 1–32. New York: Russell Sage Foundation and Levy Economics Institute.

Rockquemore, Kerry Ann, and David Brunsma. 2008. *Beyond Black*. 2nd ed. Thousand Oaks, CA: Sage.

Roth, Wendy D. 2005. "The End of the One-Drop Rule? Labeling of Multiracial Children in Black Intermarriages." *Sociological Forum* 20, no. 1: 35–67.

Saperstein, Aliya. 2006. "Double-Checking the Race Box: Examining Inconsistency between Survey Measures of Observed and Self-Reported Race." *Social Forces* 85, no. 1: 57–74.

———. 2012. "Capturing Complexity in the United States: Which Aspects of Race Matter and When?" *Ethnic and Racial Studies* 35, no. 8: 1484–502.

Schilt, Kristen. 2010. *Just One of the Guys? Transgender Men and the Persistence of Gender Inequality*. Chicago: University of Chicago Press.

Schilt, Kristen, and Laurel Westbrook. 2009. "Doing Gender, Doing Heteronormativity: Transgender People, 'Gender Normals,' and the Social Maintenance of Heterosexuality." *Gender and Society* 23, no. 4: 440–64.

Spencer, Jon. 1997. *The New Colored People*. New York: New York University Press.

Spencer, Rainier. 2003. "Census 2000: Assessments in Significance." In *New Faces in a Changing America: Multiracial Identity in the Twenty-First Century*, edited by Loretta I. Winters and Herman L. DeBose, 99–110. Thousand Oaks, CA: Sage.

Stryker, Susan. 2008. *Transgender History*. Seattle: Seal.

Tafoya, Sonya M., Hans Johnson, and Laura E. Hill. 2004. *Who Chooses to Choose Two?* Washington, DC: US Census Bureau.

Thompson, Debra. 2012. "Making (Mixed-)Race: Census Politics and the Emergence of Multi- racial Multiculturalism in the United States, Great Britain, and Canada." *Ethnic and Racial Studies* 35, no. 8: 1409–26.

Thernstrom, Abigail. 2010. "Obama's Census Identity." *Wall Street Journal*, April 20. online.wsj .com/article/SB10001424052702303720604575169783989253108.html.

Yang, Tseming. 2005. "Choice and Fraud: Race Choice and Fraud in Racial Identification: The Dilemma of Policing Race in Affirmative Action, the Census, and a Color-Blind Society." Unpublished Manuscript.

Surveying Nepal's Third Gender
Development, Implementation, and Analysis

KYLE G. KNIGHT, ANDREW R. FLORES, and SHEILA J. NEZHAD

Abstract This article discusses research undertaken in the wake of Nepal's 2011 federal census, the world's first to include a gender category in addition to male and female. It presents the methodology and initial findings of a new survey of 1,178 sexual and gender minorities in Nepal conducted to determine inclusive and locally relevant methodologies for demographic information gathering. Nepal has legally recognized a third gender since 2007 and in 2011 added that category to the census. However, due to confusion and discrimination among census enumerators and a data entry system that only allowed for two genders, those who identified as third gender were not accurately measured. Beyond those limitations, the term *third gender* is contested, and by itself it may not fully represent the many sexual and gender minorities in Nepal, including people who are gender nonconforming. This article discusses the development of new survey data measuring the identity, behavioral, and attraction dimensions of gender and sexuality across different terms that are in use in Nepal. Initial findings show that seven distinct groups of respondents can be described, and this article discusses how to expand the concepts and considerations for inclusive data collection in Nepal.
Keywords Nepal, third gender, gender, survey research

The 2011 Nepali census was the world's first to allow citizens to identify as a third gender (Shrestha 2011). However, as enumerator guidelines lacked a definition of the category, some respondents who identified as third gender reported being denied the opportunity to be registered as such by enumerators, and many who were registered on the paper forms as third gender were lumped into data sets disaggregated by male/female, because the analytical software the government used only allowed two gender options (Knight 2012).[1] Approximately one year after initial analysis of the 2011 census was published excluding third-gender-identified people (i.e., the results were disaggregated as male-female only), the Williams Institute of University of California, Los Angeles, School of Law partnered with Blue Diamond Society (BDS), a Nepali sexual health and rights organization, to design and implement a survey for collection of data about sexual and gender minority (SGM) identities in Nepal and to provide best

TSQ: Transgender Studies Quarterly ∗ Volume 2, Number 1 ∗ February 2015   **101**
DOI 10.1215/23289252-2848904   © 2015 Duke University Press

practices for future inclusive survey design. The survey instrument focuses on four key areas: demographics and socioeconomic status, self-identification with sexual orientation and gender identity terms, experiences of discrimination, and access to HIV services.

This article focuses on the research conducted in Nepal in 2012 and 2013 and preliminary analysis of the data collected. We begin by providing the context for legal establishment of Nepal's third gender category. We then describe the development of the survey instrument, the data collection, and initial analytic results. Our analysis indicates seven distinct subpopulations among the assigned-male-at-birth sample. We examine two variables within these subpopulations: outness and experiences of discrimination. Due to limitations in the sampling design, the assigned-female-at-birth sample was small and not included in the current analysis.

The Legal and Social Recognition of a Third Gender Category in Nepal

The social and legal recognition of people who identify as and/or express non-binary genders has occurred throughout history in a variety of cultural and political contexts (Herdt 1996: 22). Scholars have explored in detail whether these identity groups constitute a third gender category. Many identity groups do not explicitly self-identify as third gender but define their identities behaviorally (e.g., being sexually penetrated) or relationally (e.g., being nonmale). As the majority of research on gender-nonconforming people has been conducted on populations of those assigned male at birth, it has been critiqued for doing a poor job of separating the experiences of those assigned male and those assigned female at birth (Valentine 2007: 156).

Nepal's contemporary third gender category is heterogeneous, reflecting what anthropologist David Valentine understands as the spatial, temporal, and cultural specificity of the very concepts of gender and sexuality that may be "organized in very different ways and be understood through other kinds of orderings" (165). A Nepali who was assigned male at birth described this cultural ordering: "I am biologically male, but I am not a man. I do not desire women sexually. Men in my culture desire women sexually. Therefore I am third gender" (Bochenek and Knight 2012: 23). As legal scholar Holning Lau explained, "Some identity categories in Nepal simultaneously convey an individual's sex, gender identity, sexual orientation, and preferred role in intimacy" (2013: 487).

As sexual and gender minority activism swelled in public spaces, "third gender" has been employed in Nepali political discourse. Over the course of several years, a popular Nepali reformist politician referred to an opposition party (the United Marxist-Leninsts, or UML) as "third gender" as an insult, suggesting the party's impotence (Adhikari 2013). The usage stuck in popular memory and was repeated years later—this time more symbolically—in a political cartoon published after a group of activists led by an openly gay former parliamentarian joined politics. It read: "365 third genders enter UML. Only now has our party's sex been assigned" (Knight 2014).

Nepal first legally recognized a third gender category in 2007 when the Supreme Court ruled in *Pant v. Nepal*: "Legal provisions should be made to provide for gender identity to the people of transgender or third gender, under which female third gender, male third gender and intersexual are grouped, as per the concerned person's self-feeling" ("Decision of the [Nepal] Supreme Court" 2008: 281). The judgment in *Pant v. Nepal* does not firmly define to whom the third gender category refers. It references foreign legal precedent and the Yogyakarta Principles and mentions "transgender," "intersex," and "homosexuality" in reference to the third gender category. In some instances the court distinguishes between "homosexuals" and "people of the third gender," but in other references it employs the two terms together. The court specifically points to the census as a method for inclusion in Nepali society: "According to the data published by the Center Bureau of Statistics/Government of Nepal in 2005 . . . there are 102 identified races and castes in Nepal. . . . The male and female have been clearly mentioned under the category of 'sex' in the data published by the Center Bureau of Statistics whereas the identity of third gender has not been accepted there" (278).

This breadth and flexibility in the definition and the court's direction to determine legal gender based solely on self-identification perhaps created more of a query than a directive; however, debates over who is included in the third gender category remain unresolved. While thorough consideration of the social and cultural construction of gender and sexuality in Nepal is beyond the scope of this article, a brief discussion of identity dynamics is helpful to illustrate the complexities of establishing the new (third) category in data collection efforts.

Shivananda Khan's explanation of a framework in India, similar to that in Nepal, sheds light on sexuality and gender dynamics (as well as two of the terms, *kothi* and *panthi*, used on our questionnaire):

> [The] gendered framework is constructed within a *kothi/panthi* dynamic, where the *kothi* perceives himself and his desire for other males in the context of gender roles in South Asia, i.e., the "penetrated" partner. *Kothis* construct their social roles, mannerisms and behaviors in ways which attract what they call *panthis*— "real men"—identifying as feminised males. In this context *kothis* are usually the visible MSM in a range of public environments and neighborhoods, but *panthis* are not, for they could potentially be any "manly" male. (Khan quoted in Cohen 2005: 287)

Explaining how such identities challenge the very distinctions between gender and sexuality, Gayatri Reddy, in a reflection on her fieldwork in India, wrote: "My persistent questions about the criteria for differentiating kotis from other men almost always elicited the following answer: 'all kotis desire pantis.' This explanation positions the identity category 'koti' as one not only understood or expressed through gender non-conformity but also through sexual desire (and, ostensibly, behavior) toward a distinctly gender-conforming category" (Reddy 2005: 47). As a result, such identity categories do not necessarily fall under a sexuality or gender heading discretely and can simultaneously inhabit and challenge both categories in various ways. As Sumit Baudh argued with regard to *hijaras* in India, the term applies to male-assigned people and concerns gender more than sexual identity, possibly including "men who cross-dress, castrated men, or intersexed individuals. . . . A *hijara's* sexual acts (for instance, with men) therefore defy understanding of both heterosexual and homosexual" (Baudh 2008: 98).

Metis and *tas*, two Nepali identity groups, identify in a similar dynamic, with *metis*—the counterpart to *kothis*—being the principal target population for BDS from its inception. The term *meti* is reported to have originated in Darjeeling, India, and is derived from the phrase "to quench one's thirst," with the connotation that the role of the *meti* is to satiate men's (sexual) desires (Tamang 2003: 240). Calling both *ta* and *meti* "social and porous construction[s]," political scientist Seira Tamang noted: "Not all *metis* dress in drag. Indeed two *metis* interviewed had tried it and said they didn't really enjoy it. If they did dress in drag, they only did it once in a while at the behest of friends" (241). In Nepal, sexual and gender minorities, including *metis* and others who present as gender nonconforming, do not necessarily present as such in all settings. Ethnographic studies of *metis* in Kathmandu showed that a "high percentage" were married to women (Boyce and Pant 2001). Some are open with their partners and families, others are not. In this regard, we understand that the challenges of outness and disclosure in Nepal's context can lead people who identify with gender-nonconforming identities to sometimes present as the gender they were assigned at birth.

In this context of multiple identities and types of expression, bureaucratic implementation of the 2007 judgment's third-gender category has barreled ahead. Piecemeal achievements have included adding a third-gender tick box to voter registration documents after 2008 and to citizenship documents in 2013. The most widespread implementation of a third gender category, however, was the 2011 census. Nepal's census was launched in June 2011, and forty thousand secondary school teachers were hired as enumerators. It was a politically charged event, being the first since the end of a decadelong civil war that was bookended by populist uprisings and demands for an inclusive democracy. The census was widely viewed as an opportunity to correct longstanding practices of government exclusion (Thapa 2001). While inclusion of a third gender category was promising, technical issues and discriminatory enumerator behavior marred the process and resulted in data that were only disaggregated by male and female, leaving space for follow-up studies (Knight 2011).

The Blue Diamond Society and Williams Institute's
Nepal Sexual and Gender Minorities Survey

The partnership between Williams Institute and BDS began in the aftermath of the census, in light of both the desire of Nepali activists to have the SGM population counted and the lack of best-practices models from the region. The joint effort developed a survey that allows respondents to self-identify using SGM terms including and beyond "third gender."

Following initial consultations with BDS representatives, the Williams Institute produced a questionnaire based on the set of four focus areas noted above: socioeconomic status, inclusive and accurate identity terms, experiences of discrimination, and access to HIV services. Questions were drawn from survey instruments used to measure Nepal's general population as well as from instruments used elsewhere, which were selected for their relevance to the four focus areas of the study and comparability to Nepali national data sets.[2]

Survey administrators underwent a two-day training with Williams Institute researchers and BDS team leaders who would supervise the survey administrators during the implementation phase. A second field location–based "refresher training" was led by BDS team leaders a month later, the day before the launch of data collection in all five regions of the country.

Four community consultations convened with Williams Institute researchers and BDS representatives. The aim of these discussions was to revise and refine the survey instrument and its translation; the final meeting indicated that the survey construction was coherent and understandable. A text translator was present for the first two meetings to receive feedback on his translation of the survey instrument. During the remaining two meetings, issues of content were debated, which not only led to revisions but also informed the survey administrator/interviewer training program. For example, during one of the consultations, a BDS staff member who identifies as third gender raised an issue about a question on the survey (see appendix 1), that asked respondents to self-identify with a range of terms on a sliding scale for each one, noting that strong identification should preclude identifying with more than one term.[3] As the participant explained, "Once someone answers positively [strongly identifying] with a term, we can move to the next question. People cannot identify with more than one term. If someone is TG [third gender], she cannot also be a lesbian."

The discussion sparked by this comment gestures at the language of gender and sexuality identity in Nepal. Participants in that meeting debated whether multiple identities existed or "were possible," and various participants argued for borders around the third-gender (*tesro lingi*) identity category to be understood along presentation and appearance, while others asserted the category was more comprehensive and based solely on identity (*pahichaan*). Another participant explained: "I am a transgender woman by identity but I also call myself *meti* and I have a wife so in some places because I appear as a man and do the duties of a husband many people perceive me to be heterosexual."

English language identity terms used on the survey instrument were translated in consultation with BDS. "Transgender" became *tesro lingi*, which translates literally to "third gender." During one community discussion, it was raised that the direct and exclusive ascription of *tesro lingo* to "transgender people" is contested by some, as the term is sometimes used to refer to all sexual and gender minorities. However, participants agreed that the term most directly corresponded with the English word "transgender" while not excluding those who understood their identity—regardless of terminology—as a nonmale or nonfemale third position. During discussions, participants asserted that because there were multiple options for self-identifying, including an open-ended answer space, those who wished to identify as *tesro lingi* (in Nepali) regardless of their identification with "transgender" (in English) would be able to do so. It is worth mentioning, however, that the Nepali *tesro lingi* in Deva Nagri script was listed next to the English "transgender." It was discussed whether the survey instrument should include a transliterated "transgender" in Deva Nagri; however, participants argued that it was potentially confusing and might unfairly suggest the superiority of English by transcribing it as such. It was noted by some participants that after national consultations with BDS members and meetings with government officials, in 2012 it was decided that on official documents henceforth, "third gender" was no longer to be used. The term was replaced on documents by "other" (*anya*), which was deemed more inclusive of gender-nonconforming people, especially those who did not speak Nepali as their mother tongue (according to census figures, only 48 percent of Nepalis speak Nepali as their first language). Both "other" and "third gender" remain in use on official documents, depending on when they were issued by the government; but community participants agreed that using "other" on the survey instrument would not gather specific enough data. These discussions and decisions informed the survey administrator training program by calling attention to the need for repeated emphasis on self-identification as the core methodology for the survey, including people who identified with multiple terms.

Interviewers were trained to conduct interviews while sitting next to the respondents and to use Nepali and English as well as other regional languages where necessary. Portions of the questionnaire are shown in the appendixes.

Question 16 (appendix 1) captured one of the three conceptual dimensions of sexual orientation—self-identification—as defined by the Williams Institute (SMART 2009). To supplement this information, we added questions that addressed the other two dimensions, sexual attraction (appendix 2) and sexual behavior (appendix 3). These questions used the same identity terms as the self-identification question. For this study, we focus solely on responses to self-identification. The importance of gathering information regarding identity, attraction, and behavior about sexual orientation and gender identity is underscored by the fluidity and hybridity of sexual and gender terms used in Nepal (as elsewhere), the diversity of identities and experiences the third-gender category might capture, and the fact that measuring any type of identity is complicated by cultural, spatial, temporal, and privacy factors. In addition to collecting demographic information about identity categories (the focus of this article), sexual behavior, and attraction, the research team developed a series of questions related to experiences of discrimination and practices of identity disclosure.

Study procedures were approved by the UCLA Institutional Review Board. Survey administrators were recruited from BDS's drop-in center staff, as BDS felt the people in these positions would have the broadest access to and understanding of local community networks of SGM. Five BDS staff members and one staff member from the Federation of Sexual and Gender Minorities–Nepal, an umbrella network of community-based organizations, were hired as team leaders. Team leaders underwent an online ethical research certification program through UCLA, and a summary of this material was included in the training program for all survey administrators. After a pilot of fifty survey interviews was conducted in Kathmandu in July 2013, the survey underwent a final revision. Survey interviews were conducted during September and October 2013. Administrators approached people who accessed drop-in centers and through community networks, including with e-mail and SMS text message recruitment. Participants were reimbursed 300 Nepali rupees (USD $3) for transportation. Team leaders conducted a monitoring and evaluation mission to each of the five development regions of Nepal and evaluated each interviewer's initial ten completed surveys, giving feedback and authorizing continuation.

Table 1. Distribution of the current gender of the Nepal Sexual and Gender Minorities Survey respondents

Current Gender	Sample Size	Percent
Third gender	516	43.9%
Male	391	33.3%
Male and other	123	10.5%
Female	80	6.8%
Kothi	22	1.9%
Gay	12	1.0%
Lesbian	6	0.5%
Mougiya	6	0.5%
Female and other	5	0.4%
Bisexual	5	0.4%
Intersex	4	0.3%
Natuwa	2	0.2%
Bisexual, Kinnar	1	0.1%
Hijara, Kinnar	1	0.1%
Meti	1	0.1%
MSM	1	0.1%
Total	1,176	100%

Note: Percentages may not sum to 100 due to rounding.

Analysis

The final study has a sample size of 1,178 respondents.[4] Respondents were asked to self-identify their current gender in an open-ended question. Table 1 shows how all of respondents answered this question (including male-born and female-born respondents). Of the assigned-male-at-birth respondents who answered this question, 44.2 percent ($n = 446$) identify as "third gender," 38.5 percent ($n = 388$) identify as "male," 12.1 percent ($n = 122$) identify as "male" and another gender identity, and 5.3 percent ($n = 53$) identify with a variety of other identity terms.

The limitation of using convenience sampling in this context is that, by virtue of using a network of HIV outreach workers, survey administrators primarily recruited those who might benefit from these programs—people who were assigned male at birth. In addition, people assigned female in Nepal experience layers of social exclusion that people assigned male do not necessarily experience, meaning access to public life (including opportunities to participate in research) can be limited for those assigned female (Rankin 2010; Forum for Women, Law and Development 2011). As such, this sample reflects those people assigned female at birth who were a part of or came in contact with HIV outreach/ LGBTI activism networks, which is not representative of the general population of SGM who are assigned female at birth.

Citizenship Documentation Recognition of Nepal's third-gender category on citizenship certificates has been a central point of BDS advocacy since the 2007 judgment (see Al Jazeera 2013). Seventy-one (7.8 percent) male-assigned-at-birth respondents report that they tried to change the gender on their citizenship documents. Fifty-one (71.8 percent) of these respondents identify with gender-nonconforming identities. Of respondents who report making an attempt to change their documents, only four (5.6 percent) have been successful. They are third-gender-identified people who were assigned male at birth.

Identification across Multiple Identities This article analyzes how respondents identify with the multiple identity terms that the previously conducted community consultations determined to be relevant among SGM in Nepal. The survey provides an opportunity for respondents to select to what degree they feel an identity label represents them. Responses range from not at all, to somewhat, to strongly. Ten different labels are evaluated by the respondents, which creates 59,049 potential combinations of response patterns. An initial question is whether we can reduce these potential combinations to the observed response patterns. If so, then respondents can be classified into discrete groups based on these patterns by using multivariate statistics, and we use latent class analysis. We then make inferences on these groups, including: the size of one group relative to the others, how respondents in each group tend to self-identify, whether and when respondents have specific patterns of identity disclosure, and unique experiences of discrimination connected to perceived nonconformity for each group.[5] Our use of statistical models that incorporate the varying ways in which respondents may identify in terms of gender identity and sexual orientation provides an opportunity to examine whether, in Nepal, sexual orientation and gender identity may not be mutually exclusive concepts. We do not address here the potential complexity of multiple identities that may exist among other axes of identity such as caste, which likely also relate to experiences of discrimination.

The responses to question 16 are provided in figure 1.[6] A majority of respondents identify with terms associated with gender nonconformity—namely, *meti*, *kothi*, or third gender. Very few respondents identify as *ta*, *panthi*, *hijara*, heterosexual, or bisexual. What remains to be investigated is whether subsets of the sample identify strongly with *meti*, *kothi*, and third gender, making them

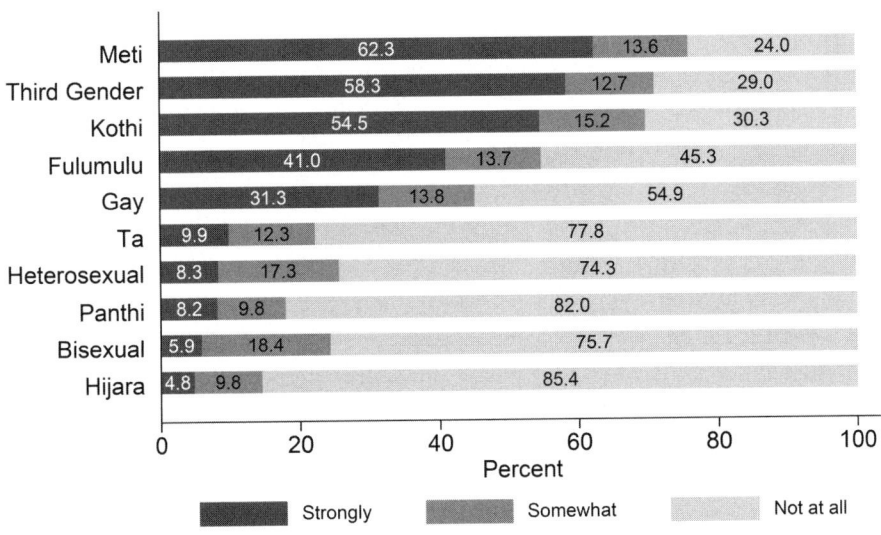

Figure 1. Overall responses to question 16 of the Blue Diamond Society and Williams Institute Sexual and Gender Minority Survey, asking respondents how much each identity label applies to them

potentially exchangeable categories, or whether there are subsets that do not identify with these terms interchangeably.

To reduce the number of potential combinations, we clustered respondents using latent class analysis (LCA), which is a form of mixture modeling. The respondents in this sample likely represent numerous subpopulations. Finite mixture modeling is a process that examines, for example, whether respondents who strongly identify as *meti* do also strongly identify as *kothi* and third gender while not identifying with the other terms listed. If so, then respondents who exhibit this pattern can be classified into one subpopulation. LCA uses the responses to question 16 to evaluate all of the respondents in order to situate them into distinct groups.

This process provides a more detailed view of a sample of the sexual and gender minority population in Nepal while permitting respondents to have multiple attachments to identity labels. A note of caution should be expressed in this analysis, as the number of subpopulations must be specified by the researcher a priori or be model driven.[7] We chose the latter option in this analysis, which resulted in seven distinct subpopulations. Since the determination of the number of classes is model driven, this type of analysis is considered exploratory. Though a second study should be conducted to confirm the number of classes, we did evaluate this finding by conducting two hundred replications of the analysis and determining whether there were significant differences between the distributions of the observed data and what would be predicted by the model. In this assessment, we observed no difference between any of the replicated distributions and the observed distribution.

In figure 2, we provide the results of the LCA. Rows are grouped by the likely response pattern of one of the seven classes. The bars represent the likely response given by a member of that class to each of the identity items. We provide names for each group along each row, determined by the likely response patterns observed in figure 2. We also provide the estimated size of each group.

The largest group in the LCA is one that we label "Strongly Gender Nonconforming" because this group of respondents tends to strongly identify with each term that refers to identifying as gender nonconforming. The respondents also have an open-ended question to indicate the term that they primarily use to identify their sexual orientation or gender identity; 91.8 percent of the respondents in this group primarily identify with gender-nonconforming identities (e.g., third gender, *meti*, *kothi*, and/or *hijara*). This measure provides some indication that the classification process accurately identifies this group. *Hijara* is the only exception to the pattern in figure 2.

We categorized another group as "Somewhat Gender Nonconforming." This group tends to somewhat identify with each of the gender-nonconforming terms (except *hijara*). We do observe some stronger identification with the third-gender item relative to *meti*, *kothi*, or *fulumulu*, but the overall pattern of this group is a weaker identification with gender-nonconforming labels relative to the previous group. This group is 8.1 percent of the sample. We observe that 79.5 percent of the respondents in this group primarily use a gender-nonconforming identity label, with third gender being the most common, followed by *meti*, then *kothi*.

The third group that is identified by the LCA represents a small group of respondents who strongly identify with the gender-nonconforming identifiers and have some identification with the labels heterosexual and bisexual. The primary terms that respondents in this group use in the open-ended question are: MSM, which refers to males who have sex with males (an HIV intervention term), and third gender. This group makes up 3.5 percent of our sample.

The next group that manifested in the data is particularly interesting because the respondents in this group had some level of attachment to all of the identity labels, except for *hijara*. We categorize this set of respondents as "Evenly Affiliated." Though the group makes up only 4.3 percent of the sample, these respondents have a uniform set of attachments to multiple identities—even combinations that may seem contradictory, such as *meti*, *kothi*, and *ta*. In the open-ended identity question, this set of respondents tends to primarily use third gender or MSM.

The final group in the set of respondents who appear to have some attachment to gender-nonconforming identity is the one that had greater levels of attachment to particular gender-nonconforming labels over others. This group, which we named "Third Gender/Meti," makes up 11.3 percent of the sample, and the respondents in this group tend not to identify heavily with *kothi* or at all with *fulumulu* as labels representing them. Of the respondents in this group, 94.7 percent primarily identify as third gender or *meti*.

Alongside the respondents who have varying levels of attachment to gender-nonconforming identity labels, there are two groups in the data where respondents identify more strongly with gender-conforming identities. The respondents belonging to the first of these groups ("Gay Identified") tend to more strongly identify as gay. This group makes up 16.8 percent of the sample, and 94.9 percent of the respondents in this group name their primary identity as gay, bisexual, or MSM. The second group of respondents ("Ta Identified") makes up 9 percent of the sample, and this group tends to strongly identify with a *ta* identity. Those who identify as *ta* are traditionally known to be gender-conforming men who have penetrative sex with men or gender-nonconforming people assigned male at birth. We find that 91.3 percent of the respondents in this group name their primary identity as gay, bisexual, or MSM.

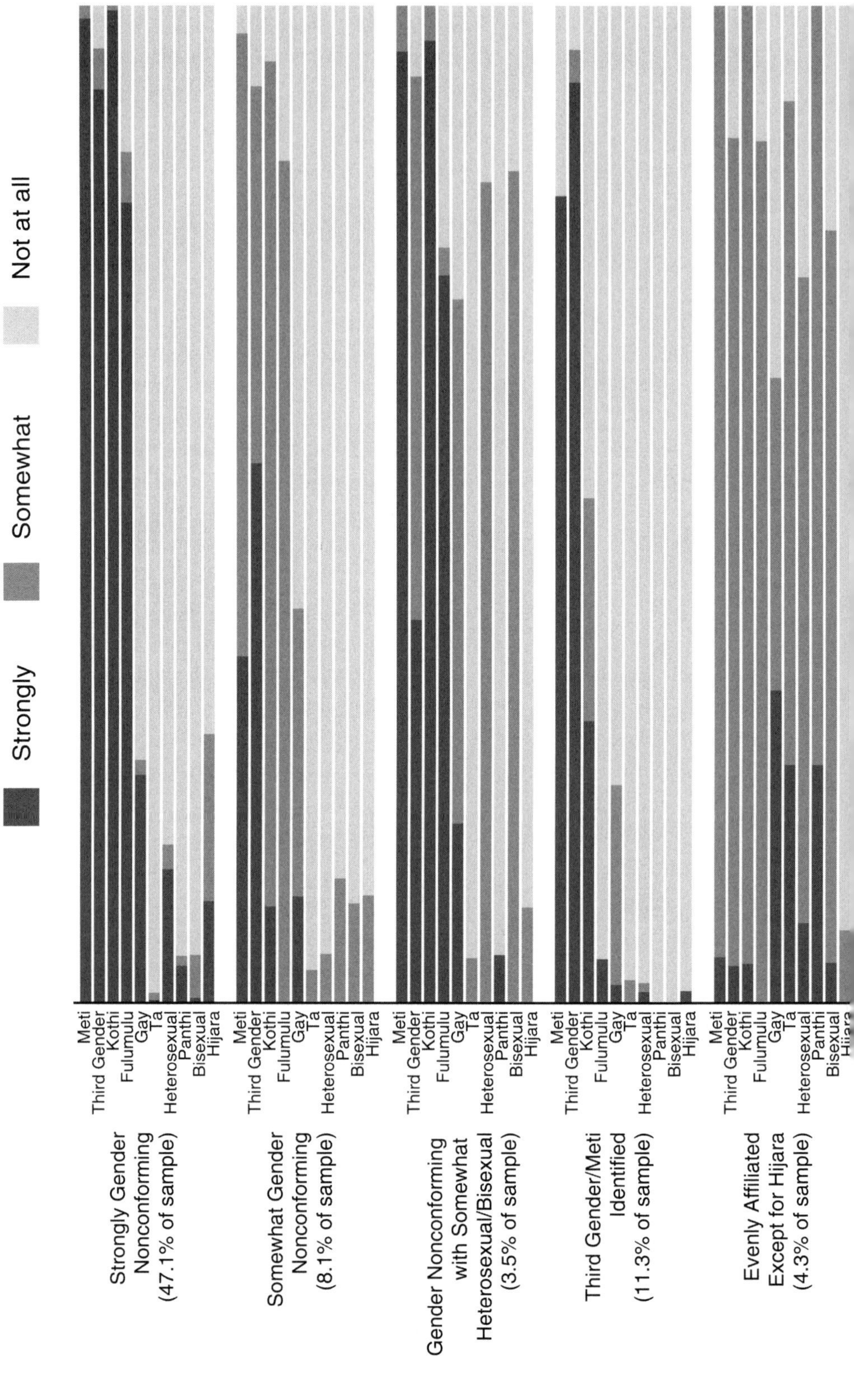
Strongly
Somewhat
Not at all
Meti
Third Gender
Kothi
Fulumulu
Gay
Ta
Heterosexual
Panthi
Bisexual
Hijara
Strongly Gender Nonconforming (47.1% of sample)
Somewhat Gender Nonconforming (8.1% of sample)
Gender Nonconforming with Somewhat Heterosexual/Bisexual (3.5% of sample)
Third Gender/Meti Identified (11.3% of sample)
Evenly Affiliated Except for Hijara (4.3% of sample)

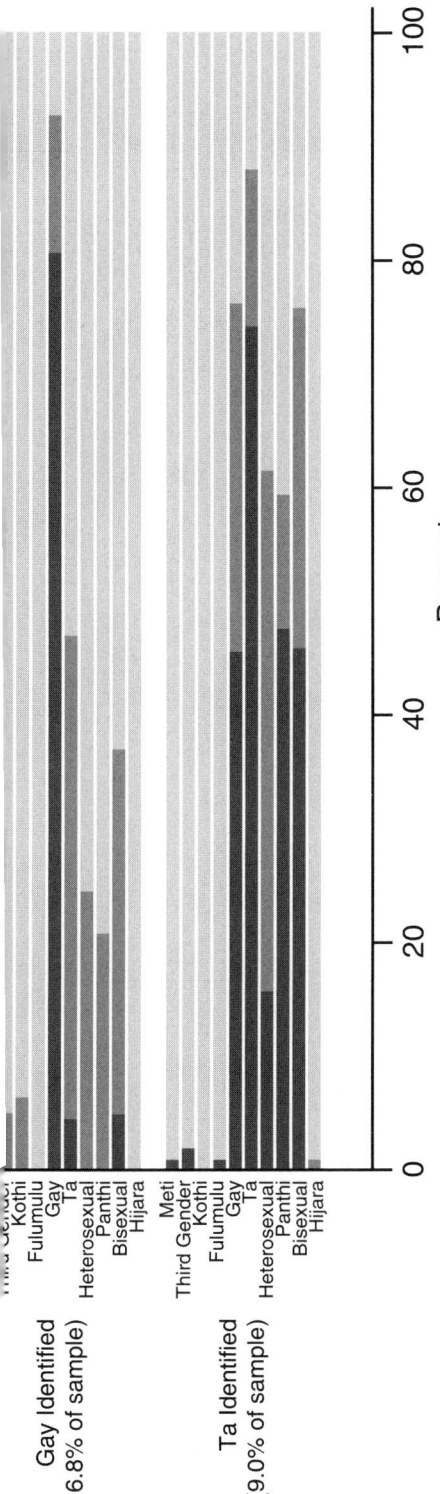

Figure 2. The seven groups from the latent class analysis of the Nepal Sexual and Gender Minorities Survey. Column of identifiers represents identity questions asked in question 16. Bars represent the likely responses of respondents in that group to each identity question.

We find in this analysis a confirmation of what was discussed in the earlier meetings and in previous studies. There are many different terms that gender and sexual minorities use in Nepal, and they have varying levels of attachment to some terms over others. The potential for respondents to indicate multiple attachments to these labels compels us to use analytic techniques that explicitly incorporate all of these potential attachments. We note that the Third Gender/ Meti group is an indication of a subpopulation in the data that would be overlooked in other data collection efforts if surveys relied on a single term such as *kothi* to measure the gender-nonconforming population in Nepal. By our analysis, such occurrences would potentially undercount the sexual and gender minority population by 11.3 percent. We should note that this sample is not intended to be representative of the sexual and gender minority population in Nepal, but it does provide greater insight.

A majority of our respondents tend not to strongly identify with both gender-nonconforming identities and gender-conforming identities simultaneously. This indicates that one's sexual orientation and gender identity may not be discrete in the Nepal context, which has been discussed in previous qualitative studies (e.g., Lau 2013). In bivariate analyses of these identity terms, there is consistently a negative relationship between strongly identifying with gender-nonconforming labels and strongly identifying with gender-conforming labels.

Disclosure and Visual Nonconformity As a further indication of how these groups allow for reasonable and insightful inference on our sample of SGM in Nepal, we examine a set of questions regarding the level of identity disclosure, or "outness," that the respondents report having in multiple venues. If we observe distinct patterns of outness by the seven subpopulations, then we have some confirmation that the LCA may indicate that the experiences of SGM are not necessarily uniform. Each outness question asks respondents how many people know about their sexual orientation and/or gender identity at (1) home, (2) work, and (3) school; and (4) whether their supervisor knows. Respondents select among five options: none, a few, some, most, or all (except for the supervisor item, which is a yes-or-no question).

As plotted in figure 3, a clear distinction emerges in outness patterns among the groups that have a degree of identification with gender-nonconforming terms versus the gender-conforming "Gay Identified" and "Ta Identified" groups. The respondents in the gender-nonconforming groups tend to report higher levels of outness than respondents in the Gay and Ta groups. We do observe variation across venues, with third gender respondents who attend school reporting less outness than third gender respondents who have occupations.[8] The patterns are quite distinct, and they suggest that respondents who identify more strongly with gay or *ta* are less likely to be out than respondents who more strongly identify with gender-nonconforming identity terms.

Being perceived as visually conforming may reduce experiences of discrimination among gender and sexual minorities (Grant, Mottet, and Tanis 2011: 27). We compare how a respondent's outness corresponds with the likelihood that they report not facing discrimination because they were perceived as heterosexual and/or gender conforming in certain settings. Outness may decrease or increase the risk of experiencing discrimination: in the US context, coming out may be empowering while at the same time could result in experiences of workplace or social discrimination (Grant et al.: 28). We investigate visual nonconformity by analyzing a series of questions regarding whether respondents face discrimination or abuse in seven areas: (1) at a store or market, (2) in a transit system (e.g., bus, airplane), (3) in a hospital or clinic, (4) by a police officer or station, (5) by a judge, (6) by a government office or agency, and (7) by a school or college. Respondents choose from a series of options to describe whether they faced discrimination, and if not, why they did not. Some respondents report not experiencing discrimination because people in that setting do not know about their sexual orientation and/or gender identity; that is, they are perceived as visually conforming. We find

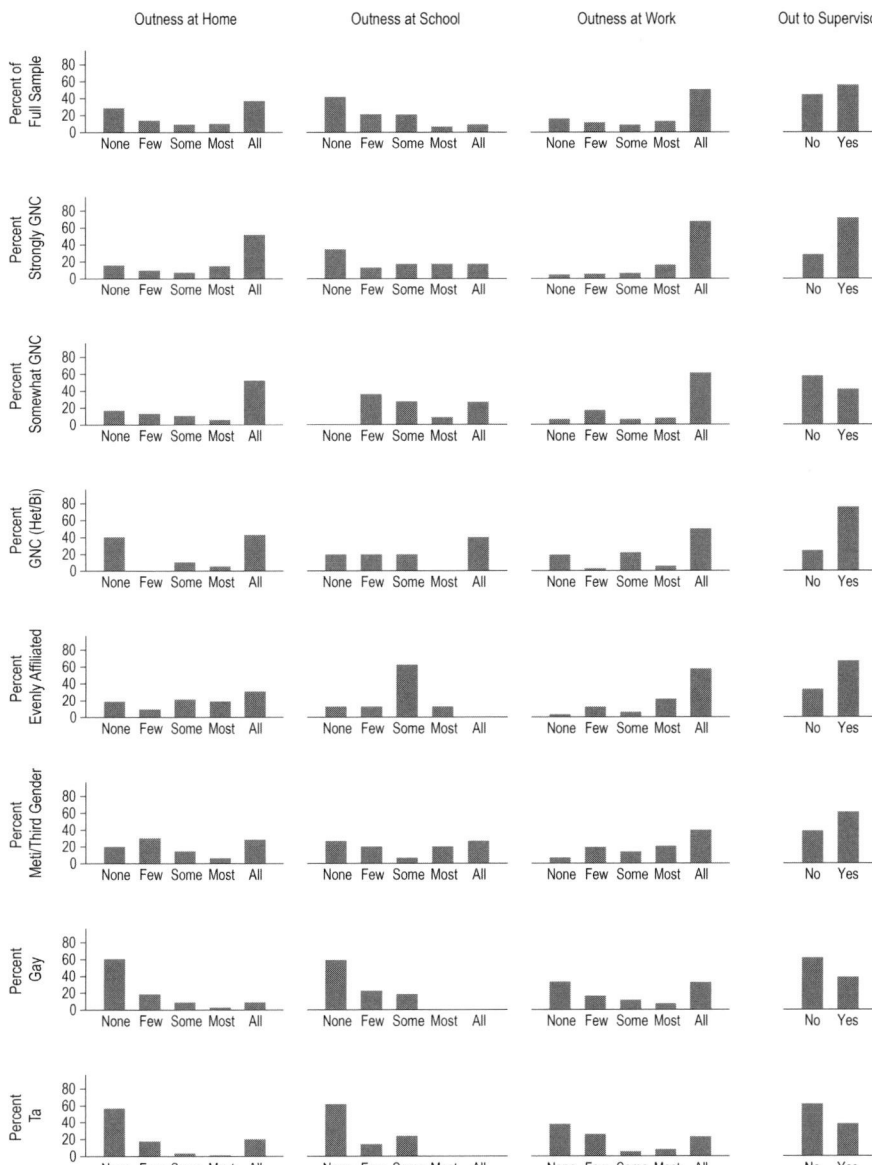

Figure 3. Levels of outness across multiple venues by the full sample and the seven groups from the latent class analysis of the Nepal Sexual and Gender Minorities Survey. GNC = gender nonconforming.

differences in how outness relates to perceived conformity among the groups. Respondents in the groups Strongly Gender Nonconforming and Somewhat Gender Nonconforming who are out to more people at home are less likely to report not experiencing discrimination while at the market due to perceived conformity. About half of the respondents in the Gay and Ta groups report not facing discrimination at a store or market, and there is no clear relationship between outness at home and not experiencing discrimination. We observe a somewhat negative relationship between outness and not facing discrimination due to perceived conformity for the respondents belonging to the group Strongly Gender Nonconforming (Kendall's $\tau = -.22$) and the group Somewhat Gender Nonconforming (Kendall's $\tau = -.33$). This indicates that in this context, respondents in the group Strongly Gender Nonconforming who are out to everyone at home rarely report not facing discrimination at a market due to perceived visual conformity.

We investigate the relationship between the multiple forms of outness and tendency to report not facing discrimination due to perceived visual conformity for the seven areas of social life.[9] While in some instances there is a relationship between levels of disclosure and experiences of discrimination, many of the relationships are not statistically significant. On average fewer than half of the respondents of *any* group report not experiencing discrimination due to perceived conformity. We also observe that the gap between the "Ta" and "Gay" groups in relation to the other groups tends to remain. We find that, in many areas of social life, those who are less likely to report not facing discrimination due to perceived visual conformity are those who have a stronger identification to gender-nonconforming identities.

We find that the LCA groups do offer additional insight into the experiences of sexual and gender minority people in our sample. We observe distinct levels of outness for each group by each of the venues. This also indicates that data collection efforts that administer surveys only in households may potentially undercount the population of sexual and gender minority people in Nepal. The respondents who do not belong to the groups "Strongly Gender Nonconforming" or "Somewhat Gender Nonconforming" tend to be less out at home, meaning that depending on survey administration processes, it is reasonable to expect a survey to miss sexual and gender minorities in its count. Alongside observing varying levels of outness, we find that it is highly unlikely for gender-nonconforming respondents to report that they did not face discrimination due to perceived visual conformity, and while the same is true for cisgender gay respondents, there is a measurable difference in how many report visual conformity as a reason for not experiencing discrimination.

Limitations

As noted earlier, the generalizability and applicability of this sample are limited due to its bias in the sampling procedure. Because the survey outreach strategy was conducted from HIV service provider offices, which have a primarily male-assigned-at-birth clientele, a very small proportion of our sample is female-assigned-at-birth respondents. Therefore, our analysis is limited to people who were assigned male or intersex at birth. For the purposes of this article, we have decided not to analyze data about female-assigned respondents because that sample was small, and combining it with the male-assigned sample could potentially lead to conclusions that would be inconsistent if we analyzed them separately.

We chose to limit the focus of this article to the methodology of collecting data on sexual and gender minority identities in Nepal and the correlation of these demographic factors to identity disclosure and experiences of discrimination. Although the discrimination question explicitly asks about discrimination related to sexual or gender minority status, the authors recognize that socioeconomic or other factors may affect the likelihood that a person experiences discrimination, and these factors would be important to include in a broader analysis of these data.

Recommendations

This study demonstrates the importance of community engagement (Tindana et al. 2007) and the early and frequent involvement of representatives from, in this case, sexual and gender minority communities to create an inclusive and nuanced survey instrument. Community consultations, particularly those that discussed translation and terminology, provided crucial feedback—ranging from discussions of sexual and gender identity language to decisions on how to phrase and order other elements in the survey. Repeated engagement with Nepali partners during the translation and revision process led to increased mutual ownership of the survey instrument design process and accuracy and applicability of the language used. Every small adjustment carried significant meaning for those involved in the process. For example, after two rounds of translation, it was requested that Nepali sexual orientation and gender identity terms be put at the top of the list in question 16 (appendix 1), because listing English terms such as "Gay and Lesbian" higher sent a message that those terms should be prioritized.

The design, implementation, and analysis process of this project suggests that future national surveys in Nepal, such as the 2021 Population and Housing Census, can be inclusive of SGM beyond adding a third column in the gender section—regardless of what it is called. In order to take into account the variety of ways in which Nepali people experience and express sexuality and gender, officials involved in designing survey instruments should consult with representatives from sexual and gender minority groups. Definitions provided for survey implementation staff should acknowledge the diversity among sexual and gender minority populations. Training programs should contextualize the reasons for asking the questions, normalize the process of asking, involve briefings on terminology, and explain special considerations for identity disclosure, such as privacy while interviewing (SMART 2009).

The findings of the LCA reinforce the observation that many SGM tend to not identify with a single identity term. Instead, of the seven distinct groups that emerged, five identified with gender-nonconforming identities and two identified with gender-conforming "Gay" and "Ta" identities. The "Evenly Affiliated" group indicates that it is possible to display the same level of association with multiple identities. Although this group was a small part of our sample, it provides an important reminder that SGM may not fit into, or remain in, discrete identity categories.

The distinctions among experiences of identity-based subgroups are important considerations for service providers and government offices engaged in programming with SGM populations. For example, interventions that focus on same-sex behavior (e.g., HIV prevention) need to consider ways to reach people using messaging that does not necessarily invoke *tesro lingi* or other SGM terminology in order to reach people who are not open about their identity or do not identify with any specific term. Experiences of discrimination in public places and bias against gender-nonconforming people should be similarly considered when designing programs and advocacy strategies. Refined data collection methods will enable civil society groups and policy makers to adequately serve and track the progress of SGM across various social-welfare contexts.

Kyle G. Knight was a 2012–14 visiting international fellow at the Williams Institute, UCLA School of Law. He lived and worked in Nepal for more than three years.

Andrew R. Flores, PhD, is public opinion and policy fellow at the Williams Institute, UCLA School of Law.

Sheila J. Nezhad is a Public Policy Fellow at the Williams Institute, UCLA School of Law. She holds a master's of development practice degree from the University of Minnesota.

Acknowledgment

This research was supported in part by the United Nations Development Programme under the Multi-Country South Asia Global Fund Programme (MSA-910-G02-H) and by the Norwegian Embassy in Nepal. We are very thankful to Jody L. Herman, Brad Sears, the anonymous reviewers, and the editors for their comments and recommendations on previous versions of this article. Any remaining errors are our own.

Notes

1. "Third gender" is sometimes used to refer to gender-nonconforming people and sometimes as an umbrella term to refer to the many sexual and gender minority identities in Nepal, either specifically or symbolically (*Pant v. Nepal*, Writ No. 917 of the Year 2064 BS [AD 2007], translated in *NJA Law Journal* 2008 at 262). That is, in some instances "third gender" (*tesro lingi* in Nepali) is translated to mean "transgender" specifically; in other instances, it includes a range of sexual and gender minorities (there is only one word for sex/gender in Nepali, *lingi*).

2. The full questionnaire and question sources are available from Andrew R. Flores upon request.

3. It should be noted that question 16.1 allowed respondents to list any term they preferred, whether it was listed in question 16 or not.

4. Forty-seven cases were dropped because they were incomplete. The data have been translated by BDS team leaders and entered into SurveyMonkey software in Nepal. Researchers at the Williams Institute have downloaded the data for analysis. Data cleaning and summary statistics are conducted using STATA 13.0 (College Station, TX). Multivariate analyses are performed in Mplus (Muthén and Muthén 1998–2014), and the R package poLCA is used to confirm the multivariate analyses (Linzer and Lewis 2011).

5. We use the terms *perceived nonconformity* and *perceived conformity* as language to describe whether respondents believe instances of discrimination are due to the perception of others as viewing the respondent as a gender and/or sexual minority. We borrow and slightly modify these terms from Jaime M. Grant, Lisa A. Mottet, and Justin Tanis (2011), who use *visual nonconformity* as a term to describe "whether respondents believed their gender presentation matched their gender identity" (27).

6. We focus solely on respondents who had male sex assigned at birth. The size of our female-sex-assigned-at-birth sample would make it unreasonable to include them in this analysis, as this would lead to conceptual stretching in this case. We will discuss and provide results for that subset of the sample in our subsequent studies.

7. The model-driven approach selects the number of classes that minimizes the Bayesian Information Criterion (BIC) to its lowest level. The BIC is an estimate that examines how well a model explains the variation present in the data while issuing a penalty for too many parameters. This approach has been validated as a reliable way to determine the number of classes in an LCA (Nylund, Asparouhov, and Muthén 2007). We conducted the initial LCA in Mplus version 7 (Muthén and Muthén 1998–2014) and reconducted it in poLCA to confirm the findings (Linzer and Lewis 2011). The BICs for the separate LCAs are: two classes 13469.137, three classes 12716.438, four classes 12473.018, five classes 12379.387, six classes 12307.614, seven classes 12272.76, eight classes 12339.767, and nine classes 12395.734.

8. Note that not all respondents attend school or have occupations, so sample sizes vary across venues. The smallest sample is of respondents who are in school, which increases the instability of those estimates.

9. To estimate these rates, the R package poLCA (Linzer and Lewis 2011) was again used to estimate the bivariate relationship. The analysis applies LCA to generate reliable estimates in highly stratified contingency tables (Linzer and Lewis 2011). For each estimate, we identify the modal response that each of the seven classes would give to each of the identity questions, and we then estimate the bivariate contingency table for the relationship between disclosure and not facing discrimination due to perceived visual conformity. Contact Andrew R. Flores for full results.

References

Adhikari, Gyanu. 2013. "Family Matters." *Kathmandu Post*, February 25. www.ekantipur.com/the
-kathmandu-post/2013/02/25/related_articles/family-matters/245712.html.

Al Jazeera. 2013. "Citizenship Cards for Nepal's 'Third Gender.'" February 5. www.aljazeera
.com/video/asia/2013/02/20132518501198693.html.

Baudh, Sumit. 2008. "Human Rights Interrupted: An Illustration from India." In *Development
with a Body: Sexuality, Human Rights, and Development*, edited by Andrea Cornwall,
Sonia Corrêa, and Susie Jolly, 93–107. New York: Zed.

Bochenek, Michael, and Kyle Knight. 2012. "Establishing a Third Gender Category in Nepal:
Process and Prognosis." *Emory International Law Review* 26, no. 1: 11–41.

Boyce, Paul, and Sunil Pant. 2001. "Rapid Ethnography of Male to Male Sexuality and Sexual
Health—Kathmandu, Nepal." Family Health International. www.hivpolicy.org/Library
/HPP000564.pdf.

Cohen, Lawrence. 2005. "The Kothi Wars: AIDS Cosmopolitanism and the Morality of Classification." In *Sex in Development: Science, Sexuality, and Morality in Global Perspective*,
edited by Vincanne Adams and Stacy Leigh Pigg, 269–303. Durham, NC: Duke University
Press.

"Decision of the [Nepal] Supreme Court on the Rights of Lesbian, Gay, Bisexual, Transsexual, and
Intersex (LGBTI) People [*Pant v. Nepal*]." 2008. *NJA Law Journal* 2, no. 1: 261–86. www
.gaylawnet.com/laws/cases/PantvNepal.pdf.

Forum for Women, Law, and Development. 2011. "Shadow Report on the Fourth and Fifth
Periodic Report by the Government of Nepal on CEDAW." www2.ohchr.org/english
/bodies/cedaw/docs/ngos/FWLD_NepalCEDAW49.pdf.

Grant, Jaime M., Lisa A. Mottet, and Justin Tanis. 2011. "Injustice at Every Turn: A Report of the
National Transgender Discrimination Survey." National Center for Transgender Equality
and National Gay and Lesbian Taskforce. www.thetaskforce.org/downloads/reports
/reports/ntds_full.pdf.

Herdt, Gilbert. 1996. *Third Sex, Third Gender: Beyond Sexual Dimorphism in Culture and History*.
New York: Zone.

Knight, Kyle. 2011. "What We Can Learn from Nepal's Inclusion of 'Third Gender' on Its Census."
New Republic, July 18. www.newrepublic.com/article/world/92076/nepal-census-third
-gender-lgbt-sunil-pant.

———. 2012. "Dividing by Three: Nepal Recognizes a Third Gender." World Policy Institute,
World Policy (blog), February 1. www.worldpolicy.org/blog/2012/02/01/dividing-three
-nepal-recognizes-third-gender.

———. 2014. "The Spark: How Sunil Pant Ignited a Queer Rights Movement in Nepal." *Caravan*,
March 1. www.caravanmagazine.in/reportage/spark.

Lau, Holning. 2013. "Law, Sexuality, and Transnational Perspectives." *Drexel Law Review* 5, no. 2:
479–95. drexel.edu/ ∼ /media/Files/law/law%20review/Spring-2013/Lau.ashx.

Linzer, Drew A., and Jeffrey B. Lewis. 2011. "poLCA: An R Package for Polytomous Variable Latent
Class Analysis." *Journal of Statistical Software* 42, no. 10: 1–29.

Muthén, Linda K., and Bengt O. Muthén. 1998–2014. *Mplus User's Guide*. 7th ed. Los Angeles:
Muthén and Muthén.

Nylund, Karen L., Tihomir Asparouhov, and Bengt O. Muthén. 2007. "Deciding on the Number
of Classes in Latent Class Analysis and Growth Mixture Modeling: A Monte Carlo
Simulation Study." *Structural Equation Modeling* 14, no. 4: 37–41.

Rankin, Katharine. 2010. "Cultures of Economies: Gender and Socio-spatial Change in Nepal." *Gender, Place, and Culture* 10, no. 2: 111–29.

Reddy, Gayatri. 2005. *With Respect to Sex.* Chicago: University of Chicago Press.

Shrestha, Manesh. 2011. "Nepal Census Recognizes 'Third Gender.'" CNN, May 31. edition.cnn .com/2011/WORLD/asiapcf/05/31/nepal.census.gender.

SMART (Sexual Minority Assessment Research Team). 2009. "Best Practices for Asking Questions about Sexual Orientation on Surveys." Williams Institute. williamsinstitute.law.ucla.edu /research/census-lgbt-demographics-studies/best-practices-for-asking-questions-about -sexual-orientation-on-surveys.

Tamang, Seira. 2003. "Patriarchy and the Production of Homo-erotic Behavior in Nepal." *Studies in Nepali History and Society* 8, no. 2: 225–58. martinchautari.org.np/files/2_%20Seira %20Tamang.pdf.

Thapa, Deepak. 2001. "Ties That Bind." *Kathmandu Post*, July 21. www.ekantipur.com/2011/07/21 /related-article/ties-that-bind/337746.html.

Tindana, Paulina O., et al. 2007. "Grand Challenges in Global Health: Community Engagement in Research in Developing Countries." *PLoS Medicine* 4, no. 9: e273.

Valentine, David. 2007. *Imagining Transgender: An Ethnography of a Category.* Durham, NC: Duke University Press.

Appendix 1. Question 16 from the Nepal Sexual and Gender Minorities Survey, asking respondents how they identify (English and Nepali)

16 ٩६	There are many terms people use to identify their sexual orientation and gender identity. Now I am going to read some terms to you and I'd like to know to which degree do the following terms apply to you? For each term you must answer "not at all" "somewhat"or "strongly" *(circle answers)* आफ्नो यौनिक अभिमुखीकरण तथा लैङ्गिक पहिचानलाई चिनाउनका लागि मानिसहरूले धेरै शब्दहरू प्रयोग गर्दछन् । म अब केही शब्दहरू पढ्छु र जान्न चाहन्छु कि तपाईँको लागि कुन हदसम्म यी शब्दहरू लागू हुन्छन् ।हरेक शब्दको लागि तपाईँले "हुँदै होइन","केही हदसम्म हो" वा "धेरै नै हो" भन्ने जवाफ रोज्नु पर्नेछ ।(उत्तरमा गोलो घेरा लगाउनुहोस्)	Meti			मेटी		
		not at all	somewhat	strongly	हुँदै होइन	केही हदसम्म हो	धेरै नै हो
		Ta			टा		
		not at all	somewhat	strongly	हुँदै होइन	केही हदसम्म हो	धेरै नै हो
		Kothi			कोथी		
		not at all	somewhat	strongly	हुँदै होइन	केही हदसम्म हो	धेरै नै हो
		Panthi			पन्थी		
		not at all	somewhat	strongly	हुँदै होइन	केही हदसम्म हो	धेरै नै हो
		Hijara			हिजडा		
		not at all	somewhat	strongly	हुँदै होइन	केही हदसम्म हो	धेरै नै हो
		Fulumulu			फुलुमुलु		
		not at all	somewhat	strongly	हुँदै होइन	केही हदसम्म हो	धेरै नै हो
		Transgender			तेस्रो लिङ्गी		
		not at all	somewhat	strongly	हुँदै होइन	केही हदसम्म हो	धेरै नै हो
		Gay or lesbian			पुरुष समलिङ्गी वा महिला समलिङ्गी		
		not at all	somewhat	strongly	हुँदै होइन	केही हदसम्म हो	धेरै नै हो
		Heterosexual or straight			विपरित लिङ्गी वा स्ट्रेट		
		not at all	somewhat	strongly	हुँदै होइन	केही हदसम्म हो	धेरै नै हो
		Bisexual			द्विलिङ्गी		
		not at all	somewhat	strongly	हुँदै होइन	केही हदसम्म हो	धेरै नै हो

Appendix 2. Question 17 from the Nepal Sexual and Gender Minorities Survey, asking respondent about their sexual attraction (English and Nepali)

17	People are different in their sexual	Metis	मेटी
१७	attraction to other people. Which best	Kothis	कोथी
	describes your feelings? Are you attracted	Panthis	पन्थी
	to? (multiple answers possible)	Hijaras	हिजडा
	मानिसहरू यौनिक रूपमा अन्य मानिसहरूप्रति	Males	पुरुष
	फरक-फरक किसिमले आकर्षित हुन्छन्। तपाईँको भावनालाई	Females	महिला
	सबैभन्दा उत्कृष्ट तरिकाले कुन कुराले बुझाउँछ ?	Transgender men	तेस्रो लिङ्गी पुरुष
	तपाई यिनीहरूप्रति आकर्षित हुनुहुन्छ ? (एकभन्दा धेरै	Transgender women	तेस्रो लिङ्गी महिला
	उत्तरहरू सम्भव छन्)	Other	अन्य

Appendix 3. Question 18 from the Nepal Sexual and Gender Minorities Survey, asking respondents about their sexual behavior (English and Nepali)

18	In the past 12 months, who have you had	Metis	मेटी
१८	sex with? (multiple answers possible)	Kothis	कोथी
	विगत १२ महिनामा तपाईँले कोसँग यौन सम्पर्क राख्नुभयो ?	Panthis	पन्थी
	(एकभन्दा धेरै उत्तरहरू सम्भव छन्)	Hijaras	हिजडा
		Males	पुरुष
		Females	महिला
		Transgender men	तेस्रो लिङ्गी पुरुष
		Transgender women	तेस्रो लिङ्गी महिला
		Other	अन्य
		I have not had sex	यौन सम्पर्क राखेको छैनँ

Making Transgender Count in Poland
Disciplined Individuals and Circumscribed Populations

ANNA M. KŁONKOWSKA

Abstract The article examines the criteria for determining which individuals become legible as transgender in Poland and how expert medical and legal discourses normalize the gender identity, sexuality, and gender performativity of this group. Only those transgender people who fit the outdated model of the "true transsexual" are allowed to (in fact expected to) undergo a physical transition. Once transitioned, they are expected to blend into society and present heteronormative, socially conforming gender roles. In Poland, only those people who have been diagnosed as so-called true transsexuals are counted in the estimated number of transgender people. After describing the convoluted legal and medical processes that individuals are required to follow, the article presents qualitative research describing how transgender people in Poland have responded to these normalizing systems. The article concludes with proposals that would make trans populations more legible to policy makers and the mass media without imposing outdated medical norms on the trans community.

Keywords transgender, transsexual, Poland, expert discourse, heteronormativity, exclusion

The social aspects of the transgender phenomenon are well grounded in the English-language literature concerning the topic (e.g., Currah 2009; Devor 1989; Ekins and King 2006; Feinberg 1999; Hines 2007; Stone 1991; Stryker 2008; Whittle 2002; Wilchins 1997). In Poland, transgender studies has only recently been acknowledged in the field of social sciences. Previously, it has been the domain of sexological and psychiatric studies (e.g., Imieliński and Dulko 1988, 1989) and presented mostly in the essentialist paradigm. This essentialist approach in Polish studies on gender identity, which would limit transgender variation to transsexualism only, has strongly influenced the social reception of the transgender phenomenon. However, the emergence of transgender studies and approaches associated with it, such as feminist and queer theory and social constructionism, has transformed thinking on transgender phenomena in much of the social sciences in Poland (e.g., Bieńkowska 2012; Dynarski 2012b; Kłonkowska 2013; Kochanowski 2008).

DOI 10.1215/23289252-2848931   © 2015 Duke University Press

Although many scholars in social science fields and activists in trans organizations do not subscribe to the essentialist approach, it continues to govern most legal and medical discourses on gender identity in Poland. Consequently, it is the narrow medical view of transsexualism that still frames the policies of government agencies and health services as well as the representation of trans people in the mass media. Only people who meet the criteria for "true transsexuals" count (Benjamin 1966): those whose desired gender entirely matches a gender socially recognized as the opposite of the one assigned them at birth; those who are heterosexual in relation to their gender identity; and those who want to legally change their gender markers and seek sex reassignment surgery. Moreover, the most common term appearing in Polish medical discourse and legal documents is *transsexualism* (*transseksualizm*) (as in the commentaries on Article 1, paragraph 1, of the Family and Guardianship Code; see Jędrejek 2013; ISAP 2010). The frame of reference for the treatment of transsexuality in Poland remains based on the medical and sexological discourse of the 1980s and early 1990s (Imieliński and Dulko 1988, 1989). The centrality of the term *transsexualism* in Polish medical discourse reflects the language of the tenth edition of the International Classifications of Diseases (*ICD*), first published in 1990, and earlier editions of the Diagnostic and Statistical Manual (*DSM*) of the American Psychiatric Association. This framework precludes the possibility of recognizing the wide range of individuals exhibiting gender-nonconforming attitudes and behaviors.

Narrowing the transgender phenomenon to "true transsexuals" circumscribes who gets classified as trans, what health-related transition services they will receive, and whether or not an individual's gender identity will be legally recognized by the state. By setting out medicalized limits to the threshold criteria, it also radically limits *who* gets counted and thus plays an important role in determining the estimated size of the trans population. Counting only "true transsexuals" rather than the much larger group of people whose gender identity or gender behavior does not comport with the sex assigned at birth results in a much smaller number. Thus how the trans population is measured influences the degree to which its members and their interests will seem to matter. This has significant consequences for the trans community: the smaller the population seems to be, the less importance is attached to policies affecting it and the more invisible it remains.[1]

Although there is no official count of the trans population in Poland, in academic publications, as well as in mass-media discourse, some speculations are endlessly circulated. One estimate is based on statistics from the earlier editions of *DSM* on the prevalence of transsexuality. According to the *DSM*-IV (American Psychiatric Association 1994), often cited in Polish academic publications and mass-media discourses (which consider the terms *gender identity disorder* and *transsexualism* as equivalent), for every 30,000 individuals assigned male at birth, one will seek gender reassignment (MTF). For trans men (FTM), the prevalence rate suggested in the *DSM*-IV is one per 100,000 individuals assigned female at birth (Fajkowska-Stanik 2001: 33). Given a population of 38,501,000 (Central Statistics Office of Poland 2011), these ratios would suggest there are only 614 trans women and 201 trans men in all of Poland (Bieńkowska 2012: 39). Based on these outmoded assumptions concerning prevalence, there are 815 trans men and women in all of Poland. The credibility of these numbers is called into question by studies finding that in Poland, like in the rest of the ex-communist East European countries, trans men outnumber trans women (Strzelecka 2007; Imieliński and Dulko 1988: 168). Even more problematic, the trans population is also measured by literally adding up the number of people who have successfully managed to navigate the heavily policed processes for gender transition. The only available data refer to court records concerning the number of people who have applied for legal gender recognition. According to this metric, from 2009 to 2012, 223 applications were submitted, and 203 were successful (Węgrzyn 2013). According to the slightly more generous methodology of counting successful gender recognition cases, a couple of hundred trans people come into legal existence every four years. In Poland, the estimated percentage of transgender people in the population is severely underestimated because only those people who have been diagnosed as "true transsexuals" and have succeeded in having their legal gender markers changed count as transgender.

I have conducted more than thirty qualitative in-depth interviews with trans people in Poland between 2010 and 2013. If one subscribed to the prevalence ratios cited with authority in Poland, one would be forced to conclude that I have talked at length with almost four percent of the entire trans population in the country. Many of these individuals, however, would not be legible as trans because they have not successfully navigated the medical and legal obstacles to transition. Many more of them would not care to attempt such a feat, because their gender identity or gender behavior falls outside the bounds of the "true transsexual." At this point, it is perhaps obvious that the meanings attached to the terms *trans* and *transgender* in this discussion are not stable. Indeed, I use the terms to signal the disagreement between those who hold an expansive view of gender nonconformity (trans people, social scientists, and trans allies) and official discourses that work to preserve the rigid and heteronormative definition of transsexual. Social scientists and trans people in Poland seek to expand the field of what and who gets counted—transgender rather than transsexual.

Medical and Legal Processes for Gender Transition

To demonstrate the narrowness of the classification and the many points at which transgender people can fail the test of "true transsexuals," I now describe the convoluted legal and medical procedures that govern gender reassignment. The process starts with psychological and psychiatric evaluations and a "Real Life Test," which supposedly enables the diagnostician (usually a sexologist) to establish whether one is "truly" transsexual and thus able to undertake the social aspects of transitioning to a different gender role. Afterward, the diagnostician commissions physical examinations to rule out some medical conditions and to determine one's fitness for medical transitioning. Although there is no official list of the advised medical examinations, usually they include: an electroencephalogram, genetic tests such as karyotype test, an X-ray or computed tomography scan of the head, an ophthalmoscopy exam, liver and kidney puncture lab tests, blood morphology, tests of luteinizing and follicle-stimulating hormone levels, an abdominal ultrasound, and a urological/gynecological examination.[2] During the psychiatric part of the diagnostic stage, individuals should prove to the satisfaction of the clinician that after transition they will be heterosexual and that they will and can conform to traditional gender roles and expressions. Those who will not pretend that after transition they will be attracted to the opposite gender and those who fail to convincingly portray their future selves as unfailingly heteronormative will not receive the needed diagnosis and will go no further in the transition process. If medical tests indicate no health issues, and if the individual receives a psychiatric diagnosis of transsexuality, the diagnostician will likely prescribe feminizing or masculinizing hormones (Dynarski 2012a). Those who do not receive the diagnosis or who have problematic results from the medical tests are denied the opportunity to transition medically or socially.

The legal aspects of the process do not begin until a medical transition is already underway. At this stage, those who have passed the medical and psychological evaluations must prove their consistent and explicit gender identity and their commitment to live in the new gender role permanently by undergoing feminizing or masculinizing medical procedures, including hormone therapy and, in the case of trans men, a double masectomy and chest reconstruction. As a result, transgender people who do not wish to or do not feel a need to undergo those medical procedures either are forced by the system to accommodate the requirements by medically masculinizing or feminizing their bodies or find themselves prevented from having their gender identity legally recognized (Kryszk and Kłonkowska 2012: 243–44).

Moreover, trans people seeking medical services face another dilemma. Article 156 of the Polish Criminal Code (ISAP 1997a) criminalizes medical treatments that interfere with an individual's "procreation abilities," and transsexuality is not one of the serious medical conditions exempted from this provision. As Wiktor Dynarski, a researcher and president of Poland's Trans-Fuzja Foundation, points out, providers have interpreted "procreation ability" to include chest surgery on trans men. "As a result, a vicious circle is created in which a person is required to undergo a mastectomy, but some health care providers refuse to carry out such an operation because of the fear of legal consequences. This situation drastically limits the offer of medical help to transgender people and creates a corruption-friendly environment" (Dynarski 2012a).

Those who have made it this far in the process now must initiate the legal procedures for changing one's gender markers. According to Article 156 of the Polish Criminal Code (ISAP 1997a), genital surgeries such as phalloplasties or vaginoplasties can be performed only after a court has issued a positive verdict on one's gender recognition and the individual has been issued a new birth certificate and a new personal identification number. To secure this court ruling, individuals (usually adults) must file a lawsuit against their parents to meet Article 189 of the Polish Criminal Code (ISAP 1997a). Dynarski describes the problems this adversarial process can create:

> Because a person's parents are involved in the court process, the procedure can be irrationally prolonged, especially when parents do not accept their child's decision. . . . Since the Polish court system does not educate its judges on the subject of gender recognition, the court hears out both of sides and (usually) calls an expert witness . . . who is expected to check whether the first diagnosis was carried out accordingly. As a result, this process can take up to several years. (2012a)

Although an applicant's post-transition heterosexuality will have already been confirmed during the diagnostic stage, judges will often query trans people about their sexual orientation before issuing their verdict.

If the court verdict on one's gender recognition is positive, the individual's birth certificate is amended to reflect the new gender marker. The given name and the form of the surname are also changed, as most Polish surnames indicate the person's gender. Unfortunately, however, the old information remains: anyone who views the full certificate can easily discover a transgender person's past. At this point, one may apply for new identity documents (e.g., ID card, driver's license, university diploma). Since the successful applicant has already convinced their diagnostician of their commitment to live a post-transition life in a (hetero) normative gender role once the gender markers are changed, married individuals must divorce their pretransition husbands or wives. Same-sex marriages are banned in Poland according to Article I, Part I, of the Family and Guardianship Code (ISAP 1964) and Article 18 of the Constitution of the Republic of Poland (ISAP 1997b). It is only at this stage that an individual can undergo genital and other surgeries that would, in the view of the state, complete their transition. But there is yet a final barrier: the National Health Fund does not cover the cost of those medical procedures. At the moment of writing (September 2014), legislation to reform this system of gender recognition, which Dynarski describes as among the worst in Europe (2012a), is under discussion in the Polish parliament (Olczyk 2014).

Transgender Strategies of Resistance and Assimilation

I now turn to a discussion of the response of trans people to this classification regime. Since 2010, as noted, I have conducted more than thirty in-depth interviews with transgender people in Poland. I have collected the biographical stories of my respondents and studied Internet forums (transseksualizm.pl) populated by transgender people (Kłonkowska 2012, 2013; Bojarska and Kłonkowska 2014). Given the predominance of the myth of the "true transsexual" in both the mass media and expert discourses, it is important to contest that narrative with the voices of trans people. My respondents spoke of the imposition of traditional gender norms, compulsory heterosexuality, whether to resist or assimilate, and most important, how transgender should be defined.[3]

Marcin, a trans activist, addressed the need to deceive in order to meet the pathologizing criteria:

> In the whole official process of sex reassignment the most frustrating is the constraint of lying in order to fit the heteronormative pattern of a poor, unhappy misfit who, with the help of God-doctors, can finally become an ordinary Mr. Smith. Not only do we have to beg successive institutions to give us a chance of a normal, decent life but we don't even get the right to be ourselves—no, we have to be almost a perfect example of dysfunction.

According to Igor, some doctors are aware of this common practice:

> I read a comment from a doctor who claimed that only statements of transsexuals after transition are worth something (i.e., are honest), because only a transsexual who is independent of a doctor will tell the truth. So doctors are aware that we stretch the truth to achieve our goal.

Respondents also took issue with the impossible ideals they were measured against, norms that cisgender people can fail to meet without losing their status as men or women. According to Konrad:

> Not every man has short hair. Why should an FTM? Not every woman has long hair. Why should an MTF? Not every man is tough and has a typically masculine hobby. Why should an FTM? Not every woman wears makeup and feminine

clothes. Why should an MTF? There isn't one person in the world who fits an ideal image of a man or a woman.

Respondents also took issue with the role sexual orientation plays in the diagnosis of transsexuality. Cisgender people in Poland most certainly experience the social pressure to be heterosexual. But again, the legal gender of homosexual cis individuals does not depend on their sexual orientation. But for noncisgender LGB people, their gender identity can be invalidated by their (post-transition) sexual orientation.

> Iza: My trans colleagues who identify themselves as gay lied to their doctors. . . . They had a choice of saying they're straight and getting their medicines right away or admitting they're gay or bisexual and be forced to undergo psychotherapy. . . . It was clear what they would choose.

> Sławka: Such doctors [diagnosticians] draw a conclusion that *all* trans people are straight. This is what they tell their next patient, that's what they write in their publications, and this is how their publications are being cited in the Internet. And as a result, a few years later, a poor little trans person who is looking for some knowledge and identity discovers that since their sexual orientation is different, it means that they must be some kind of a "pervert" and will not qualify for treatment.

Social and expert pressure exerted on transgender people concerning their declared sexual orientation also affects their self-perception. Some transgender people, especially those identifying as transsexual, view heterosexuality as confirmation of one's gender identity and status as a "true transsexual." They remain confined by the socially constructed, heteronormative matrix defining femininity and masculinity. This is especially true for transgender people who have not had body modifications.

> Zdzisław, who was assigned female at birth: I live with a woman. I can't imagine a man touching me . . . as long as I have my present body. If [my body] were "proper" I wouldn't have such objections.

> Janek, also assigned female at birth: Oh, God, I like men, so maybe I'm not a true transsexual.

Only by subscribing (or pretending to) to the norms of the disciplinary apparatuses governing transsexuality can hetero- and gender-normative trans people succeed in becoming legible, first as transsexuals in the diagnostic process and later, post transition, as "proper" men and women. These assimilating subjects not only reproduce the common perception of transgender individuals; they influence the self-perception of other transgender people as well, and they reinforce the demand to conform. Of course, it is ultimately the expert discourses of participating sexologists, psychiatrists, psychologists, and physicians that produce the power/knowledge regime that certifies (through diagnosis and legal proceedings) who in Poland can change their gender.

From Gender-Disciplined Individuals to Circumscribed Transsexual Populations

The disciplining of trans individuals through measurement and evaluation of their identifications, bodies, gestures, desires, and everyday activities also has effects at the level of the population. Norms, Michel Foucault explains, "circulate between the disciplinary and the regulatory" (2003: 252). While disciplinary knowledges center on an "anatomo-politics of the human body," regulatory controls are interventions on the "biopolitics of the population" (Foucault 1978: 139). Transposed onto the regulatory realm, the norms governing whether, how, and when individuals in Poland may transition from one gender to another also become metrics for estimating the number of transsexuals in the population. As a result, only a tiny fraction of the number of people who identify as transgender, broadly construed, become legible as trans. A class of individuals constituting 0.00001 percent to 0.00003 percent of the entire population can be labeled as a mere anomaly, their needs easily ignored. Moreover, the existence of this small group will have little effect on challenging hegemonic notions of sex and gender. This is especially true because the individuals classified as trans are perceived as only moving from one pole of the gender binary to another instead of challenging the notion of dichotomous gender.

As in most other countries, transgender people in Poland are also rendered invisible by government data collection efforts. Questions about assigned birth sex, current gender identity, and transgender identification have never been included in any census conducted by Central Statistical Office of Poland. But it is not impossible to do a much better job at counting the trans population. Rather than using criteria originating in medicalized models of transsexuality, a census could ask people to simply state their gender identity, the sex they were assigned at birth, or transgender identification. This would allow people to make declarations about their gender identity in the same way they now can declare an ethnic identity or languages spoken. Adding one or two questions to the census questionnaire should not be problematic and would have a number of significant consequences. First, allowing individuals to simply declare their gender would begin to undermine the authority of the expert medical and legal discourses empowered to determine individuals' gender. Second, letting people declare their own identity instead of letting the expert discourse decide for them could also precipitate changes in social attitudes about gender. Moving away from the essentialist approach to sex and gender identity could result in diminishing the now widespread perception of transgender identities as exceptions, norm violations, illnesses, or deviations. Third, transgender people would be more likely to have a voice in decisions concerning the health, safety, and public welfare of the population. Fourth, it might also begin to transform language, the bedrock of many social attitudes about gender. In the Polish language, not only pronouns but also the noun, adjective, verb, and numeral forms express the gender of the person speaking and the person to whom the speech is addressed.

Finally, over time, the transgender category itself might be productively destabilized. As people recognize that many cis people exhibit gender-nonconforming expressions and behaviors, the heavily policed borders between cisgender and transgender and between gender identity and expression could be breached. As one of my respondents, Konrad, suggested:

> There is not a single person in the world who would totally fit the ideal model of a man or a woman. Partly because there is not just one single model of a man or a woman. Everything depends on where we actually are, where we come from, what our attitude is toward the things we were taught in childhood. So, isn't it true that everybody is trans, at least in a tiny little part?

In moving away from rigid expert discourses and disciplinary norms and toward ways of figuring trans that are no longer bounded in essentializing notions of sex and gender, bodies and identities, other questions arise. At which point does a nonconforming attitude to gender performance consolidate into a transgender identity? Kasia, one of my respondents, pointed out that being transgender may be a temporary identification, not a permanent one:

> I'm wondering if now—when I've completed all these changes and transformations, when I have new documents and when I finally have the body that fits who I am; when I do not only feel like a woman, but I also am acknowledged to be female on my new birth certificate and in all my documents, and when I have a female body and I like this gender role—so I'm wondering, am I still being transgender? Maybe I am no longer transgender, maybe I'm cisgender now? Because now I don't feel like transgender anymore.

As Richard Ekins and Dave King explain, "Transgendering . . . refers to the idea of moving across (transferring) from one preexisting gender category to another (either temporarily or permanently); to the idea of living in between genders; and to the idea of living 'beyond gender' altogether" (2006: xiv). Transgender will mean different things to different people. Wiktor, one of my respondents, explains:

> After shifting and blending different roles, being identified in another . . . speaking about myself beyond the known linguistic categories . . . I feel an explicit need to point out how very individual my own experience is and that it absolutely doesn't mean that all of us see the issue of transgender identity in the same way.

Since it is not easy to draw a distinction between cis- and transgender identity, since being transgender may mean different things to different people, since it can be permanent identity change, a temporary stage, or an ongoing lifelong process, no one but the individuals themselves should be able to declare what their gender identity is. Experts and officials should not have the power to decide whether an individual's gender identity will be recognized by the state.

Anna M. Kłonkowska, an adjunct professor in the Department of Social Sciences at the University of Gdansk and a visiting scholar at the Center for the Study of Men and Masculinities, Stony Brook University, is a sociologist, psychologist, and philosopher, publishes in the field of transgender studies, and is the editor in chief of the sociological journal *Miscellanea Anthropologica et Sociologica*. She also has facilitated one of the few support groups for transgender people in Poland since 2010 and cooperates with the Trans-Fuzja Foundation.

Acknowledgments
I would like to thank Paisley Currah for his editorial guidance, Amanda Kennedy for linguistic corrections, Wiktor Dynarski for his helpful comments, and the individuals who shared their stories with me in interviews.

Notes

1. The Polish terminology applied to the transgender phenomenon is not equivalent to the English terminology. First, there is no Polish word for gender. The Polish word *płeć* is equivalent to the English term *sex*, and the lack of a correlate for the English word *gender* implies that there is no differentiation between sex and gender. Thus *płeć* has a determined and determining essential character. With regard to trans, the lack of a Polish term for gender results in a confusing situation. The term used for transsexualism is *transseksualizm*, a literal copy of the English term. But the term used for transgender (understood as broader than transsexualism and including gender-nonconforming identities and practices) is *transpłciowość*, and that term is in fact also derived from "transsexualism" (instead of "transgender"), as the word *płeć* means "sex," not "gender."

Thus, in Polish, the difference between the terms *transpłciowość* (transgender) and *transseksualizm* (transsexualism) seems insignificant from the linguistic point of view, even though they are defined differently. Nevertheless, of concern here is that only the term *transseksualizm*, not *transpłciowość*, appears in Polish legal and medical discourse concerning the transgender population. The latter is used only by social scientists and trans advocates. Also, *transpłciowość* is sometimes replaced by Polish social scientists and by trans activists with the English term *transgender* to signify "individuals . . . whose personal identities [are] considered to fall somewhere on a spectrum between 'transvestite' . . . and 'transsexual'" (Stryker 2006: 4). Using the English term avoids the essentialism conveyed by the Polish word *płeć*. In this article, I use the word *transgender* as it is used in the contemporary English-language social sciences: as an umbrella term broadly encompassing a whole variety of gender-nonconforming identities and practices.

2. This list of tests is based on accounts of members of a support group for transgender people that I have been running since 2010.

3. Interview quotations have been translated by the author. The names of respondents have been changed. Polish first names always reveal the gender: If the name ends in an *a*, it is a female name. If the name ends with a consonant, it is a male name.

References

American Psychiatric Association. 1994. *Diagnostic and Statistical Manual of Mental Disorders*. 4th ed. Washington, DC: American Psychiatric Association.

Benjamin, Harry. 1966. *The Transsexual Phenomenon*. New York: Julian.

Bieńkowska, Małgorzata. 2012. *Transseksualizm w Polsce: Wymiar Indywidualny i społeczny przekraczania binarnego systemu płci* (*Transsexualism in Poland: Individual and Social Dimensions of Overstepping the Gender Binary System*). Białystok: Wydawnictwo Uniwersytetu w Białymstoku.

Bojarska, Katarzyna, and Anna M. Kłonkowska. 2014. "TRANSgresja płci, TRANZycja ciała, TRANSwersja tożsamości: Czym jest TRANSpłciowość?" ("Gender Transgression, Body Transition, Identity Transversion: What Is Transgenderism?") In *Psychospołeczne, prawne i medyczne aspekty transpłciowości* (*Psychosocial, Legal, and Medical Aspects of Transgenderism*), edited by Anna M. Kłonkowska and Katarzyna Bojarska, 63–82. Gdańsk: Wydawnictwo Uniwersytetu Gdańskiego.

Central Statistics Office of Poland. 2011. *Narodowy spis powszechny ludności i mieszkań* (*General National Census of Population and Housing*). www.stat.gov.pl/cps/rde/xbcr/gus/lud _raport_z_wynikow_NSP2011.pdf.

Currah, Paisley. 2009. "The Transgender Rights Imaginary." In *Feminist and Queer Legal Theory: Intimate Encounters, Uncomfortable Conversations*, edited by Martha Albertson Fineman, Jack E. Jackson, and Adam P. Romero, 245–58. Surrey, UK: Ashgate.

Devor, Aaron H. 1989. *Gender Blending: Confronting the Limits of Duality*. Bloomington: Indiana University Press.

Dynarski, Wiktor. 2012a. "Poland's Route to a Transgender Revolution." *V4/Revue*, December 21. visegradrevue.eu/?p=750.

———. 2012b. "Wszyscy jesteśmy hetero: Homonormatywności lęk przed transpłciowością" ("All of Us Are Straight: Homonormativity's Transgender Fears"). In *Transpłciowość— androgynia: Studia o przekraczaniu płci* (*Transgenderism—Androgyny: The Studies of Transgressing Gender*), edited by Anna M. Kłonkowska, 147–61. Gdańsk: Wydawnictwo Uniwersytetu Gdańskiego.

Ekins, Richard, and Dave King. 2006. *The Transgender Phenomenon*. London: Sage.

Fajkowska-Stanik, Małgorzata. 2001. *Transseksualizm i rodzina: Przekaz pokoleniowy wzorów relacyjnych w rodzinach osób transseksualnych* (*Transsexualism and Family: Intergenerational Transmission of Relational Patterns in Transsexual Families*). Warsaw: Wydawnictwo SWPS.

Feinberg, Leslie. 1999. *Trans Liberation: Beyond Pink or Blue*. Boston: Beacon.

Foucault, Michel. 1978. *An Introduction*. Vol. 1 of *The History of Sexuality*, translated by Robert Hurley. New York: Random House.

———. 2003. *"Society Must Be Defended": Lectures at the Collège de France, 1975–76*. Translated by David Macey. New York: Picador.

Hines, Sally. 2007. *TransForming Gender: Transgender Practices of Identity, Intimacy, and Care*. Bristol, UK: Policy.

Imieliński, Kazimierz, and Stanisław Dulko. 1988. *Przekleństwo Androgyne; Transseksualizm: Mity i rzeczywistość* (*The Curse of Androgyne; Transsexualism: Myths and Reality*). Warsaw: Państwowe Wydawnictwo Naukowe.

———. 1989. *Apokalipsa płci* (*Apocalypse of Sexes*). Szczecin: Glob.

ISAP (Internetowy System Aktów Prawnych). 1964. *Kodeks rodzinny i opiekuńczy* (*Family and Guardianship Code*). isap.sejm.gov.pl/DetailsServlet?id=WDU20120000788.

———. 1997a. *Kodeks karny* (*Polish Criminal Code*). isap.sejm.gov.pl/DetailsServlet?id=WDU19970880553.

———. 1997b. *Konstytucja Rzeczpospolitej Polskiej* (*Constitution of the Republic of Poland*). isap.sejm.gov.pl/DetailsServlet?id=WDU19970780483 (English version: www.senat.gov.pl/en/about-the-senate/konstytucja/).

———. 2010. Rozporządzenie Ministra Obrony Narodowej z dnia 8 stycznia 2010 r. w sprawie orzekania o zdolności do zawodowej służby wojskowej oraz właściwości i trybu postępowania wojskowych komisji lekarskich w tych sprawach (Regulation of the Minister of National Defense of 8 January 2010 on adjudication of capability of professional military service and features and procedures of military medical committees in such cases). isap.sejm.gov.pl/DetailsServlet?id=WDU20100150080.

Jędrejek, Grzegorz. 2013. *Kodeks rodzinny i opiekuńczy—małżeństwo: Komentarz do art. 1–61* (*Family and Guardianship Code—Marriage: Commentary on Art. 1–61*). Lex. Warsaw: Wolters Kluwer Polska.

Kłonkowska, Anna M. 2012. "Czy potrzebna nam płeć? Zjawisko androgynii wobec dychotomii płci" ("Do We Truly Need Gender? The Phenomenon of Androgyny as Opposed to Gender Dichotomy"). In *Transpłciowość-androgynia: Studia o przekraczaniu płci* (*Transgenderism—Androgyny: The Studies of Transgressing Gender*), edited by Anna M. Kłonkowska, 11–32. Gdańsk: Wydawnictwo Uniwersytetu Gdańskiego.

———. 2013. "'Kobiety z wyboru': O społecznym wykluczeniu trans-kobiecości" ("'Women by Choice': About the Social Exclusion of Trans-Women"). In *Społecznie wykluczeni: Niewygodni, nienormatywni, nieprzystosowani, nieadekwatni* (*The Socially Excluded: Inconvenient, Nonnormative, Inappropriate, Inadequate*), edited by Anna M. Kłonkowska and Marcin Szulc, 131–51. Gdańsk: Wydawnictwo Uniwersytetu Gdańskiego.

Kochanowski, Jacek. 2008. "Poza funkcję falliczną: Płeć w perspektywie społecznej teorii queer" ("Beyond Phallicism: Sex and Gender in Social Queer Theory Perspective"). In *Teatr płci: Eseje z socjologii gender* (*Theatre of Sexes: Essays in Sociology of Gender*), edited by Małgorzata Bieńkowska and Jacek Kochanowski, 237–61. Łódź: Wydawnictwo Wschód-Zachód.

Kryszk, Kinga Radosław, and Anna M. Kłonkowska. 2012. "Sytuacja społeczna osób transpłciowych: Analiza danych z badania ankietowego" ("The Social Situation of Transgender People: Analysis of the Survey Research"). In *Sytuacja społeczna osób LGBT: Raport za lata 2010 i 2011 (The Social Situation of LGBT People in Poland: Report for 2010 and 2011)*, edited by Mirosława Makuchowska and Michał Pawlęga, 228–77. Warsaw: Wydawnictwo KPH.

Olczyk, Magdalena. 2014. "Problematyka zmiany płci metrykalnej osób transpłciowych w działalności Rzecznika Praw Obywatelskich" ("The Changes in the Gender Recognition Process in Light of Activities Taken by the Polish Human Rights Defender [Ombudsman]"). In *Psychospołeczne, prawne i medyczne aspekty transpłciowości (Psychosocial, Legal, and Medical Aspects of Transgenderism)*, edited by Anna M. Kłonkowska and Katarzyna Bojarska, 141–64. Gdańsk: Wydawnictwo Uniwersytetu Gdańskiego.

Stone, Sandy. 1991. "The *Empire* Strikes Back Again: A Posttranssexual Manifesto." In *Body Guards: The Cultural Politics of Gender Ambiguity*, edited by Julia Epstein and Kristina Straub, 280–304. New York: Routledge.

Stryker, Susan. 2006. "(De)Subjugated Knowledges: An Introduction to Transgender Studies." In *The Transgender Studies Reader*, edited by Susan Stryker and Stephen Whittle, 1–17. New York: Routledge.

———. 2008. *Transgender History*. Emeryville, CA: Seal.

Strzelecka, Alicja. 2007. "Związek pomiędzy poczuciem płci psychicznej a biologicznej" ("The Relation between Psychological Identity and Biological Sex"). Trans Fuzja. transfuzja .org/pl/artykuly/zwiazek_pomiedzy_poczuciem_plci_psychologicznej_a_zachowaniami _typowymi_plciowo/rozdzial_iii_transseksualizm.htm.

Węgrzyn, Wojciech. 2013. Odpowiedź podsekretarza stanu w Ministerstwie Sprawiedliwości—z upoważnienia ministra—na zapytanie nr 5487 w sprawie udostępnienia informacji o liczbie orzeczeń sądów okręgowych na terenie Polski rozpoznawanych na podstawie art. 189 K.p.c., dotyczących zmiany oznaczenia płci wpisanej do aktu urodzenia (Answer of the Undersecretary of State in the Ministry of Justice—under the authority of the Minister—to inquiry no 5487 on the accessibility of information about the number of decisions of district courts in the Republic of Poland distinguished in accordance with Art. 189 Code of Civil Procedure on changing gender marking in the birth certificate). www.sejm.gov.pl/Sejm7.nsf/InterpelacjaTresc.xsp?key=5804023C.

Whittle, Stephen. 2002. *Respect and Equality: Transsexual and Transgender Rights*. London: Cavendish.

Wilchins, Riki Anne. 1997. *Read My Lips: Sexual Subversions and the End of Gender*. Ann Arbor, MI: Firebrand.

Counting Trans* Patients

A Community Health Center Case Study

NATALIE INGRAHAM, VANESSA PRATT, and NICK GORTON

Abstract With the Affordable Care Act revolutionizing the US health care system, the importance of collecting clinical, demographic, operational, and utilization data has exponentially increased for community health centers (CHC). Data collection of gender and gender identity presents a unique set of challenges for medical settings. One central challenge is the conflict between, on one hand, the need to know and use patients' preferred names, gender identities, and pronouns to establish trust and safety and, on the other hand, institutional requirements to know and use patients' legal names and gender markers with insurance companies and pharmacies. This essay examines how a community-based LGBTQ community health center, Lyon-Martin Health Services, collects and reports data about gender identity and how this process has changed over time. Lyon-Martin strongly supports the use of the two-step gender data collection method, which allows clinicians to have necessary information related to patients' anatomy-based health care while simultaneously honoring and respecting patients' gender identity and preferred pronouns. Collecting precise information about patient sex and gender is vital to providing not only respectful care but also medically appropriate care. The ability to quantify and justify the services provided by CHCs is a key part of keeping clinics open and thriving, from securing grant support to implementing internal quality improvement efforts to provide the best care for trans* patients. The shift toward electronic medical records and electronic practice management systems is also highlighted, including billing and clinical practice challenges due to narrowed gender options written into practice-management and billing software.
Keywords trans* health care, health technology, community health center, trans* data collection

W ith the Affordable Care Act revolutionizing the US health care system, the importance of collecting clinical, demographic, operational, and utilization data has exponentially increased for community health centers. Being able to quantify what we, as a community health center, do and whom we serve is expected, if not required, for governmental reporting, private funders, and quality improvement efforts. This type of data collection generally includes basic demographic information like gender, sexual orientation, race/ethnicity, and income. For clinics and hospitals, this information may also inform the type of health care received. Data collection of gender and gender identity presents a

TSQ: Transgender Studies Quarterly ★ Volume 2, Number 1 ★ February 2015
DOI 10.1215/23289252-2848922 © 2015 Duke University Press

unique set of challenges for medical settings for a variety of reasons. One central challenge is the conflict between, on one hand, the need to know and use patients' preferred names, gender identities, and pronouns to establish trust and safety and, on the other hand, institutional requirements to know and use patients' legal names and gender markers with insurance companies and pharmacies. These challenges persist and perhaps even increase with the proliferation of electronic medical records and electronic health systems.

Gender Identity: One- versus Two-Step Method

The World Professional Association for Transgender Health (WPATH) Electronic Medical Record (EMR) working group recommends the two-step method of gender collection adopted by the US Centers for Disease Control and Prevention in 2011 (Deutsch et al. 2013). The two-step, or two-question, method involves asking on demographic forms about current gender identify *first*, then about previous gender (and/or sex) assignment, to honor the importance of current identity over past assignment.

This method of assessing gender in the social and medical sciences is considered more robust than a single-gender question (Tate, Ledbetter, and Youssef 2013). The authors recommend first asking "What is your current gender identity?" followed by "What gender were you assigned at birth?" This is opposed to a single-question assessment—for example, "What is your gender?" Charlotte Chuck Tate, Jay N. Ledbetter, and Cris P. Youssef argue that the two-step method allows for greater identification of transgender subjects (almost three times as many as the single-step question), less missing data, higher response rate (there was seven times more missing data in the one-step method than the two-step one), and specific identification of cisgender subjects,[1] a data point that is impossible to extract without the two-step method. While previous studies of transgender health have reported using the two-step method (Deogracias et al. 2007; Melendez et al. 2006), it is not commonly found in other large-scale data collection efforts.

This essay examines how a community-based LGBTQ community health center, Lyon-Martin Health Services, collects and reports data about gender identity and how this process has changed over time. First we present a brief review of Lyon-Martin's history, current services, and patient demographics followed by a short examination of how gender-identity data collection has changed over time. Then we highlight specific gender-identity data collection and reporting challenges. Finally, we explore future directions and challenges based on the implementation of electronic medical records and other automated health systems.

Lyon-Martin Health Services

Lyon-Martin Health Services (LMHS) is a nonprofit community health center founded in 1979 by a group of medical providers and health activists.[2] Today, as a federally qualified health center,[3] Lyon-Martin offers an integrated model of primary care and behavioral health to patients who identify as women and/or transgender, regardless of ability to pay. LMHS currently has twenty-five full- and part-time staff members and serves approximately two thousand patients a year. It serves a highly diverse patient population, including 32 percent trans*,[4] 49 percent LGBQ (lesbian, gay, bisexual, and queer), 43 percent people of color, and approximately 80 percent patients below the federal poverty line. LMHS is also well-known for its transgender health education program, Project HEALTH, a joint program with the Transgender Law Center that aims to expand health care access for trans* patients.[5]

LMHS Gender Data Collection Changes over Time

As mentioned above, Lyon-Martin's origin was as a service for cisgender lesbian women. However, its mission statement and patient population have shifted over time. Figure 1 reflects the total number of patients from data available from 2003 to 2013.

These data from the California Office of Statewide Health Planning and Development (OSHPD) also include gender categories, although there are only two genders available in these reports. The figure reflects an increasing number of LMHS patients who are categorized as male. These reports are an example of the potential inaccuracies in gender data collection. Not only are there only two genders available in the report; it is impossible to know, based on these reports, if these numbers reflect patients' sex assigned at birth or patients' gender identity. For example, the increase in male patients could reflect an increase in FTM or trans male patients if these reports reflect current gender identity. Alternatively, if these reports reflect sex assigned at birth, the increase in male patients reflects the increasing number of trans women in the patient population.

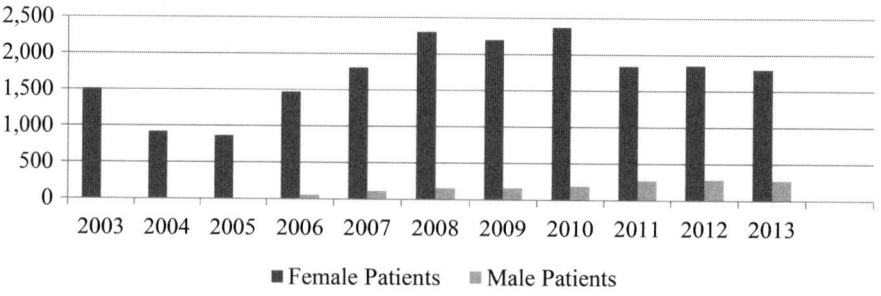

Figure 1. LMHS patient population by gender, 2003–2013

Our past patient demographic forms reflect a shift in gender data collection as well. Based on a review of past forms, table 1 shows changes in our assessments of gender, sex assigned at birth, sexual orientation, and pronoun preference in the last fifteen years. These are based on charts from trans* patients who have had LMHS as their primary-care home for five or more years. Forms used before 1999 were not available.

Additional gender categories (such as genderqueer) were added over time based on patients' response to the open-ended "Other" option. Patients are also increasingly reporting "my name" as a preferred pronoun, though this has not yet been formalized into our data collection forms. Our most recent revision includes the addition of a third gender assessment: "For billing purposes if you have insurance, what gender do they have on record for you?" This allows us to bill insurances without rejection, since every piece of demographic information entered for a patient must match what the insurance company has on file before a bill can be processed and paid.

Current LMHS Gender and Sexual Orientation Data Collection Procedures

Lyon-Martin collects patient gender identity and sexual orientation data at various stages of the clinical encounter. New patients or patients reestablishing care after more than three years are asked to complete a patient intake demographic form that asks about gender identity, sex assigned at birth, insurance gender marker, sexual orientation, and pronoun preferences, all as separate questions. These forms are available in English and Spanish (see fig. 2).

Additionally, patients complete update forms (given at an annual exam or more often if the patient notes a change in contact information), where we ask questions related to gender identity (see fig. 3).

Lyon-Martin strongly supports the use of the two-step gender data collection method. This method allows clinicians to have necessary information related to patients' anatomy-based health care while simultaneously honoring and respecting patients' gender identity and preferred pronouns. Additionally, this method also allows for more complete data collection information from a quality-management and data-reporting perspective. For example, in an analysis of patients seen from May to November 2013, if we asked only about gender identity, 30 percent of our patients would be counted as trans*. Compare this to the two-step method, where, instead, 32 percent of our patients are counted as trans*. It is also important to note that these two figures reflect a collapse of noncisgender gender identities (such as transgender, genderqueer, or nonbinary) under one trans* umbrella term. In addition, the two-step method also makes another option available to our patients: that one can be trans* without

Table 1. Changes in LMHS data collection forms (1999–2013)

Year	Form Type	Gender Identity Assessed (Yes/No)	Gender Identity Answer Options	SAAB[a] Assessed (Yes/No)
1999–2001	Health history	No (see sexual orientation)	N/A	No
2002	Patient registration	Yes ("Gender")	Female Transgender (M-F/F-M) Other _____	No
2005	Grant data form	No	N/A	No
2006[b]	Patient demographic	Yes ("What is your gender?" [mark one])	Female Male Transgender/ transsexual MtF Transgender/ transsexual FtM Other _____ Decline	Yes ("What is your sex?" [mark one])
2010	Patient intake	Yes	Female Male Decline	Yes
2012–now	Patient intake	Yes	Female Male Transgender MtF Transgender FtM GenderQueer Other _____ Decline	Yes

[a]SAAB = sex assigned at birth.
[b]2006 is the first record of the two-step gender assessment's use at LMHS.
[c]2006 is the first year intersex appears as an option for SAAB.

necessarily having a trans identity (e.g., marking male for sex and female for gender). For example, a trans woman can choose female as her gender versus transgender or MTF on an intake form while still indicating that she was assigned male at birth. This flags the staff to give this patient trans*-specific health care while respecting her preferred gender identity. While this possibility has not been

SAAB Answer Options	Sexual Orientation Assessed (Yes/No)	Sexual Orientation Answer Options	Pronoun Assessed (Yes/No)	Pronoun Answer Options
N/A	Yes ("How do you identify yourself, sexually?")	Lesbian Bisexual Heterosexual Transgender Celibate	No	N/A
N/A	No	N/A	No	N/A
N/A	Yes (open-ended with "sexual orientation" as prompt)	Some patients wrote in transgender as sexual orientation	No	N/A
Female Male Intersex[c] Other _____ Decline	Yes (Decline option introduced)	Lesbian Gay Bisexual Heterosexual/straight Queer Celibate Other _____ Decline	Yes	She/Her He/Him Sie/Zie/Hir Other _____
Male Female Intersex Other _____ Decline	Yes	Lesbian Queer Bisexual Gay Celibate Heterosexual	Yes	She/Her He/Him Zee/Hir
Male Female Intersex Other _____ Decline	Yes	Lesbian Gay Queer Bisexual Heterosexual Celibate Other _____ Decline	Yes	She/Her He/His They/Them/Their Ze/Hir Other _____

noted in other literature on the two-step method, we believe that it allows patients to most clearly express their preferred gender identity.

LMHS Gender Data Collection Challenges

Even the more accurate two-step method of gender data collection brings challenges when collapsing gender categories for internal quality control analysis as well as when reporting to outside entities, such as funding agencies, foundations, and health departments. For example, genderqueer patients or those who utilize the self-defined "other" category are routinely combined with both trans men and trans women in data analysis under one trans* umbrella for reporting purposes. Additionally, outside entities often want or need sex data in order to match our records to other databases. We know internally that sex data do not translate

Lyon-Martin Health Services
Patient Demographic Information

Date: ______________ *LMHS Chart #:* ________

Preferred Name: ______________ Legal Name: ______________

Home Address (including city, state, and zip): ______________

Mailing Address (including city, state, and zip): ______________

Date of Birth: ______________ SSN: _____-_____-_____

Phone Number: ______________ Email Address: ______________

Can we leave you a confidential message at this phone number? Yes No

If you don't have contact information, what other social service agencies do you frequent?

____

What type of insurance(s)/coverage(s) do you have? *We treat everyone regardless of ability to pay.*

☐ None ☐ CDP ☐ San Francisco Health Plan ☐ Medicare
☐ Healthy SF ☐ Family Pact ☐ Medi-Cal ☐ Other: ________

For billing purposes, if you have insurance, what gender do they have on record for you? ☐ Female ☐ Male

If you have been seen at San Francisco General Hospital, what is your medical record number? ________

My head of household is: ________, & additional # members: ______. My household's annual income is: ______

Due to Federal Regulations, we must ask all patients their household size and income, regardless of health insurance status. Household members include those persons living in the same home who are related by birth, marriage, registered domestic partnership, or adoption. If you are interested in applying for our Sliding Scale Program, please request an application from the Front Desk as providing this information here does not constitute an application.

My gender identity is:
☐ Female
☐ Male
☐ Trans (MTF)
☐ Trans (FTM)
☐ Genderqueer
☐ Other: ______
☐ Decline

My sex assigned at birth is:
☐ Female
☐ Male
☐ Intersex
☐ Other: ______
☐ Decline

My marital status is:
☐ Single
☐ Married
☐ Divorced
☐ Registered Domestic Partner
☐ Widowed
☐ Unmarried Partner
☐ Legally Separated
☐ Other: ______
☐ Decline

My sexual orientation is:
☐ Lesbian
☐ Gay
☐ Queer
☐ Bisexual
☐ Heterosexual
☐ Celibate
☐ Other: ______
☐ Decline

My pronoun preference is:
☐ She/her
☐ He/his
☐ They/Them/Their
☐ Zie/Hir
☐ Other: ______

I live (please check all that apply):
☐ In a house or apartment or SRO or hotel
☐ In an RV or vehicle
☐ On the street
☐ In a shelter
☐ In a transitional or treatment program
☐ My situation is temporary and/or unstable

I am Hispanic/Latin@: Yes No

My race is:
☐ Native American and/or Alaskan Native
☐ Hispanic or Latin@
☐ Black/African American
☐ Caucasian or White
☐ Native Hawaiian
☐ Asian
☐ Other Pacific Islander
☐ More than one race
☐ Other: ______
☐ Decline

I am a veteran: Yes No

I am a seasonal agricultural worker: Yes No

Emergency Contact: ______________

Relationship: ______________

Phone Number: ______________

My preferred language is:
☐ English
☐ Spanish
☐ Other: ______
☐ Decline

For Office Use Only:
Entered into EPM by: ________ *on:* ________

Figure 2. Lyon-Martin Health Services demographic forms (as of August 2014)

automatically to our patients' current gender identities or pronoun preferences, but other agencies with less transgender cultural competency may not consider or understand this. Thus we ran into a customer service debacle earlier this year when patient data, including sex but not gender, provided for a utilization analysis was then used to infer pronoun preferences for a mailed patient satisfaction survey. Since we had such robust data from the two-step method and collecting pronoun preferences, we were able to quickly identify which patients had been misgendered and place outreach calls. Nonetheless, it was a poignant reminder of how challenging collecting patient-centered gender data can be when one has to translate them for outside entities that do not have the same diverse understanding of gender.

While it is known that binary gender options (male/female) offered by entities such as insurance companies or government agencies directly conflict with the wideness of the gender spectrum, we find that this is also true for other agencies tracking LMHS patients or patient outcomes. Required reporting for grant-giving foundation and health department data rarely accommodates patient gender information beyond the binary gender options. This sometimes means that nonbinary (genderqueer, identifying by name only) patients either get left out of data collection completely or are misgendered in the data reporting process by reversion to their sex assigned at birth for data purposes, especially if they are a part of specific reporting populations such as homeless patients or

Lyon-Martin Health Services
Patient Demographic Update

Date: ________ *LMHS Chart #:* ________

Preferred Name: ________ Legal Name: ________

Address (including city, state, and zip): ________

Phone Number: ________ Email Address: ________

Can we leave you a confidential message at this phone number? Yes No

If you don't have contact information, what other social service agencies do you frequent?

____

What type of insurance(s)/coverage(s) do you have? *We treat everyone regardless of ability to pay.*

☐ None ☐ CDP ☐ San Francisco Health Plan ☐ Medicare
☐ Healthy SF ☐ Family Pact ☐ Medi-Cal ☐ Other: ________

For billing purposes, if you have insurance, what gender do they have on record for you? ☐ Female ☐ Male

My head of household is: ________, & additional # members: ______. My household's annual income is: ______

Due to Federal Regulations, we must ask all patients their household size and income, regardless of health insurance status. Household members include those persons living in the same home who are related by birth, marriage, registered domestic partnership, or adoption. If you are interested in applying for our Sliding Scale Program, please request an application from the Front Desk as providing this information here does not constitute an application.

My gender identity is: ☐ Female ☐ Male ☐ Trans (MTF) ☐ Trans (FTM) ☐ Genderqueer ☐ Other: ______ ☐ Decline

My pronoun preference is: ☐ She/her ☐ He/his ☐ They/Them/Their ☐ Zie/Hir ☐ Other: ______

My sexual orientation is: ☐ Lesbian ☐ Gay ☐ Queer ☐ Bisexual ☐ Heterosexual ☐ Celibate ☐ Other: ______ ☐ Decline

I live (please check all that apply):
☐ In a house or apartment or SRO or hotel ☐ On the street ☐ In a transitional or treatment program
☐ In an RV or vehicle ☐ In a shelter ☐ My situation is temporary and/or unstable

For Office Use Only: Entered into EPM by: ________ *on:* ________

Figure 3. Lyon-Martin Health Services demographic update form (as of July 2014)

HIV-positive patients. Additionally, patients who may not choose to identify as trans* on their intake forms, such as the example in the previous section, still need to be counted as transgender for specific grant programs to provide an accurate reflection of the amount of transgender health care we provide.

LMHS Electronic Practice Management and Electronic Health Records Challenges

As implementation of electronic medical records and other automated health systems increases, we anticipate continued challenges for accurate collection of gender data for patient populations like those at Lyon-Martin and, indeed, all health organizations. The challenge we faced in 2013 with misgendering of patients during a utilization analysis with an outside agency is one example of the ways in which automated health systems like those in electronic practice management (EPM), electronic medical records (EMR), or electronic health records (EHR) may not be sophisticated enough to deal with more than two genders (male and female). We have worked closely with the software designers during our ongoing EHR implementation process to make the systems as flexible as possible for patient demographic data collection. However, the software has its own limitations and thus we continue to adapt by making clinic-level procedural changes or work-arounds in order to ensure that health center staff identify our patients by their current preferred name and pronoun. Many EHRs also automate functions based on patient gender, such as which anatomical systems providers should review with patients. For example, a patient with gender marked female would have a provider prompt to review for pap smears and breast exams, while a male patient would be prompted for prostate screenings. Discrepancies between a patient's preferred gender identity and anatomical medical needs created by automated health systems provide a significant barrier to trans* patients' ability to receive safe, competent medical care.

M. B. Deutsch and colleagues (2013), from the World Professional Association for Transgender Health EMR working group, provide specific recommendations for EMR and transgender patients, including utilization of optional data collection fields within the software as well as means for tracking patients' gender-related medical treatments and current anatomy. LMHS has utilized these optional data fields within our current EPM software; we chose to add sex assigned at birth, patient preferred name, preferred pronoun, and sexual orientation. However, only four optional fields could be added for the entire patient record, limiting our ability to collect more detailed information on other demographics beyond what is built into the existing program. The main challenge is incongruence between preferred gender and the gender reflected on patients' insurance cards. From April 2013 to February 2014, our schedule pulled from the preferred name, but this resulted in billing staff having to change individual patient gender for each bill. This system was not sustainable with our patient load and resulted in increased billing errors and automatically denied claims based on "incorrect" patient information. Currently, the system pulls a patient's legal name for all billing documents in order to interface properly with outside systems such as pharmacies or outside labs. This issue also resulted in the most recent edits to our demographic form to assess insurance-identified gender. The preferred-name field is used for appointment interfacing such as searching for a patient within EPM or appointment reminder calls.

Future Directions and Challenges

We agree with Deutsch and colleagues' recommendations and hope that providing information about the challenges we have faced will help other clinics and hospitals move forward with respectful, accurate gender and sex data collection. Collecting precise information about patient sex and gender is vital to providing not only respectful care but also medically appropriate care. The sweeping changes in health care as a result of the Affordable Care Act have already started to impact transgender individuals, especially those who were previously unable to access health care. However, this change also comes with the challenges highlighted in this essay, including clashes between legal gender, preferred gender, and insurance companies and the necessity for individual providers to work around the binary-focused private or public insurance systems (Murtha 2014). Our ability to quantify and justify the services we provide and the individuals we serve is a key part of keeping our clinic open and thriving, from securing grant support to implementing internal quality improvement efforts to provide the best care for our patients. The Affordable Care Act's expanded insurance coverage for trans* patients also means that the two-step method may need to evolve into three or more steps in the health care setting, as our most recent demographic form revisions indicate. All the pieces of demographic data for a patient must match across systems for the insurance billing process to work smoothly or even to work at all. For us, that means that we lost the most accurate patient data because of EPM limitations in number of optional fields; sex assigned at birth was replaced with sex assigned to insurance so that billing requests would move forward. This loss of accuracy is small but significant and will become increasingly so as more and more trans* individuals interact with the health care system under the Affordable Care Act.

Natalie Ingraham is a project coordinator at Lyon-Martin Health Services and a PhD candidate in sociology at the University of California, San Francisco.

Vanessa Pratt is currently a project manager in the Practice Improvement Program at the San Francisco Health Plan. She contributed to this paper as the quality manager at Lyon-Martin Health Services.

Nick Gorton is a primary care provider at Lyon-Martin Health Services. He is an openly transgender physician.

Acknowledgments

The authors would like to thank LMHS Medical Director Dr. Dawn Harbatkin for her review and guidance on this article and Elizabeth Sekera for her insight on the EPM/EHR processes at LMHS.

Notes

1. The website for Basic Rights Oregon, an LGBT rights organization, defines cisgender (or cissexual) as a term that describes "people who, for the most part, identify as the gender they were assigned at birth" (Basic Rights Oregon 2011).
2. For a full history of Lyon-Martin, see Lyon-Martin Health Services 2014.
3. Federally Qualified Health Centers (FQHCs) must serve an underserved area or population, offer a sliding fee scale, provide comprehensive services, have an ongoing quality assurance program, and have a governing board of directors (see HRSA 2014).
4. The use of the term *trans** reflects an adaptation of web-based language taken up by the trans* community. The * (asterisk) is used as a wildcard in web searches by acting as a placeholder or a fill-in-the-blank symbol. This symbol or representation has been applied to gender identification to expand and include "folks who identify as transgender and transsexual (the terms usually understood as included when the prefix trans is used on its own) as well as other identities where a person does not identify with the gender they were assigned at birth" (Jones 2013).
5. For more information about Project HEALTH, see Project HEALTH 2014.

References

Basic Rights Oregon. 2011. "Trans 101: Cisgender." www.basicrights.org/uncategorized/trans-101 -cisgender/.

Deogracias, Joseph J., et al. 2007. "The Gender Identity/Gender Dysphoria Questionnaire for Adolescents and Adults." *Journal of Sex Research* 44, no. 4: 370–79. doi:10.1080 /00224490701586730.

Deutsch, M. B., et al. 2013. "Electronic Medical Records and the Transgender Patient: Recommendations from the World Professional Association for Transgender Health EMR Working Group." *Journal of the American Medical Informatics Association* 20, no. 4: 700– 703. doi:10.1136/amiajnl-2012-001472.

HRSA (Health Resources and Services Administration). 2014. "What Are Federally Qualified Health Centers (FQHCs)?" HRSA, US Department of Health and Human Services. www .hrsa.gov/healthit/toolbox/RuralHealthITtoolbox/Introduction/qualified.html (accessed November 4, 2014).

Jones, Nash. 2013. "Bridging The Gap—Trans*: What Does the Asterisk Mean and Why Is It Used?" The Q Center, *Bridging the Gap* (blog), August 8. www.pdxqcenter.org/bridging -the-gap-trans-what-does-the-asterisk-mean-and-why-is-it-used.

Lyon-Martin Health Services. 2014. "The Lyon-Martin Story." lyon-martin.org/about-us/the -lyon-martin-story (accessed November 4, 2014).

Melendez, Rita M., et al. 2006. "Health and Health Care among Male-to-Female Transgender Persons Who Are HIV Positive." *American Journal of Public Health* 96, no. 6: 1034–37. doi:10.2105/AJPH.2004.042010.

Murtha, Tara. 2014. "The Problem with Obamacare for Some Transgender Policyholders." RH Reality Check. rhrealitycheck.org/article/2014/03/12/problem-obamacare-transgender -policyholders.

Project HEALTH. 2014. "About Project HEALTH." project-health.org/about-project-health (accessed November 4, 2014).

Tate, Charlotte Chuck, Jay N. Ledbetter, and Cris P. Youssef. 2013. "A Two-Question Method for Assessing Gender Categories in the Social and Medical Sciences." *Journal of Sex Research* 50, no. 8: 767–76. doi:10.1080/00224499.2012.690110.

Who Counts as "Transgender"?

Epidemiological Methods and a Critical Intervention

HALE THOMPSON and LISA KING

Abstract This article draws on the work of Michel Foucault to critique epidemiological methods in general and transgender HIV prevention research in particular. Funding for transgender HIV prevention research and programs is often directly connected to widely accepted, yet often problematic, practices of data collection and analysis. The authors believe that attending to the needs of those who do not conform to a binary gender system requires analyzing the ways in which epidemiology research produces and reifies the gender system itself. In order to understand the relation between a trans "identity" and a trans "population," the article employs as analytics Foucault's concepts of normalizing power and biopower. It reviews the history and techniques of epidemiology and then briefly the ways in which normalizing power produces specific identity categories such as gender and gender identity as inherent to an individual, followed by an examination of how those socially produced identities operate at the level of population regulation. Finally, it explores some resistant practices that both epidemiologists themselves and the targets of their research might engage in order to at least mitigate some of these difficulties.

Keywords transgender, biopower, normalizing power, critical epidemiology, population, HIV prevention

This article is a critical engagement with research aimed precisely at "making transgender count" in the global fight against HIV/AIDS. Recognizing the dearth of HIV prevention resources accessible to those referred to as "transgender,"[1] this work critiques epidemiological research that seeks to respond to this lack of resources. Through the generation of quantitative data, the research provides evidence in support of prevention resources aimed specifically at persons referred to as "transgender women." We identify two main problems with this approach, one methodological and one philosophical: the first questions particular uses of epidemiological methods that invoke a "transgender population" in order to make inferences. Here we argue that these methods reproduce specifically Western gender categories, in contexts where they may not fit, with detrimental effects of restigmatization and a reification of transgender as a type of

TSQ: Transgender Studies Quarterly ★ Volume 2, Number 1 ★ February 2015 **148**
DOI 10.1215/23289252-2848913 © 2015 Duke University Press

individual universally at high risk for HIV. We argue here that even on its own terms and with its own goals in mind, epidemiology fails to serve the individuals it claims to be serving. The second problem we address is about the power-laden nature of identity categories themselves: the very insistence that particular persons be classified and counted as transgender positions them as abnormal and subject to greater scrutiny and social surveillance within the binary gender system. We approach both problems through Michel Foucault's work on biopower and normalizing power, drawing attention to the discursive and material practices involved in the creation of subjects, or individuals with particular identities, as well as to the categories that render them objects of scientific knowledge and targets of population control and political and biomedical technologies.

We understand the high stakes of the research we critique here: funding for both HIV prevention research and programs is often directly connected to the practices of data collection that we call into question. But we believe that attending to the needs of those who do not conform to a binary gender system requires analyzing the ways in which research produces and reifies the gender system itself, even if that means challenging accepted epidemiological practices. Put differently, it is imperative to examine how statistical and medical knowledge about gender-nonconforming persons, as well as the biopolitical grid that circumscribes it, may perpetuate the forms of invisibility and violence it aims to remedy. One question that emerges, then, is how epidemiology as a field might respond to the problems we identify. To that end, we explore some resistant practices that both epidemiologists themselves and the targets of their research might employ in order to at least mitigate some of these difficulties.

Epidemiological studies on transgender HIV prevention invariably and problematically assume an a priori transgender population. While this research has the laudable goal of trying to promote health and expand services to individuals whom HIV prevention research tends to overlook, the means by which it attempts to identify those individuals perpetuates the very problem it seeks to address. It assumes that a trans identity is both natural to an individual and globally universal; such an assumption leads to problematic data collection practices that erase trans and gender-nonconforming people's needs and lives and perpetuate global dynamics of injustice and inequality. In order to understand the relation between a trans "identity" and a trans "population," it is key to analyze the mutually reinforcing interactions of normalizing and biopower. We will first review the history and techniques of epidemiology and then briefly review the ways in which normalizing power produces specific gender identity categories as inherent to an individual. We will then turn to examining how those socially produced identities operate at the level of population regulation.

Epidemiology, the Population, and (Ab)Normality

Epidemiology is generally understood as the study of the distribution of health and disease among various human populations (Aschengrau and Seage 2008; Szklo and Nieto 2007). Though its logics can be traced to the seventeenth century and the scientific revolution, epidemiology emerged as a science in the nineteenth century and then as an academic discipline in the early twentieth century (Aschengrau and Seage 2008; Krieger 2012). According to Nancy Krieger (2012), social scientists extrapolated mathematical principles from astronomy in order to infer notions of the "average man." The key difference, however, was that "for a star, the location of the mean referred to the location of a singular real object, whereas for a population, the location of its population mean depended on how the population was defined" (642). Krieger's essay "Who and What Is a Population?" traces the problematic ways in which epidemiology has continued to deploy the "population" as an a priori fact, simultaneously neglecting to define it with any precision or acknowledge the relational, extrinsic, and dynamic qualities that shape populations (660). Statistics, etymologically defined as the science of the state, is a primary epidemiological technique to derive means, probabilities, and complex risk profiles from sufficiently large samples to make comparisons between and inferences about various imprecisely defined populations as well as subgroups within a population. Without conceptual precision, the statistics derived from population research are, at best, approximations of societal patterns and, at worst, dangerous and essentialist knowledge claims.

The problem is widespread, and it is clear that from the beginning, epidemiology has operated in biopolitical and normalizing ways. Krieger (2012) and other scholars (Lorway and Khan 2014; Spade and Rohlfs, forthcoming) have highlighted how epidemiology and its use of statistics have progressed in the context of specific social, economic, and political developments such as the eugenics movement in the early twentieth century and the Gates Foundation's global epidemiological research that has merged with Harvard Business School metrics in the early twenty-first century. In both contexts, epidemiology and statistics are deployed to make visible populations with distinct sets of bodily and behavioral traits that are linked to potential illness or potential threats to national and economic security. Here, too, the pathologizing mechanisms of normalizing power operate implicitly and largely invisibly, precisely by leaving unquestioned the ways in which so-called abnormal populations are created through the techniques used to measure and "fix" them.

Consider Geoffrey Rose's seminal work *Preventive Medicine* ([1993] 2008), which fails to provide a nuanced definition of population despite the centrality of the construct to his argument (for a more in-depth critique of Rose's conceptualization, see Krieger 2012). Rose famously makes the case that health promotion and disease prevention are most effectively and efficiently achieved via population-based analyses of and interventions on what he terms the "normal majority" rather than via an approach that targets those few who are most at risk and what he refers to as abnormal (94). Foucault's (1990) analysis of normalizing power suggests that leaving unexamined the use of the very terms *normal* and *abnormal* masks complex systems of social, economic, cultural, and political power relations that actually create and enforce the very categories so named. Extending Rose's approach to HIV prevention research today, one can easily anticipate the ways in which epidemiological analyses may exclude the most vulnerable or, alternatively, encourage the construction of "abnormal populations" in order to justify research and interventions on the social margins.

Indeed, in the latter half of the twentieth century, epidemiology devoted its resources to large cohort studies that examined health risks and behaviors of predominantly white, middle-class America and Europe such as the Framingham Heart Study and the British Doctors Study. This methodological approach exemplifies Rose's prioritization of what he deems a "normal majority." In so doing, it advances social and economic interests of the state through the quantification and normalization of health and behaviors without any identification of the ways in which state apparatuses may harm the health of persons in its wake, particularly those on the margins.

Epstein (2003, 2007) illuminates how, in the wake of the civil rights era, advocates on the social margins, rather than respond to the erasures and potential harms that state-centered methods and population-based research created, lobbied instead for state-centered research on "special populations," including women, persons of color, and lesbian and gay ones initially, and much later, bisexual and transgender ones. He argues tha this "state-centered approach takes categorical identitites to be the foundation of a health promotion and biomedical research strategy" (2003: 132). Janet Shim (2000) argues that, through this emphasis on individual characteristics of a sample—assumed to be fixed and static categories—such as race, class, and gender and their relationship to poor health outcomes, population-based methods place the burden of change upon individuals, masking and even reproducing the power relations that circumscribe the health disparities in question. Shim observes, for example, how nonwhite and poor racial and class statuses are routinely cited as individual, additive risk factors for poor health outcomes, while white and middle-class statuses are viewed as protective factors (179). This framework, though it may acknowledge the role of social stigma and discrimination, casts intersections of race, class, gender, and sexual orientation as individual and essential rather than as a relational and social process.

Excluded by lesbian and gay as well as HIV research agendas, transgender health and HIV prevention research have navigated a unique trajectory. In "Counting

Us In," Hanssmann (2010) reviews this trajectory thoroughly and highlights the community-based research conducted by US researchers—including trans community members—in the 1990s and early 2000s that estimates HIV disease burdens, among other health risks, unique to US urban transgender communities. In the twenty-first century, many of these small studies have been pooled into a meta-analysis (see Herbst et al. 2008) so as to achieve a sufficiently large sample and establish population-level evidence on which to justify the funding of state-centered HIV prevention programs and research. Based on the ostensible success of the 2008 study by Herbst and colleagues, researchers concerned with transgender HIV prevention have gone global with the meta-analysis, attempting to make visible and declaring an HIV crisis among a global, universal transgender population (Baral et al. 2013). The use of the meta-analysis has become widely accepted in transgender health research (see also Operario, Soma, and Underhill 2008). Unfortunately, through its construction of population-level data about trans and gender-nonconforming bodies, it perpetuates the problems of normalization and social control. To illustrate this problem and to explore transgender health research issues in depth, we turn first to Michel Foucault's work (2007) and then to the 2013 meta-analysis of Stefan Baral and colleagues in the following section.

Biopower: Epidemiology and Reifying Transgender

It is in the Baral and colleagues' 2013 global meta-analysis and its cascade of effects that understanding the connection between normalizing power and biopower becomes crucial. Whereas normalizing power targets individuals for social surveillance and control, biopower targets "the population." Biopower regulates subjects with a goal of promoting overall health. In order to do so, it collects data and enumerates events like mortality, birth, teenage pregnancy, drug use, criminality, and, of course, the spread of disease. The data seem like objective evidence of what they track, but Foucault's analysis makes clear that the data collection processes themselves create the populations they claim simply to identify. Biopower, he argues, is a mechanism of governmentality, the construct known as a population itself being a tool of management and containment, functioning as a mechanism to manage the health and life of its members, whose bodies are generally viewed as an economic resource that requires governing. He provides a helpful way of thinking about public health's slippery use of this construct (2007). Foucault observes that the population is not a natural taxonomy to be discovered, ordered, counted, and made visible. Rather, the population is produced through statistics, which are understood to make visible "a set of elements in which we can note constants and regularities even in accidents, in which we can identify the universal of desire . . . and with regard to which we can identify a number of modifiable variables on which it depends" (75). Those statistical effects help produce a "nature" inherent to the population and against which the state can intervene and manage individuals. Interventions and management arise from multiple sites within the state, of course, including government-funded research but also nongovernmental projects and corporations with a perceived stake in the issue at hand. In relation to HIV/AIDS, biopower flows through various government agencies and private foundations that track data and fund research projects at local, national, and international levels as well as through the World Health Organization (WHO) and various pharmaceutical companies involved in HIV/AIDS treatment and prevention. In this case, being considered a legitimate member of the priority population is key to receiving services; when normalizing identities become part of data collection, normalizing power's exclusionary and coercive mechanisms may induce more harm than good.

To underscore the work of normalizing power and biopower, we turn to the *Lancet* and Baral and colleagues' 2013 "Worldwide Burden of HIV in Transgender Women: A Systematic Review and Meta-analysis." This study exemplifies the methods by which a transgender population and its nature are produced ex post facto through the work of the study itself. The authors define transgender through a reification of the sex and/or gender binaries whereby the gendered subject is viewed as fixed, coherent, and nonambiguous. They posit, "Transgender women [are] defined here as people who were assigned male at birth but who identify as women" (Baral et al. 2013: 214) and then later, with no explanation, as "people who were born male but identify as a different gender" (215). The authors pool the results of thirty-nine studies conducted in fifteen different countries in order to determine the "relative burden of HIV in all transgender women worldwide" (214). Several of the studies do not describe the research participants as transgender at all and suggest contextually and temporally specific sets of classifications and comparisons that shine light on additional conceptual ambiguities. For example, Altaf (2008) compares *hijras* with male sex workers whereas Shaw and colleagues (2011) compare *hijra* sex workers with male sex workers in urban Pakistan. A 2008 study in Ho Chi Minh City that recruited men who have sex with men from popular sites for public or commercial sex compares "four distinct groups: transvestites (. . . known as 'bong lo'), non-transvestites (. . . known as 'bong kin') . . . , bisexuals who had both male and female partners (known as 'da he') . . . , and sex workers (heterosexuals selling sex to men to earn money)" (Nguyen et al. 2008: 3). In South America, Grandi and colleagues (2000) recruited male sex workers in São Paulo, Brazil, between 1992 and 1998—as much as fourteen years prior to Shaw and colleagues—and compared the HIV epidemiology of transvestites to hustlers; in Montevideo, Uruguay, in 1999, Russi and colleagues (2003) conducted a seroepidemiologic study of 200 male transvestite commercial sex workers.

The vast amounts of slippage across time, space, and social categories call into question the basic legitimacy of the conclusions. The notion that throughout the world today transgender women's odds of having HIV is forty-nine times that of the general population is questionable precisely because of the assumptions and techniques used to "count" them. Indeed, the researchers themselves seem to understand the problem here when they note that "gender identities are complex and fluid"; yet despite contradictions with the original definition, they maintain that "a full explication of gender identities is beyond the scope of this text" (Baral et al. 2013: 214). This acknowledgment masks the insidious nature of the category of transgender in this context, erasing culturally specific experiences of gender and conflating a broad range of gender expressions and experiences into one term that is supposed to capture them all.

The *hijra* category in Pakistan and India, for example, long precedes the late twentieth-century category of transgender and has operated in contexts that others have argued are quite different from those of the Western gender binary (see, for example, Cohen 2005 and Reddy 2005). Yet this study reorganizes *hijra* as a subset of a global transgender population. The accuracy and function of the term *transgender* thus become highly suspect. There are quite practical effects of such categorizing that undermine the very goals of the researchers doing the study. Similar to Cohen (2005), anthropologist Aniruddha Dutta (2012) observes that HIV-prevention funding streams for nongovernmental organizations (NGOs) in India have now been parsed in the same way as in the United States, despite a very different understanding and set of practices around sexuality and gender. Funders have been eager to separate gender and sexuality in India, where they have been understood as intertwined, overlapping, and fluid, and to standardize Western models of "MSM" (men who have sex with men) and "transgender" funding streams. Dutta notes, "The MSM-TG division may not only exclude people who do not 'fit' these labels, but also splinter existing marginalized communities of gender/sexually variant people into narrow identitarian groups. This particularly affects communities and community-based organizations in non-metropolitan and rural areas, which are more dependent on such funding than metropolitan middle class LGBT groups."

Consider as well WHO, the authority on health for the United Nations, which recently released its HIV prevention, treatment, and care guidelines for key populations, "Values and Preferences of Transgender People: A Qualitative Study" (Schneiders 2014). Based on interviews with only fourteen "transgender men and women" from six of the seven WHO regions, the guidelines also cite Baral and colleagues (2013) and another US-focused meta-analysis (Herbst et al. 2008) as key evidence for transgender persons' disproportionately high HIV burden. Noting a failure to use condoms consistently despite availability, the guidelines restate the recommendations of Baral and colleagues for more research on bio-medical interventions such as pre-exposure prophylaxis (PrEP) and postex-posure prophylaxis (PEP) for HIV-negative transgender persons (Baral et al. 2013; Schneiders 2014). These recommendations target those perceived as trans-identified individuals throughout the world for greater scrutiny from govern-mental organizations, NGOs, and researchers as well as from pharmaceutical corporations, not to mention those informed by the (mis)interpretations of these studies' findings by mainstream and LGBT media sources.

Epidemiologists Greta R. Bauer and Ayden I. Scheim attempted to inter-vene on the flattening and stigmatizing effects of Baral and colleagues' study. In a letter to the *Lancet*'s editor (Bauer and Scheim 2013), they flag both the sampling bias—that the Baral analysis pooled only studies that focused almost exclusively on street-based sex workers—as well as their extrapolation of the study results to all transgender women rather than to transgender, street-based sex workers (832). They do not, however, question the Eurocentric, positivist use of the cat-egory itself.

In a subsequent article, Bauer (2014) builds on the work of Krieger and proposes that epidemiologists adapt intersectionality theory in order to address inequality more precisely. Kimberle Crenshaw (1989, 1994), among other black feminist scholars, developed intersectionality theory for use in qualitative and legal research to identify and intervene, not upon populations or individuals, but upon the contextually (e.g., legally) specific ways in which marginalized persons, such as black women, experience systemic erasures that can result from the notion of unitary categories of identity (1994). Bauer calls for a quantitative adaptation and more precisely specified, multilevel models that account for intersecting social identities, social positions, and related social policies in order to "reduce measurement bias and improve construct validity" and, ultimately, advance health equity on a population level (2014: 15). Bauer offers a more critical epide-miology as she recommends models that account for unstable identities, encourages triangulation with qualitative results, and makes room for structural interventions such as policy change. Nonetheless, this intersectional approach—that quantifies and compares ever more data about types of people—continues along the path of individualizing people into narrow identitarian subpopulations and runs "the risk of continuing to reinforce the intractability of inequity" (12).

It is important to remember that normalizing power is a tool of biopower: the specification of individuals allows them to be more readily controlled and regulated through the various social bodies—medicine, law, psychiatry, as Foucault suggests, but also WHO and various other bodies monitoring and managing health within nations and around the globe. Our analysis suggests that while these various bodies are trying very hard to do good in the world, they ultimately perpetuate the problems of stereotyping and oppression that they aim to overcome. And they do so precisely by using the terms of normalizing and biopower: fixed identities, invasive scrutiny of individuals, and the imposition of dominant cultural norms on individuals who often do not fit into them. As noted above and by others (Dutta 2012; Lorway and Khan 2014), many individuals are not "counted" precisely because they do not fit the definitions of identity categories at play. Valentine's (2007) ethnographic research in New York City identified how "transgender" only gained traction as an identity among primarily white, college-educated, activist trans women in the 1990s, a pattern that emerged simultaneously with its use in social-service agencies, where the same trans-identified women may have worked as peer counselors and outreach workers. Meanwhile, he observed that among persons of color, particularly within ball culture, it was "more common to hear participants refer to themselves as gay, fem queens, girls, and sometimes (though often jokingly) as women" (105). These multiple forms of self-identification can be seen as resistance to a system that requires conformity to the identity "transgender." The solution is not to specify individuals ever more carefully—that is the path of ever-increasing normalization. The solution, rather, is to question the system itself.

Conclusion

We believe that research aimed at expanding resources for trans individuals should itself seek to understand the various biopolitical and normalizing social, economic, and political components that contribute to the marginalization and invisibility of trans and gender-nonconforming individuals within the HIV prevention and treatment complex rather than merely acknowledge structural problems as complicating the process. That is, if social stigmatization and economic marginalization contribute to a lack of access to resources, as numerous trans health and HIV studies have suggested, then those practices need to be understood, challenged, and changed. It seems clear here that simply being gender nonconforming cannot explain an individual's exclusion from resources; the system and the research that position the individual as abnormal are complicit in the problem. So first, researchers need to ask a different set of questions that might include: How are identities produced within the sex/gender binary as abnormal? How do funding streams assume these identities as a foundation? How can we work across disciplines to interrogate with more precision how socioeconomic and geopolitical inequalities intertwine with the gender binary system and the exclusions it generates? This means that researchers should be educated about our own role in broad social, political, and economic power relations, and we should also lobby for changes in the research system along these lines. In short, researchers themselves need to find modes of resistance to the system of which we are a part.

Second, if researchers need to understand what drives sex work or intravenous drug use, a structural analysis of poverty is in order rather than a classification of identities. Focusing research on understanding structures and structural violence, coupled with broader engagements with gender-nonconforming individuals as partners in the mutual task of undermining structural oppression, may begin to move research beyond biopolitical and normalizing mechanisms of regulation and social control. Relatedly, researchers need to pay more attention to the resistances that inevitably arise from participants themselves, who may either implicitly or explicitly resist the research in which they agree to participate. While these forms of resistance may not transform the normalizing and biopolitical systems they seek to alter, they may mitigate some of their worst effects and open up spaces of questioning within the research itself.

Hale Thompson is a PhD candidate in public health at the University of Illinois at Chicago. He is a National Science Foundation predoctoral fellow in electronic privacy and security.

Lisa King is associate professor of philosophy at Edgewood College. Her research and teaching interests include feminist, queer, and gender theory, continental philosophy, and political philosophy.

Acknowledgments

We thank the editors of *TSQ*, our anonymous reviewers, and Fred Harrington, Laini Kavaloski, Lauren Lacey, Zhivka Valiavicharska, Nicole VanKim, and Ashley Byock for feedback on earlier drafts. This work was partially supported by the National Science Foundation IGERT grant CNS-1069311.

Note

1. Throughout the article, we use the terms *transgender*, *trans*, and *gender nonconforming* to refer to any individual who violates the alignment of sex-assigned-at-birth and gender expression of their culture. Similar to Christoph Hanssmann (2010) and David Valentine (2007), we intentionally vary our usage of these terms, knowing well that any term we choose poses potential problems and does not necessarily resonate with those to whom we have applied them.

References

Altaf, Arshad. 2008. "Explosive Expansion of HIV and Associated Risk Factors among Male and Hijra Sex Workers in Sindh, Pakistan." Poster presented at the Eleventh Annual International Meeting of the Institute of Human Virology, Baltimore, September 11–13.

Aschengrau, Anne, and George R. Seage III. 2008. *Essentials of Epidemiology in Public Health.* Sudbury, MA: Jones and Bartlett.

Baral, Stefan, et al. 2013. "Worldwide Burden of HIV in Transgender Women: A Systematic Review and Meta-Analysis." *Lancet Infectious Diseases* 13, no. 3: 214–22.

Bauer, Greta R. 2014. "Incorporating Intersectionality Theory into Population Health Research Methodology: Challenges and the Potential to Advance Health Equity." *Social Science and Medicine* 110: 10–17. doi:10.1016/j.socscimed.2014.03.022.

Bauer, Greta R., and Ayden I. Scheim. 2013. "Sampling Bias in Transgender Studies." *Lancet Infectious Diseases* 13, no. 10: 832. doi:10.1016/S1473-3099(13)70242-1.

Cohen, Lawrence. 2005. "The Kothi Wars: AIDS Cosmopolitanism and the Morality of Classification." In *Sex in Development: Science, Sexuality, and Morality in Global Perspective*, edited by Vincanne Adams and Stacy Leigh Pigg, 269–303. Durham, NC: Duke University Press.

Crenshaw, Kimberle. 1989. "Demarginalizing the Intersection of Race and Sex: A Black Feminist Critique of Antidiscrimination Doctrine, Feminist Theory, and Antiracist Politics." *University of Chicago Legal Forum* 1989: 139–68.

———. 1994. "Intersectionality, Identity Politics, and Violence against Women of Color." In *The Public Nature of Private Violence*, edited by Martha Albertson Fineman and Rixanne Mykitiuk, 1:93–118. New York: Routledge.

Dutta, Aniruddha. 2012. "Between Aid Conditionality and Identity Politics—The MSM-Transgender Divide and Normative Cartographies of Gender vs. Sexuality: Aniruddha Dutta." *Kafila*, April 5. kafila.org/2012/04/05/between-aid-conditionality-and-identity-politics-the-msm-transgender-divide-and-normative-cartographies-of-gender-vs-sexuality-aniruddha-dutta/#more-12257.

Epstein, Steven. 2003. "Sexualizing Governance and Medicalizing Identities: The Emergence of 'State-Centered' LGBT Health Politics in the United States." *Sexualities* 6, no. 2: 131–71.

———. 2007. *Inclusion: The Politics of Difference in Medical Research*. Chicago: University of Chicago Press.

Foucault, Michel. 1990. *An Introduction*. Vol. 1 of *The History of Sexuality*, edited and translated by Robert Hurley. New York: Vintage.

———. 2007. *Security, Territory, Population: Lectures at the Collège de France, 1977–78*. Edited by Michel Senellart, translated by Graham Burchell. New York: Palgrave McMillan.

Grandi, João Luiz, et al. 2000. "HIV Infection, Syphilis, and Behavioral Risks in Brazilian Male Sex Workers." *AIDS and Behavior* 4, no. 1: 129–35. doi:10.1023/A:1009553211416.

Hanssmann, Christoph. 2010. "Counting Us In: Problems and Opportunities in Health Research on Transgender and Gender Nonconforming Communities." *Seattle Journal for Social Justice* 8, no. 2: 541–77. digitalcommons.law.seattleu.edu/cgi/viewcontent.cgi?article=1095&context=sjsj.

Herbst, Jeffrey H., et al. 2008. "Estimating HIV Prevalence and Risk Behaviors of Transgender Persons in the United States: A Systematic Review." *AIDS and Behavior* 12, no. 1: 1–17. doi:10.1007/s10461-007-9299-3.

Krieger, Nancy. 2012. "Who and What Is a 'Population'? Historical Debates, Current Controversies, and Implications for Understanding 'Population Health' and Rectifying Health Inequities." *Milbank Quarterly* 90, no. 4: 634–81. doi:10.1111/j.1468-0009.2008.00538.x.

Lorway, Robert, and Shamshad Khan. 2014. "Reassembling Epidemiology: Mapping, Monitoring, and Making-up People in the Context of HIV Prevention in India." *Social Science and Medicine* 112: 51–62. doi:10.1016/j.socscimed.2014.04.034.

Nguyen, Tuan Anh, et al. 2008. "Prevalence and Risk Factors Associated with HIV Infection among Men Having Sex with Men in Ho Chi Minh City, Vietnam." *AIDS and Behavior* 12, no. 3: 476–82. doi:10.1007/s10461-007-9267-y.

Operario, Don, Toho Soma, and Kristen Underhill. 2008. "Sex Work and HIV Status among Transgender Women: Systematic Review and Meta-analysis." *Journal of Acquired Immune Deficiency Syndromes* 48, no. 1: 97–103. doi:10.1097/QAI.0b013e31816e3971.

Reddy, Gayatri. 2005. *With Respect to Sex: Negotiating Hijra Identity in South India.* Chicago: University of Chicago Press.

Rose, Geoffrey. (1993) 2008. *Rose's Strategy of Preventive Medicine.* 2nd ed. Oxford: Oxford University Press.

Russi, Jose C., et al. 2003. "Sexual Transmission of Hepatitis B Virus, Hepatitis C Virus, and Human Immunodeficiency Virus Type 1 Infections among Male Transvestite Commercial Sex Workers in Montevideo, Uruguay." *American Journal of Tropical Medicine and Hygiene* 68, no. 6: 716–20. www.ajtmh.org/content/68/6/716.short.

Schneiders, Mira. 2014. *Values and Preferences of Transgender People: A Qualitative Study.* New York: World Health Organization.

Shaw, Souradet Y., et al. 2011. "The Descriptive Epidemiology of Male Sex Workers in Pakistan: A Biological and Behavioural Examination." *Sexually Transmitted Infections* 87, no. 1: 73–80. doi:10.1136/sti.2009.041335.

Shim, Janet. 2000. "Bio-Power and Racial, Class, and Gender Formation in Biomedical Knowledge Production." In *Health Care Providers, Institutions, and Patients: Changing Patterns of Care Provision and Care Delivery*, edited by Jennie Jacobs Kronenfeld, 173–95. Stamford, CT: Jai.

Spade, Dean, and Rori Rohlfs. Forthcoming. "Legal Equality and the (After?)Math of Eugenics." *The Scholar and Feminist Online.*

Szklo, Moyses, and F. Javier Nieto. 2007. *Epidemiology: Beyond the Basics.* 2nd ed. Sudbury, MA: Jones and Bartlett.

Valentine, David. 2007. *Imagining Transgender: Ethnography of a Category.* Durham, NC: Duke University Press.

Information Systems
and the Translation of Transgender

JEFFREY ALAN JOHNSON

Abstract Using the data systems of Utah Valley University as a representative case study, this research note discusses the sociotechnical process, which I term the *translation regime*, through which data systems interpret and construct the world, focusing on gender nonconformity as a paradigmatic instance of that process. Through both the technical structures of data systems and the social knowledge within which they operate, such regimes impose multiple substantive translations on the conditions that they purport to represent, translations that come with important political consequences for those who are gender nonconforming. So understood, information technology becomes an important locus for action in the pursuit of social justice for gender-nonconforming people.
Keywords data systems, justice, translation

I t should by now be clear that, contrary to the common perception of data as an objective representation of reality, the content of data systems is an interpretation. Using the data systems of Utah Valley University (UVU) as a representative case study, this research note discusses the sociotechnical process, which I term the *translation regime*, through which data systems interpret and construct the world, focusing on gender nonconformity as a paradigmatic instance of that process. Such regimes impose multiple substantive translations on the conditions that they purport to represent, translations that come with important political consequences for those who are gender nonconforming. So understood, information technology becomes an important locus for action in the pursuit of social justice for gender-nonconforming people.

The Data Translation Regime
The ubiquity of data obscures the fact that it is a form of knowledge unique to the modern, bureaucratic organization (whether in the state, the economy, or civil society) and rooted in such organizations' needs to make knowledge of its subjects

TSQ: Transgender Studies Quarterly ★ Volume 2, Number 1 ★ February 2015 **160**
DOI 10.1215/23289252-2848940 © 2015 Duke University Press

legible. What James C. Scott (1998) terms "legible knowledge" represents a transformation of reality into standardized, aggregated, static facts that are capable of consistent documentation and limited to the matters in which there is official interest. Such facts emerge from a process of creating common representations into which cases are classified and can then be aggregated to create new facts on which the organization will rely in making decisions (80–81). But while the process of producing legibility probably requires something like the illusion of objective representation, observation alone cannot actually produce a specific data state (that is, a specific ordering of data within a data system). The relationship between a "reality" that is to be represented and a data state representing it is one-to-many. In making the relationship between an individual and the social practices of gender legible, for instance, one might classify individuals using biological sex, binary gender identity, or more complex identity systems. Hence a data system that attempts to provide a definitive representation must include a process that selects only one data state from among the many possible representations to the exclusion of all others. It also must do so systematically rather than exegetically, as the final data state chosen by such a process for any one set of circumstances must be commensurable with those states for all other possible circumstances chosen by that same process: what counts as "male" must do so consistently across all cases. These final data states are the de facto reality within which data-based decision processes operate.

I call this process as it takes place within any data system (whether public or private) the *translation regime*. Following Stephen D. Krasner's (1982: 186) definition of regimes in international relations, one might define the translation regime as the set of implicit or explicit principles, norms, rules, and decision-making procedures through which single, commensurable data states are selected to represent conditions in the world. The translation regime acts as an external source of stability for the data system and allows it to bring legibility to the represented conditions (Mitev 2005). Translation regimes are composed of two domains: a technical domain that includes the formal rules and procedures of the data system that collect, store, validate, relate, extract, and apply the data; and a social domain of implicit and explicit norms and standards that provide the content of the technical structures. In regimes shaping gender data, the technical domain might include validation tables defining acceptable values for a gender field, while the social domain would include the dominant binary system of gender representation as well as, potentially, alternative forms of representation or discourses that deny the legitimacy of such forms. The technical structures embed, enforce, and constrain the substantive worldview of the social domain while at the same time hiding the inherently social nature of data systems behind the appearance of pure technicity: every form that allows one to select only "male" or "female" resignifies the gender binary in an ostensibly apolitical framework.

There are at least three characteristic types of translations effected by translation regimes. Normalizing translations establish certain states of the world as within the realm of normalcy to the exclusion of others. Characteristics for which there are no fields in the database cease to exist analytically, while conditions that are not included in the validation table that defines the valid values for a field are errors that must be corrected. Atomizing translations fragment related characteristics into entirely distinct fields, destroying meanings and narratives that exist through relationships among characteristics. Unifying translations do the opposite, grouping several conditions into a single value that obscures differences in the effort to make the range of conditions more manageable. Commonly this occurs when reducing the diversity of conditions to a small number of values, but it also can unify temporal variability into a single value that is understood as a permanent or essential feature. Through these translations, the reality that the data system purports to represent is irrevocably changed, creating a new reality. That translated reality, not the state of the world from which it originated, informs data-driven processes of decision.

Translating Gender Nonconformity

Gender can be understood as a paradigmatic case of translation in information systems. The many possibilities of gender expression are sufficiently well recognized that Facebook has added an ever-expanding list of gender identities from which its users can choose along with a separate specification of personal pronouns that the system uses to refer to a user (Facebook 2014). In spite of this, the translation regime at work in many educational data systems takes the raw experiences of the students, staff, and faculty and, as one might expect, translates them into the gender binary.

The primary mechanisms of this translation are the single gender field and the validation table for the gender field. The single field prevents representing multiple aspects of gender (such as sex at birth, expression, and identification). Validation tables define the set of acceptable values for a field and include any additional information about that value, such as the start and end dates during which it is valid and the description of the value. That table includes only two values: "M" and "F." As described below, a third value, "U" for "Unspecified," was deprecated in 2012.

Substantively, however, this translation reflects political and social factors more strongly than technical ones, as there is no technical constraint that would prevent a broader categorization of gender. The Utah System of Higher Education

(USHE) data standard for gender allows only values representing male and female students, though it does not define either (USHE 2013: sec. S-13). The 2012 deprecation of "Unspecified" in UVU's data system was an implementation of a similar deprecation in the USHE standard that year, in principle an attempt to better coordinate USHE and federal data standards. Conversations surrounding the deprecation focused on the idea that an unspecified gender represented inherently bad data rather than circumstances that could not be captured in the binary values (i.e., all students are either permanently male or permanently female, and "unspecified" represented students who had failed to specify which of those values was true of them). But this deprecation followed legislative opposition to the installation of unisex restrooms at Weber State University as a support measure for gender-nonconforming students, an issue that strongly reinforced binary views of gender within higher education in Utah. Though a technical implementation, the translation is very much a political act.

This translation fundamentally changes the identities of gender-nonconforming students. It serves, immediately, as a unifying translation. The myriad gender identities that Facebook permits its users to express are reduced to two categories, hiding both the diversity and the temporal instability of gender expression within each of them. It also unifies the different constructs at work in gender in a single representation that assumes gender conformity. Less apparently, it also atomizes, separating gender from ethnicity and eliminating the possibility of understanding the intersectional identities of gender-nonconforming students of color.

But this is most significantly a normalizing translation. The reduction of gender identity to a gender binary—and implicitly to gender conformity—classifies gender nonconformity first as deviant and then as nonexistent. The pre-2012 standard left gender-nonconforming students in a residual category: "unspecified" is functionally equivalent to "other" as both a data value and a social identity contrasted with the self that those with gender-conforming identities express. With the deprecation of "unspecified," gender nonconformity ceased to exist analytically; all students were forced to accept a position in the gender binary that was assumed to represent gender conformity, and analysis of nonconforming and conforming students became impossible. This is not to say that such students ceased to exist in other ways, but they were invisible to the data-driven decision processes most common at the university.

The Politics of Translation

The need to exercise political control that gives rise to the legibility imperative makes the translation regime a political process. Its design presents a range of consequences for political practice and social structure. Representation and normalization are the most apparent consequences in this case. Data is not just a set of facts for satisfying curiosity; it is the fundamental basis for decision making in modern organizations. Rendering gender-nonconforming students illegible, thus invisible, and finally nonexistent in data systems undermines their representation in data-driven processes. The annual budget process expects that budget requests will be supported by data; in the absence of data identifying gender-nonconforming students, no budget request can be made for programs to support them: there can be no demonstrated need because there are no data. Even in an environment of good will, the institutional structure undermines the capacity for representation.

At the same time, the stigmatization of gender nonconformity that comes from being outside the valid data states—what one might, in line with Judith Butler (1997), think of as "hate data"—undermines gender-nonconforming students' legitimacy within political processes, limiting their ability to assert their interests through other means while increasing opposition to any decisions on the part of the administration that might support those interests. This is even more so in the case of either intersectional identities—which are fragmented and reassembled into groups where the intersectional are marginalized—or potential coalitions that could work to mutual advantage if their commonalities rather than different values were the focus of attention. It should not be lost on anyone that the outcome of such a process will almost always serve the interests of the same groups who developed the translation regime.

Information systems are thus sites of political contestation and should be viewed as important loci of efforts to promote social justice. The technical structures of data systems embed political values and relationships. These, as much as any other form of political institution, are significant contributors to social injustices affecting groups like gender-nonconforming people. But also, as much as any other form of political institution, they can be changed, designed consciously to further social justice. As data-driven decisions become increasingly the norm, attention to values, building for pluralist rather than unitary purposes, and inclusivity in the design process will become critical elements of information systems design.

Jeffrey Alan Johnson is assistant director of Institutional Effectiveness and Planning at Utah Valley University. His book, *Toward Information Justice: Principles, Policies, and Technologies,* will be published in 2015.

References

Butler, Judith. 1997. *Excitable Speech: A Politics of the Performative*. New York: Routledge.

Facebook. 2014. "How Do I Edit Basic Info on My Timeline and Choose Who Can See It?" www
.facebook.com/help/276177272409629.

Krasner, Stephen D. 1982. "Structural Causes and Regime Consequences: Regimes as Intervening
Variables." *International Organization* 36, no. 2: 185–205.

Mitev, Nathalie N. 2005. "Are Social Constructivist Approaches Critical? The Case of IS Failure."
In *Handbook of Critical Information Systems Research: Theory and Application*, 70–103.
Northampton, MA: Elgar.

Scott, James C. 1998. *Seeing Like a State: How Certain Schemes to Improve the Human Condition
Have Failed*. New Haven, CT: Yale University Press.

USHE (Utah System of Higher Education). 2013. "Student Data Submission File, 2013–2014
Submission Year." higheredutah.org/wp-content/uploads/2013/09/rd_2013DataDict
_Students.pdf.

Boxes of Our Own Creation

A Trans Data Collection Wo/Manifesto

JACK HARRISON-QUINTANA, JAIME M. GRANT,
and IGNACIO G. RIVERA

Abstract This article reports on the experience of developing and conducting the National Trans-gender Discrimination Survey (NTDS) as a grassroots community-based project that made a home for the 6,456 trans and gender-nonconforming people who chose to answer its seventy questions and created the largest quantitative data set on trans experience anywhere in the world. In order to explore the possibility of liberatory grassroots survey research, this article addresses three elements of the survey questionnaire and process. First, it discusses the convening of the team that ultimately created the instrument. Second, it describes the four qualifying questions that opened the survey questionnaire, inviting respondents to articulate their own gender identities. And finally, it looks closely at the last question of the survey, which eschewed the multiple-choice format in order to invite long-form responses about any topic respondents wished to address. This project has been unique in that it owes as much to the methodologies of activism and the history of community organizing as to the theories of survey research. Likewise, this article does not seek to offer best practices built only on citations to existing social science but rather is a record of the trail we blazed with this survey project in dialogue with women of color feminisms and trans liberation. The NTDS is a joint project of the National Gay and Lesbian Task Force and the National Center for Transgender Equality.

Keywords National Transgender Discrimination Survey, survey research, transgender

I n 1989, Audre Lorde—self-described black lesbian feminist mother war-rior poet—delivered the keynote for a conference at Georgetown University. During the question-and-answer period, a young woman posed a now very familiar question: "Why do you have to list all of those things? I really hate labels," she said. "I don't want to live in a box."

Lorde responded by drawing a distinction between labels and identities. A label is a term someone else imposes on us from the outside—and it is lim-iting. Identity, on the other hand, is something we claim for ourselves. Identities help give us a starting place to define our justice work and the communities we call home.

TSQ: Transgender Studies Quarterly ∗ Volume 2, Number 1 ∗ February 2015
DOI 10.1215/23289252-2848949 © 2015 Duke University Press

Lorde articulated her identity as a black lesbian feminist mother warrior poet at a time when each of these identities drew attack (Lorde 1982). Few believed that black women could be lesbians or that any woman, but especially a woman of color, could be a poet. Mothers could not be warriors, and describing oneself as a black warrior drew enormous state violence. By presenting these descriptors as a coherent identity, Lorde effectively resisted the constricting "boxes" that had been imposed on her in an overwhelmingly white supremacist, patriarchal, and heteronormative culture. Of course, no description can represent the totality of who we are, but trailblazers like Lorde taught us the power of illuminating invisibilized and silenced parts of ourselves.

Some twenty-five years later, grassroots researchers seeking to gather data on trans[1] experience with survey research are still debating the question of how to construct a liberating versus limiting set of "boxes" to uncover the depth and breadth of trans experience. To date, trans research frameworks have rarely been drafted by trans people and have overwhelmingly centered on pathologies. Many in the community are appropriately wary of surveys, because the limited options presented all too often collapse and marginalize trans experience rather than expand and uncover the richness and complexities of trans lives.

This article reports on our experience of developing and conducting the National Transgender Discrimination Survey (NTDS) as a grassroots community-based project that made a home for the 6,456 trans and gender-nonconforming people who chose to answer its seventy questions and created the largest quantitative data set on trans experience anywhere in the world (Grant et al. 2011).

In order to explore the possibility of liberatory grassroots survey research, this article will address three elements of our survey questionnaire and process. First, we will discuss the convening of the team that ultimately created the instrument. Second, we will describe the four qualifying questions that opened the survey questionnaire, inviting respondents to articulate their own gender identities. And finally, we will look closely at the last question of the survey, which eschewed the multiple-choice format in order to invite long-form responses about any topic respondents wished to address.

This project has been unique in that it owes as much to the methodologies of activism and the history of community organizing as to the theories of survey research. Likewise, this article does not seek to offer best practices built only on citations to existing social science but rather is a record of the trail we blazed with this survey project in dialogue with women of color feminisms and trans liberation.

Team and Process

The NTDS has been a collaboration between the National Center for Transgender Equality (NCTE) and the National Gay and Lesbian Task Force (now the National

LGBTQ Task Force). In this section, we trace the early history of the project and how these two organizations convened a diverse set of activists, researchers, and community members in order to create it. The most critical aspects of this team were the centering of trans voices—and a plethora of trans experiences—in the creation of the questionnaire and the high number of potential end users of data involved in the process.

When NCTE and the Task Force came together to create the NTDS, there was no project-specific funding. We drew only on the dedicated labor of existing staff and a cadre of volunteers. A full year prior to fielding the questionnaire, Task Force intern and trans activist Eli Vitulli developed a database of 918 trans-led or trans-serving organizations that indicated by phone an interest in receiving the link to involve their primary constituencies in the study. The 2007 excision of transgender protections from the historic House vote on the Employment Non-Discrimination Act (ENDA) created a groundswell of interest in a project to more fully explore the impacts of discrimination on trans people in the United States. Eli's outreach was enthusiastically met, and another intern, Kyla Bender-Baird, spent this stretch of the project researching other surveys and key issues facing trans people that reinforced Eli's efforts.

The seventy-question survey instrument took eight full months and countless interlocutors to develop. A mix of trans leaders and cisgender activists, lawyers and lobbyists, academics and stats geeks, feminist and antiracist organizers, theory-heads and practitioners, ENFPs and ISTJs, lesbians, gay men, bisexual and pansexual folks, revolutionaries and legal reformers, people of color and white folks, corporate-based and anticapitalist agitators, monogamists and polyamorists, youths and elders, kinksters and vanilla-identified activists all brought their passions and considerable skills to the table.

The consistent core deliberators in the drafting process were Mara Keisling and Justin Tanis, NCTE's executive director and communications director, respectively, and cisgender trans equality/liberation activists Lisa Mottet and Jaime M. Grant, the Task Force's Transgender Civil Rights Project director and Policy Institute director, respectively.

M. Somjen Frazer came to the project first as a volunteer and then as the Task Force's policy analyst. A significant weakness in the team at this stage of the process was the absence of a single person of color on the core four-person drafting team. Key volunteers in the drafting process included Dr. Scout, Dr. Susan Rankin, Marsha Botzer, Hawk Stone, Marcus Waterbury, Amy Sagalkin, Beth Teper, and significantly, Steve Aurand, a twenty-year Task Force volunteer and statistician.

Our discussions were often arduous and reflected more than one hundred years of collective experience in queer and trans community work. As we struggled with the wording of a specific question, someone would say, "Remember Janice in Oklahoma? She would be offended by that construction." Or "How would Kyle in Mississippi answer that one?" Or "If you asked it that way, my trans partner would not relate to it."

Whenever we found ourselves between a rock and a hard place in a deliberation about the relevance and/or construction of a question, trans experience and the specific (and not always congruent) needs of end users of the data ruled the day. And even this early on in the process, how we selected who was in the room, both rhetorically and physically, contributed greatly to our ultimate success.

The First Four Questions

To create a study that would facilitate the broadest possible participation of trans people across geography, race, class, age, and identity was the goal toward which we struggled. This section spotlights the first four questions of the survey, which both yielded invaluable data and created a container that made it clear that this survey was intended for people across the trans spectrum.

The lack of dedicated funding to pay participants or facilitators to improve our dissemination strategy was a significant obstacle. Just prior to fielding the questionnaire, Dr. Scout at the National LGBT Tobacco Control Network offered $3,000 to improve our outreach to impoverished trans people in exchange for impact on our questions on smoking. This funding was crucial to our distribution of 2,000 paper surveys to homeless- and health-outreach workers across the country in order to reach people unlikely to respond to an online survey. Trans researcher Sari Reisner's analysis (2013) of the differences between the online and paper respondents in the NTDS affirm that this funding provided absolutely crucial access to people in the community whose voices are least heard and who experience in many cases the most catastrophic impacts of antitrans discrimination.

Given our funding limitations, we were left strategizing mightily about ways to craft a study instrument where people would see themselves and their genders in the earliest moments of entering the study process. Our first four questions created a multilayered invitation for people to create the kind of multilayered articulation of self that Audre Lorde had famously crafted—to find a way to claim the creativity and express the nuances trans people are living out in the embodiment of their many genders.

Q1: Do you identify as transgender/gender non-conforming in any way?
☐ Yes
☐ No. If no, do NOT continue.

This question was designed to invite gender-variant people across a broad spectrum of gender, from a soft butch lesbian to a transsexual-identified woman to a male-assigned-at-birth cross-dresser and a female-assigned-at-birth genderqueer so that we could explore the distinct impacts of discrimination based on specific gender identities and expressions.

> Q2: What sex were you assigned at birth, on your original birth certificate?
> ☐ Male
> ☐ Female

Along with our first qualifying question, this question served to anchor our sample. If people checked male here and then chose male identifiers and expressions below, and if their responses to subsequent questions reported a male gender identity and experience, we disqualified them as a study participant. In this way, questions 1 through 4 helped create a nuanced qualifier for our study population.

One important finding from this question was that people who checked female-assigned-at-birth reported certain congruent impacts of being born female: they were more likely to be verbally harassed in kindergarten through twelfth-grade settings, for example, while male-assigned-at-birth respondents experienced more physical violence in the same period, regardless of current gender identity (Grant et al. 2011).

> Q3: What is your primary gender identity today?
> ☐ Male/man
> ☐ Female/woman
> ☐ Part time as one gender, part time as another
> ☐ A gender not listed here, please specify: _____

The careful construction of this question created one of the true treasure troves of information about gender identity in the study. Sixty percent of our sample identified along a transfeminine spectrum and forty percent as masculine. Masculine-identified people checked the fourth option, "a gender not listed here," much more often than their transfemale counterparts. Eight hundred forty respondents chose "a gender not listed here," offering five hundred distinct terms for their genders. This is the largest sample of third-gender or genderqueer experience anywhere in the world (Grant, Herman, and Harrison 2012).

In addition to the genderqueers, many respondents reported living part time as one gender, part time as another. The experiences of male-assigned-at-birth cross-dressers are reported in a chapter in the full *Injustice at Every Turn* report (Grant et al. 2011), and those of the female-assigned-at-birth cross-dressers are explored in an article in the 2014 Harvard Kennedy School's *LGBTQ Policy Journal* (Harrison-Quintana, Glover, and James 2014).

> Q4: For each term listed, please select to what degree it applies to you. [Not at all, Somewhat, or Strongly]
>> Transsexual
>> Transgender
>> FTM (female-to-male)
>> MTF (male-to-female)
>> Intersex
>> Gender non-conforming or gender variant
>> Genderqueer
>> Androgynous
>> Feminine male
>> Masculine female or butch
>> A.G. or Aggressive
>> Third gender
>> Cross dresser
>> Drag performer (King/Queen)
>> Two-spirit
>> Other, please specify: _____

This list was generated based on much discussion by all of the collaborators working on the survey instrument. It represents a particular moment that is fixed in time, in cultures, and in the communities of the creators, which is why it was so important for us to tap into networks of diverse activists in its creation. No list is ever perfect, and this one had the following strengths and weaknesses. On the strength side, we attempted to include culturally specific articulations of trans identity in order to be intentionally welcoming to people of color and to immigrants from other cultural contexts. We also allowed participants to distinguish between terms with which they felt partially identified from those with which they felt strongly identified, so that no one felt they had to box themselves in completely with the terms they chose. Its weaknesses included its length—the survey was long, and every time we added options and questions, we ran the risk of tiring people out and encouraging people with lower literacy or less access to computers, in particular, to stop. And, of course, as many identities as we included, we left out many. This is also why it was critical to again include the option to write in one's own response and rank the term on our Likert scale.

In conclusion, these four questions were in many ways the reason we were able to attract as many respondents as we did. We believe we created radical welcome for the 6,456 respondents who chose to participate and that our sample would have been smaller and less diverse without these questions. They enabled us to do nuanced research later, comparing nuanced specific slices of the sample, and they enabled the entire enterprise of the NTDS.

Question 70

The final question of the NTDS survey read: "Anything else you'd like to tell us about your experiences of acceptance or discrimination as a transgender/gender non-conforming person?" Here we delve into the liberatory grassroots framework of the survey process as it once again decentered the authors and placed respondents as the experts on their own experience. We asked the best questions we knew to ask given all that was poured into the process, but at the end of the day, of course, there were mistakes and gaps, and this question helped to partially make up for those.

One of the most unfortunate omissions from the survey in general was that no questions were asked concerning respondents' faith identities or their experiences of discrimination in religious settings. Fortunately, respondents caught this mistake and filled in question 70 addressing this topic more than any others. It is thanks to the respondents and to question 70 that this data set has also yielded information on military service, transition on the job, and the medical benefits of transition. Using qualitative methods of analysis, one article on military service has already been published (Herman and Harrison 2013), and three more on the other topics are to follow.

This question generated more than two hundred pages of text. Excerpted quotes were included throughout the report. We believe these narratives bring the data to life in a way that is invaluable; they present a significant untapped resource for discovering the information that this project can deliver to the scholarly and activist community.

Points of Entry, Points of Departure

The generative grassroots research model established by the principal team on this project continues to grow because the NTDS is a living, breathing enterprise that has continued to produce publications and empower trans leaders.

The decision by the team was/has been to make the data set available to researchers and activists all over the world who have the statistics software to work with it. Because we asked seventy questions, there is still so much data to utilize, comb through, crosstab, and compare, and we knew that we would never be able to do it all ourselves. In fact, just as we believed that no small research team could create the instrument without widespread input, the same applies to the results. We also did not set out on this journey to build our own careers but rather to contribute to a movement, and we are energized by the idea of a generation of trans researchers using these data as part of the process of becoming credentialed and spreading their ideas to their own academic communities.

Audre Lorde famously said, "Your silence will not protect you." The corollary to this statement is that the more we uncover and share the great diversity of experiences within our communities, the more power we grow, both individually and collectively. The watershed impacts of the NTDS speak to the crucial need for accountable grassroots research that illustrates the depth and breadth of the human rights violations trans people are surviving on a daily basis alongside the resilience, resistance, creativity, and hope we demonstrate in committing to ourselves, and our brilliant genders, day after day.

Jack Harrison-Quintana is a queer Latino activist and researcher currently serving as the manager of the Policy Institute of the National LGBTQ Task Force. In 2010, he was a contributing author for *Outing Age 2010: Public Policy Issues Affecting Lesbian, Gay, Bisexual, and Transgender Elders*, and in 2011, he was a coauthor of *Injustice at Every Turn: A Report of the National Transgender Discrimination Survey*. His other work has addressed issues of sexual liberation, racial justice, and anti-genderqueer discrimination. Before coming to the Task Force, Jack did fellowships with the National Center for Transgender Equality in Washington, DC, and Khemara in Phnom Penh, Cambodia. A native of Signal Mountain, Tennessee, Jack earned his BS and MA from Georgetown University.

Jaime M. Grant is the coauthor of *Injustice at Every Turn: A Report of the National Transgender Discrimination Survey* and "A Gender Not Listed Here: Genderqueers, Gender Rebels, and Other-Wise in the National Transgender Discrimination Survey." Previously, she served as director of the Policy Institute at the National Gay and Lesbian Task Force. She holds a PhD in women's studies from the Union Institute. For six years she directed the Union Institute's Center for Women, the nation's only academic women's center dedicated to collaborations between scholars and activists. Her articles on transformational organizations and coalition work have been published in major academic journals and anthologies.

Ignacio G. Rivera, MA, who prefers the gender-neutral pronoun "they," is an internationally known Queer, Two-spirit, Black-Boricua Taíno, lecturer, activist, sex educator, filmmaker, and performance artist whose body of work has focused on gender and sexuality, specifically on queer, trans, and sexual liberation issues within a race/class dynamic. Ignacio is currently working with John Harrison-Quintana and Jaime M. Grant on the Global Transgender Research and Advocacy Project of the National Transgender Discrimination Survey.

Note

1. The term *trans* in this article is used in the most inclusive sense to mean a range of people whose genders vary in a range of ways from the sex they were assigned at birth. At times, we use the combinatory term *trans and gender nonconforming* as well but do so with the intention of further specifically highlighting the inclusion of all gender-variant people.

References

Grant, Jaime M., et al. 2011. *Injustice at Every Turn: A Report of the National Transgender Discrimination Survey*. Washington, DC: National Center for Transgender Equality and National Gay and Lesbian Task Force.

Grant, Jaime M., Jody Herman, and Jack Harrison. 2012. "A Gender Not Listed Here: Genderqueers, Gender Rebels, and OtherWise in the National Transgender Discrimination Survey." *LGBTQ Policy Journal* 2: 13–24.

Harrison-Quintana, Jack, Julian Glover, and Sandy James. 2014. "Finding Genders: Transmasculine Crossdressers in the National Transgender Discrimination Survey." *LGBTQ Policy Journal*. www.hkslgbtq.com/finding-genders/

Herman, Jody, and Jack Harrison. 2013. "Still Serving in Silence: Transgender Service Members and Veterans in the National Transgender Discrimination Survey." *LGBTQ Policy Journal*. www.hkslgbtq.com/still-serving-in-silence-transgender-service-members-and-veterans-in-the-national-transgender-discrimination-survey/

Lorde, Audre. 1982. *Zami: A New Spelling of My Name*. Berkeley: Crossing.

Reisner, Sari. 2013. "Gender Identity as a Social Determinant of Health: Methods for Transgender Health Research." ScD diss., Harvard School of Public Health.

The Ethical Case for
Undercounting Trans Individuals

MEGAN M. ROHRER

Abstract This article makes an ethical case for celebrating the undercounting of trans individuals in surveys and studies. Despite positive motivations compelling researchers to more accurately enumerate the transgender spectrum, researchers trying to quantify the trans experience should ask themselves if their personal definition of who is trans is more or less important than the identity of trans individuals living a low/nondisclosure life.

Keywords trans identity, survey research

For much of the past fifty years, LGBT activism and "acting up" have focused on the political and social value of being out and proud. In recent years, the emphasis on publicly claiming an identity has extended to demanding that LGBT populations "stand up and be counted." At this moment, however, it is important for us to pause and examine the ethical implications of outness and the desire for accurate counts of transness.

Just because it may be possible one day to find accurate ways to count trans people, it does not mean that we always should.

A decade ago, I stood firmly on the other side of this argument. I am the pastor of Grace Evangelical Lutheran Church in San Francisco and have been the executive director of Welcome, primarily serving LGBTQ homeless individuals for twelve years. Despite being "out" about my trans identity, I, like many trans individuals, maintain a low level of disclosure about my medical choices.

Living on the autistic spectrum, I am a stickler for rules and exactness in counting. My unique way of thinking, fueled by lessons learned coming out in South Dakota, convinced me that the ability to self-identify is an intrinsic part of liberty. In the past, this has caused me to create long, elaborate counting systems and surveys that did a better job at validating people's choices than in collecting concise information.

TSQ: Transgender Studies Quarterly ∗ Volume 2, Number 1 ∗ February 2015
DOI 10.1215/23289252-2848958   © 2015 Duke University Press

Working with the homeless, I know all too well that exactitude in counting vulnerable populations not only has real and lasting budgetary implications but also has the potential to produce the political momentum needed to create safety nets and to end discriminatory policies.

Yet along with all the positive effects of accurate data on health care and public policy and in making us feel a little less alone, there is also an ethical case to be made for not counting trans individuals, particularly those who are the most vulnerable.

Each year since 2002, I have spent a week on street retreat, sleeping on the sidewalks, in shelters, or in the makeshift spaces that homeless individuals in San Francisco or Minneapolis call home. During these outings I have answered my fair share of surveys, honestly providing my financial, medical, sexual, and employment history. I have gone through the process of changing my sex marker in shelter databases and with primary care providers.

In these situations, I have found that the surveys that did the best job uncovering my sexuality and gender identity were time-consuming, were conducted orally in locations without privacy, and were used as a gateway to gain shelter or other resources designed to care for the most vulnerable. While some of these surveys make it possible for individuals engaging in high-risk behaviors to obtain much-needed health care, prevention, and harm reduction, they also require vulnerable individuals to make themselves even more vulnerable in exchange for obtaining basic food and shelter services. Regardless of the socioeconomic class of those answering the overly sexualized questions, providing unnecessary medical information to strangers can leave trans individuals feeling pathologized, overexposed, and abnormal.

In ancient biblical times, people believed that infertile women were a different sex than fertile women (Carden 2006). Can you imagine the outrage if people were asked to list their fertility status on forms in an attempt to acquire a more accurate understanding of their sex? What if menopausal women or men taking Viagra were required to state their hormonal status in parity with trans individuals? Should women who have had surgery to remove breast cancer or a hysterectomy and men who had prostate cancer removed be counted differently than others who have not? If not, then why is it considered acceptable to ask trans individuals questions about their hormones and the surgical state of their bodies?

In addition to the ethical issues about vulnerability and privacy, the full spectrum of our community will never be fully represented by these numbers. Perhaps the greatest barrier to accurate and complete data is the identity choice of some individuals to *not* come out as trans. As long as there are individuals some might describe as trans who have fully affirmed their asserted sex living as trans low/nondisclosers, studies on our community will always undercount it.

As Julia Serano points out, low/nondisclosing individuals are not hiding their true identity when they choose not to identify as transgender (2007). Rather, these individuals are asserting the identity they have always known themselves to be and/or have become. To many low/nondisclosing individuals whose transition is complete, their identity is now male or female, and there is no longer a need or desire to identify as a member of the trans community. This creates an ethical dilemma. If the ability to self-identify is an intrinsic part of liberty, then how can it be right to include this individual under a trans umbrella? But not including these individuals undercounts the number of people who *at some point* in their lives may need transgender-related health and social services and who may need policies protecting them from discrimination.

Researchers striving for accuracy may try to find better ways to include trans low/nondisclosing individuals. While this could improve understandings of the ways in which people across the trans continuum live and breathe, it may also have effects beyond the study results. For example, failing to take into account the trans low/nondisclosure experience may artificially increase unemployment and violence statistics, causing some trans individuals to believe that their lives will be safer and more productive if they choose to delay transition or not to transition at all. On the other hand, the inclusion of trans low/nondisclosing individuals in data may decrease the rate of discrimination reported and make it more difficult to use numbers to justify the need for special protection under the law.

There are many positive motivations compelling researchers to more accurately enumerate the transgender spectrum and to enable people to find their place on it. Still, the project of counting trans individuals raises hard questions. Researchers trying to quantify the trans experience should ask themselves if their personal definition of who is trans is more or less important than the identity of individuals living a low/nondisclosure life. Those who conduct surveys in social-services settings should think long and hard about the extra vulnerability they are imposing on an already vulnerable group. Does the perception that food, housing, and other benefits must be "paid for" by answering intrusive questions mean that the consent is real? If it is not yet possible to fully describe and quantify our community, what are the potentially negative consequences of survey results that say they represent the entire trans community?

We are a diverse, evolving community that cannot be generalized or captured in statistics. Instead of striving to be quantified and reduced to numbers frozen at one moment in time, we should find better ways to educate the cis community. Our strength lies beyond what can be counted by researchers. The wisdom that evolves from our lives cannot be fully understood without living them.

The Rev. **Megan M. Rohrer** is pastor of Grace Evangelical Lutheran Church in San Francisco and the executive director of Welcome. They coedited *Letters for My Brothers: Transitional Wisdom in Retrospect* (2011) and authored *With a Day Like Yours, Couldn't You Use a Little Grace* (2014) and *Queerly Lutheran* (2011).

References

Carden, Michael. 2006. "Genesis/Bereshit." In *The Queer Bible Commentary*, edited by Deryn Guest et al. London: SCM Press.

Serano, Julia. 2007. *Whipping Girl: A Transsexual Woman on Sexism and the Scapegoating of Femininity*. Berkeley, CA: Seal.

Transsexuality as a Window on and a Metaphor for Contemporary Iran

LEILA HUDSON

Professing Selves: Transsexuality and Same-Sex Desire in Contemporary Iran
Afsaneh Najmabadi
Durham, NC: Duke University Press, 2014. vii + 450 pp.

Under guise of an ethnography of transsexuality in contemporary Iran, Afsaneh Najmabadi has written a nuanced ethnography of the transition of the Iranian state and public sphere from one type (*jins*) to another. Building on Joan Scott's (1986) observation that gender is a useful category for historical analysis, Najmabadi goes beyond showing that sex and sexuality are also useful categories for historical analysis to suggest that somatic-constitutional transformation can be as well. Interestingly, these are all better categories for analysis of the pre- and post-op (Islamic revolution) state of Iran than they are for comprehending a class of transsexual Iranians. This book is a nuanced study of the ways in which the most stigmatized and least conforming of Iran's citizens evade but also embody rigid binaries of sex and gender. But it is even more an analysis of how science, law, journalism, and eventually Shi'i *fiqh* (jurisprudence) used the subjectivities, bodies, and practices of gender of sexually fluid people to shape public discourses and state institutions. In contrast to approaches that impart too much sinister agency to the state or too much creative empowerment to the individual citizen, this account shows how ever more precise articulations of transsexuality in narratives, popular culture, state certification, and medical, psychiatric, and religious discourses provide the fairly stable categories that the transforming state needs to order itself. Transsexual individuals, who seem understandably to prefer their privacy and control of their public personas, resist categorization.

TSQ: Transgender Studies Quarterly ∗ Volume 2, Number 1 ∗ February 2015   **179**
DOI 10.1215/23289252-2849144   © 2015 Duke University Press

In Najmabadi's generally readable prose, the bulk of the book (chaps. 2–6) shows the accumulated layers of discourse around nonheteronormativity. From the sediment of curiosity and scientism, Najmabadi unearths the various tropes of the twentieth century—the erotic literary, biological outlier, tragic pathology, private folly, criminal danger—that made transsexuality and its corollary homosexuality legible around the edges of Pahlavi Iran. The gender, sex, and desire phenomenologies became increasingly specific as the modern secular state developed new claims on its population, and journalists and publishers found the language and genres to market them to the public. In a couple of generations, we go from the vague language of yearning for the forbidden to competing religious theories of the disjuncture of the body, soul, and psyche.

Through the 1960s, the public sees those who are squeamishly labeled as *daujinsi*, or dual sexed (a term encompassing everything from the hermaphrodites of Islamic tradition to the queer to the gender dysphoric), as wondrous, slightly titillating evidence of the divine mystery, while the Ministries of Health and Education see them as medical challenges to be solved for the greater good of public order. The discourse of perverse criminality is a recognizable trope as well, as the well-known story of Asghar Qatil, a 1930s gay serial killer, illustrates. By the early 1970s, popular culture and journalism approach the issue through the lens of the real-life crime story of Mahin and Zahra, a lesbian/transsex affair and murder. The mainstream public lingered attentively on a lesbian "crime of passion" through a serialized investigation and pondered the question of a hypermasculine woman acting out patriarchal proprietary "love" through violence more as horrifying entertainment than enlightenment. Modern heteronormativity relished the opportunity to interpret these deviations as a kind of entertainment.

Also by the 1970s, a gay scene developed in which same-sex desire and cross-dressing coexisted fluidly in the city of Teheran. In the club culture of gayness, same-sexuality and transgendering were part of a performative counterpublic—a carnivalesque periphery to the modern, hetero, national norm. Through the 1970s, queer and transsexual were blurred together as corollary conditions that existed beyond the pale or under the radar of heteronormative society and the state. These scenes and scenarios were unspeakable transgressions or unspoken voyeurism for the mainstream. "Afflicted" families (and make no mistake, the reputation-hungry family is a much more powerful mechanism of social control than the state in this period) required no precise naming of conditions; what they could no longer ignore, they shamed and excluded. Prior to the Islamic revolution, transsexuality was part of a mélange of sexual and gender "deviance" that was dialogic and performative, not classificatory or expository. This changed when the state performed its own somatic transition from one *jins*/genus (secular nationalist) to another (radical clerical) in the 1979 Islamic revolution.

The Islamic revolution of 1979 included important acts of collective trans-vestism, expressing publicly and in embodied fashion an alternative vision of Iran's basic essence. Ayatollah Khomeini certainly worked out rationally and textually the theoretical model of the *wilayat al-faqih* (clerical state), but the people in the street who tactically embraced Shi'ite ritual expressions and forms of bodily comportment made the revolution as well. In an irony of historic pro-portions, the *chador* (Iranian full body hijab) donned by masses of not particu-larly modest Iranian women as a voluntary act of revolutionary fervor would be used to imprison them in a gender-segregated world of enforced bodily modesty complete with police power of the *basij* of which premodern Persians never could have dreamed. The new Islamic order was a somatic (as much as if not more than a rational-critical) transition in which women were folded inward, men grew protective facial hair, and power wore the robes and turbans of the clerics. The new dress code of the Islamic revolution forced and allowed "same-sex players" (or *hamjins-baz*, as homosexuals are most commonly, insultingly called in Farsi) to pass even more easily than before in the new homosocial order. Mannish women like the lesbian murderer Mahin were no longer free to perform mas-culinity in the streets with motorcycles and switchblades, and effeminate men "played" in a more restricted sphere than the club culture—in-house privacy. Their sex and sexuality were covered by the chador even as the shari'a worked to enforce gender.

But, simultaneously, same-sex playing was no longer play in any way. It became the object of serious state-building work. It triggered censure of Islamic jurisprudence and threatened the new clerical state in a way it had not before. Because of the jurisprudential constitution of the Islamic republic, the line between gayness and transsexuality based on dysphoria became a critical matter of punishing and preventing forbidden deviance while fixing unfortunate gender disorders. Same-sex playing and all the behaviors associated with it were not just stigmatized; they were criminal and subversive to the clearly stated religious law of the land. Gayness had to be named and excised. Transgender and transsexuality, given legitimacy through a legendary *fatwa* by the Ayatollah Khomeini himself, were given a pass. Transsexuality (still assumed to be a variation of intersex/ hermaphroditism) was a medical condition that the state could tolerate inter-stitially, that religion could exercise a therapeutic power on, and that allowed modern science and radical jurisprudence to cohabit and productively consult, even cross-fertilize. Where gayness and transsexuality had existed as fluidly linked sets of practices in prerevolutionary Iran, the Islamic republic developed an obsession with prying them apart.

Najmabadi as seasoned cultural historian set the stage for Najmabadi the rookie ethnographer with this clear chapter-by-chapter analysis that takes the reader from "before transsexuality," through the closet/exhibitionism of high 1970s gayness, to the clerical imperative and fetish for teasing apart willful deviance (same-sex playing and homosexuality) from congenital curable confusion (transness) in the Islamic republic. The introductory chapter of the book, in which ethnographer Najmabadi navigates the medical/juridical rituals of the state that trans persons must traverse in order to win the prized certification papers that qualify them for treatment and that stave off (totem-like) police abuse during transition, is one of the best in the book. The reader feels Najmabadi's surprise at the sophistication and tolerance of most of the professional gatekeepers (psychiatrists, doctors, jurists) who bring their own liberal, paternalistic, idiosyncratic combinations of science, religion, personal belief, well-intentioned pragmatism, and bureaucratic territoriality to the process. Indeed, it must be noted that Najmabadi's encounters with the bureaucratic gatekeepers of transness are more interesting and revealing than her encounters with trans people themselves. Najmabadi's dialogue with a cleric who specializes in filling in the blank spots between hermaphoditism and modern transsexuality is one of the most interesting sections of the book.

Given that Najmabadi's research was carried out during the years 2006 to 2008, when the world was transfixed with the perverse spectacle of a trans-friendly Iran, it was a little surprising that there was not a lot in this book about sex reassignment surgery (SRS) operations either at the micro or the macro level. During the years we might call "peak trans," the community that pays attention to such things was fascinated with the counterintuitive exoticism of prudish Iran's being second only to Thailand in SRS and with the slowly dawning horror that the Islamic republic may have forced queer people into SRS as part of their jurisprudential housekeeping. The only gatekeeper community with which Najmabadi does not really engage is that of the SRS surgeons (whose worldviews and practice have recently been illuminated through ethnography). At the same time, her complete lack of prurient interest in the genital mechanics of transness and SRS surgery is testimony also to the seriousness of her discursive study. The net effect of the work is to clearly show, without erasing doubts about the practice of nonconsensual SRS, that the difference between forbidden homosexuality and tolerated transsexuality is really a "difference that makes a difference" in Iran today. Policing the boundary between the two gives the clerical/scientific state a boost in all forms of its legitimacy, just as all boundary maintenance practices and protection discourses do.

Only at the end of the book do we actually hear the voices of Iranian transsexuals themselves. Najmabadi declares herself stunned (after her painstaking archeology of the genealogies of gender and sex categories that the state has cultivated) to find that many prefer to slide between the gay and trans poles of their repertoire. One surprises the ethnographer by declaring herself 70 percent trans and 30 percent lesbian. Another tells their tedious but well-meaning therapist that they do not have the time (or inclination) to perform "selfology," since they must keep house, stay groomed, and entertain the boyfriend. Another uses the camouflage like ambiguity to manipulate mandatory military service. Many seem to have (same-sex) played the ever more rigid system—using certification to prolong the liminal period of transition and expertly performing their public and private roles by manipulating clothing, makeup, chador, and facial hair for maximum effect within the homosocial norms of the Islamic republic. Ironically, one senses (probably unfairly) that Najmabadi almost feels that Iranian trans people she meets are unappreciative of all the hard work that modern professionals have done to recognize and clarify their status. Although she maintains an impeccable political correctness, stooping only to judge the most exploitative of tabloid journalists and the most hypocritical of "Islamic therapists," Najmabadi has more in common with the jurists and doctors who seek to stabilize categories than with the nonconforming individuals who seek to exploit structures and loopholes alike. They show a stubborn tendency to resist the labels and corresponding safely defined havens that the best efforts of gatekeeper professionals in the clinical and religious legal domains have prepared for them. Academics similarly pigeonhole their subjects; Najmabadi herself must periodically fight the urge to categorize her informants with the more descriptive and precise but hardly more flexible labels of Western queerness—butch, femme, queen, and so on. The people themselves insist on preserving their flexibility, prolonging their transition, getting their legitimizing certification papers, and engaging in self-interested *taqiyya* (dissimulation) in order to live their lives on their own terms. The emergent trans nongovernmental organization (NGO) regularly tells inquiring academics to look elsewhere for "subject" fodder for their studies. There is an almost comic moment when a gathering of Najmabadi's queer and trans informants ponder what might be called the clueless homophobe's conundrum—how and why would an FTM embrace a gay identity or an MTF be a lesbian? Just skip the middleman and stay hetero, say the assembled Iranian trans people, in what polite queer Western society would consider a shocking conflation of gender, sex, and orientation. In chapter 6, trans persons organize and jostle to take their place at the institutional table with their own NGOs. They are definitely players seeking to capitalize on their own terms on global recognition and institutional legitimacy with organizations like the Living Well Organization or the Iranian Society for Supporting Individuals with Gender Identity Disorders.

Najmabadi is an excellent guide through this world of nonconforming confirmers of the core gender categories of the Islamic Republic of Iran. Her occasional repetitive usage of *he/she* in gender-ambiguous narratives can be irritating, and the reader sometimes finds the dry and clinical FTM and MTF parsing insufficient to identify characters, let alone to convey the rich and asymmetrical performative semiotics of a *jahil i-mahall* who elbows their way into public modes of male power or a *zan-push* who channels a very different form of feminized sexual power. That the cultural spaces of transness in Iran are practical and performative ("centered on conduct—the situated, contingent, daily performances that depend not on any sense of essence about one's body and psyche," 297) rather than successfully rationalized is emphasized by the fact that the reader finishes the more than four-hundred-page tome without learning a Farsi word for transsexuality that is not either foreign or intersex referencing. This ambiguity, in spite of the best efforts of practitioners in the service of the hyperheteronormative and hyperhomosocial Islamic republic to stabilize gender and sex boundaries, makes the informants and the state itself so much more complex than the exoticizing fascination with Iranian transsexuality could have imagined.

Leila Hudson is an associate professor of Middle Eastern and North African studies at the University of Arizona. She is the author of *Transforming Damascus: Space and Modernity in an Islamic City* (2008) and coeditor of *Media Evolution on the Eve of the Arab Spring* (forthcoming).

Reference

Scott, Joan W. 1986. "Gender: A Useful Category of Historical Analysis." *American Historical Review* 91, no. 5: 1053–75.

Funny Hawaiian Toni Morrison

MORGAN M. PAGE

He Mele A Hilo: A Hilo Song
Ryka Aoki
New York: Topside Press, 2014. 310 pp.

I spent three days trying to find the words to describe Ryka Aoki's lyrical 2014 debut novel, *He Mele A Hilo*, while hawking books at the Philadelphia Trans Health Conference. On the table beside this beautiful book were seemingly more obvious choices for this particular audience: Imogen Binnie's much acclaimed *Nevada*, Casey Plett's touching *A Safe Girl to Love*, Sybil Lamb's surreal punk epic *I've Got a Time Bomb*. But as much as I wanted people to read those books, I so desperately wanted to get Aoki's novel into their hands, because I knew that it had the potential to change their lives. And by the end of those three days, these are the words I had settled on: "It's like a funny Hawaiian Toni Morrison."

Unfortunately, to my great surprise, few had actually read Toni Morrison. "What about Zora Neale Hurston meets Jorge Amado?" Still no flash of recognition passed across most of the faces in front of me.

Really, I have been searching for the right words, the magic words, for nearly two months since I originally read an advance review copy that I left battered and obsessively marked when I was finished with it. At first, I told my friends. I'm sure each and every one of them can attest to my cornering them and seemingly out of nowhere telling them that their problems, which they had not yet decided they had, would all be solved by reading *He Mele A Hilo*.

When I ran out of friends to tell, I took to the Internet. And then to Trans Youth Toronto, the social group for trans youth I facilitated for the past four years. "Oh cool," they said. "So it's about a trans woman in Hawaii?"

"Well, no," I'd say. "It's by a trans woman from Hawaii. And it's all about Hawaii and music and love and food." The group, ravenous for any scrap of trans

TSQ: Transgender Studies Quarterly ∗ Volume 2, Number 1 ∗ February 2015
DOI 10.1215/23289252-2849153 © 2015 Duke University Press

lit they could get their hands on, shrugged it off, like sure that's cool but we want trans characters.

Now, don't get me wrong. I want trans characters too. I want trans books by trans writers about trans characters talking to and for each other. *He Mele A Hilo* is, as Aoki describes it, about simple things: food, hula, music, dance. And though it does not contain any explicit trans characters, and it only contains one queer character, make no mistake: this book elevates trans literature.

I won't try to pull any of that "this is a story about people transforming their lives, so that makes it kind of a trans novel even though there aren't trans characters per se" crap. What makes this elevate trans literature is, as Emma Caterine (2014) astutely pointed out in her review/personal essay for the *Youngist*, "you are more than your trans self." Aoki knows very deeply that as much as she is a trans woman to her core, she is equally a Hawaiian woman. And this book manages to be true to her fullest self in a way most trans writers today should be aspiring to be. This work will find its place not only within the recent renaissance of trans women's literature but, I believe, within the canon of American literature as a whole.

Aoki is a master of words. *He Mele A Hilo* follows the lives of a small community in Hilo, Hawaii. The large ensemble includes Hilo residents living what some may think of as simple lives, such as Nona Watanabi, a self-described fat, perpetually mismatched older woman simply trying to find a way to blend into the background of her *halau* (hula group), and Eva Matsuoka, the conniving owner of a plate-lunch restaurant who must steal the secret of Nona's chicken recipe by any means necessary. As well, there are outsiders from the mainland such as Steve Yates, a billionaire technology giant who has moved to Hilo to care for his ailing wife, and Kam Schulman, a Jewish musician who, in a fit of midlife crisis logic, heard Hawaiian music by the legendary Bruddah Iz that inspired him to move to Hawaii and change his name from Mel to Kamakawiwo'ole.

On the surface, it seems that what Aoki does best is weave all of these many characters and their equally numerous stories and desires together into a single plot, at times funny, tragic, and tender. But, while I spent the entire book wondering about the magic secret to Nona Watanabi's chicken recipe, it was only when I finished the novel that I figured out the breadth of Aoki's true skills.

"You will spend this whole novel wondering about Nona's chicken recipe, and then you will put it down and realize you just read an incredibly nuanced critique of gentrification and colonialism," I began to tell the people visiting the table in Philadelphia. And suddenly people who had never heard of Aoki, who had perhaps never been to Hawaii, who had a moment ago been looking strictly for a reflection of their transness in the fictional worlds within the books between us—these people became interested and would give the book a second look. Often, they bought it.

What Aoki manages to do is communicate a great deal about gentrification and colonialism without ever letting you think you are reading about more than those simple things: food, hula, music, dance. The plot about what happens when rich outsiders move to a small place and think they can solve people's problems by throwing money at them simmers in the background while you become consumed with the emotional lives of the dozens of characters, and by the end you walk away with a far more complex picture of these big political issues than you could hope to get from any dry academic text.

It should also be noted that Aoki's choice to write the book entirely in Hawaiian Pidgin, a creole English, works perfectly, both by establishing the characters and setting in their own unfiltered language—much like the aforementioned Zora Neale Hurston—and also by reminding us that the perspective of this book is deeply and unapologetically Hawaiian. Though a very playful glossary is included at the back, and any non-Hawaiian reader can easily guess the meanings of words by their context, this choice to write in Pidgin firmly locates the work in a decolonial context.

So these are the words I've come up with to begin to describe Ryka Aoki's masterful debut novel, *He Mele A Hilo: A Hilo Song* from Topside Press. They are not nearly enough, so I hope you will take the time to sit down with the entire Hilo community, with Noelani Choi's *halau*, with Harry's tackle box, with the musicians of Kuʻuipo, and with Aoki herself as she tells the stories closest to her heart.

Morgan M. Page is a writer, performance artist, and activist currently living in Montreal. Her first novel, *Other People's Grief*, is forthcoming in 2015.

References

Caterine, Emma. 2014. "You Are More than Your Trans Self: Ryka Aoki's *He Mele A Hilo.*" *Youngist*, May 22. youngist.org/ryka-aoki-and-trans-identity/.

New from DUKE UNIVERSITY PRESS

Back in Print!
Cherry Grove, Fire Island
Sixty Years in America's First
Gay and Lesbian Town
ESTHER NEWTON
With a new preface
21 illustrations, paper, $24.95

"Newton shines, weaving stunning
anecdotes of violence and humiliations
among her descriptions of fabulous
parties and sex. . . . Her empathy
conveys the enormous integrity of
people whose most radical gesture was
to be fabulous in the face of hate."
—*Village Voice*

Willful Subjects
SARA AHMED
paper, $24.95

"*Willful Subjects* offers a vibrant,
surprising, and philosophically rich
analysis of cultural politics."
—**Judith Butler,** Maxine Elliot Professor
of Comparative Literature, University of
California, Berkeley

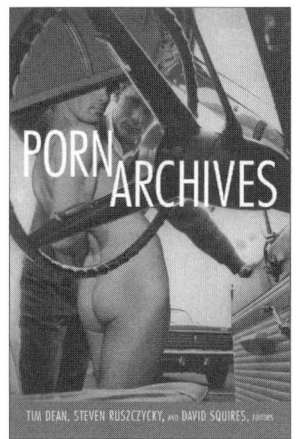

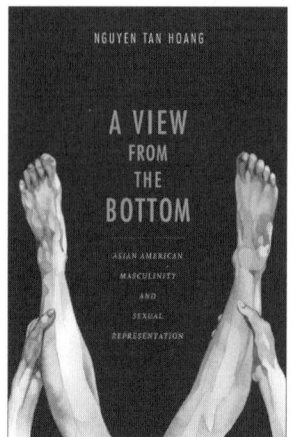